D0056168

A Vision of
the Future

ALSO BY MORTIMER J. ADLER

Dialectic

What Man Has Made of Man

How to Read a Book

How to Think About War and Peace

The Capitalist Manifesto
(with Louis O. Kelso)

The Idea of Freedom

The Conditions of Philosophy

The Difference of Man and the Difference It Makes

The Time of Our Lives

The Common Sense of Politics

The American Testament
(with William Gorman)

Some Questions About Language

Philosopher at Large

Reforming Education

Great Treasury of Western Thought
(with Charles Van Doren)

Aristotle for Everybody

How to Think About God

Six Great Ideas

The Angels and Us

How to Speak, How to Listen

A VISION OF THE FUTURE

Twelve Ideas for a Better
Life and a Better Society

MORTIMER J. ADLER

MACMILLAN PUBLISHING COMPANY
NEW YORK

COLLIER MACMILLAN PUBLISHERS
LONDON

Copyright © 1984 by Mortimer J. Adler

All rights reserved. No part of this book may be reproduced or transmitted in any form or by any means, electronic or mechanical, including photocopying, recording or by any information storage and retrieval system, without permission in writing from the Publisher.

Macmillan Publishing Company
866 Third Avenue, New York, N.Y. 10022
Collier Macmillan Canada, Inc.

Macmillan books are available at special discounts for bulk purchases for sales promotions, premiums, fund-raising, or educational use. Special editions or book excerpts can also be created to specification. For details, contact:

Special Sales Director
Macmillan Publishing Company
866 Third Avenue
New York, New York 10022

Library of Congress Cataloging in Publication Data

Adler, Mortimer Jerome, 1902–
    A vision of the future.

    1. Quality of life.   2. State, The.   3. Social justice.   I. Title.
HN60.A34   1984   301   83-24828
ISBN 0-02-500280-5

10   9   8   7   6   5   4   3   2

Printed in the United States of America

Contents

Chapter 1. Prologue: More Down to Earth   1

PART ONE: A BETTER LIFE

Chapter 2. Work and Leisure   7

    The Six Parts of Life   8

    Categorizing Human Activities   12

    Is a Particular Activity Sleep, Toil, Leisure, Play, or Some Mixture of These?   18

    The Spectrum of Work, Compensated and Uncompensated   23

    Idling and Rest   27

    The Options Open to Us for the Use of Our Free Time   30

Chapter 3. Wealth and Property   42

    The Forms of Wealth and Other External Goods   45

    How Is Wealth Produced?   50

    Property: Its Rightful Possession   55

    The Wealth of Societies: Different Economies Compared   64

Chapter 4. Virtue and Happiness   88

    Habits, Good and Bad   92

    Habits of Mind and of Character   97

Virtue and the Virtues: One or Many?   100

Virtue as an End and as a Means   105

How Can One Individual Help Another to Become Morally Virtuous?   107

Is Anyone Ever Perfectly Virtuous or Completely Happy?   112

PART TWO: A BETTER SOCIETY

Chapter 5.   State and Society   127

When States Exist, Are They Identical With Society?   132

Man, the Only Politically Social Animal   135

Is the State Natural, Conventional, or Both?   139

What Must Be Included in the Definition of the State?   143

The Goodness of the State   149

Chapter 6.   Government and Constitution   157

What Is Government and When Is Anyone Governed?   161

The Necessity of Government   165

War and Peace   169

The Modes and Forms of Government   174

The Mixed Regime   179

Resistance to Government   183

The Idea of Civil Police   185

Chapter 7.   Democracy and Citizenship   201

Why Did It Take So Long?   206

The Only Perfectly Just Form of Government   210

The Conflict Between Justice and Expediency   218

Will Democracy Survive, Spread, and Prosper?   222

Chapter 8.   Epilogue: Ideas with a Future   254

A Vision of
the Future

CHAPTER 1 Prologue: More Down to Earth

FOR MOST OF US, work occupies a considerable portion of our time. All of us who work for a living contrast that with our free time for leisure. Work, in our minds, has a close, but not inseparable, connection with the wealth we come to have and the property we come to own.

Living a good life—becoming happy—is one goal to which everyone aspires. In this connection, we may, and perhaps should, give thought to our virtues and vices. To be able to live in a good society and in a well-governed state is something we all wish for ourselves and our children. When we think of good government, most of us think of constitutional government. We praise our own constitution as one that establishes a political democracy and that secures our human rights. Most of us take pride in the fact that we are citizens of the United States.

In the foregoing sentences, I have named the twelve ideas that are the subjects of this book. They come in pairs: Work and Leisure; Wealth and Property; Virtue and Happiness; State and Society; Government and Constitution; Democracy and Citizenship.

The pairs fall into two distinct, but related, groups. The first six—from Work to Happiness—belong together because, in our consideration of them, we are concerned (as the title of Part One indicates) with what goes into making good lives for ourselves.

In dealing with the second six—from State to Citizenship—we are confronted (in Part Two) with all the problems to be solved in making progress toward a good society for ourselves, our children, and grandchildren.

If you were called upon to discuss the ideas just mentioned, you would probably not regard doing so as being highbrow. You might be much more hesitant, or beg off getting into a discussion, about Truth and Beauty, or Liberty and Justice. You might regard them as being way up there in the blue sky. Most of us would not feel that way about Work and Wealth, Government and Democracy.

All the ideas I have named are great ideas, but all great ideas are not equally great. Truth, Goodness, and Beauty are transcendental ideas, applicable to everything we think about. Liberty, Equality, and Justice are less highflown, but they, too, have a far-reaching scope that involves them in our thinking about all our practical affairs.

While ideas such as Work, Wealth, and Virtue, or State, Government, and Democracy are not as great, they are more down to earth. They are more concrete, less abstract. We can give concrete examples of one or another of the meanings we attach to these terms. The illustrations we use to exemplify them fall within the range of our ordinary perceptual experience.

Anyone who has played the game of twenty questions, using the categories of animal, vegetable, and mineral, knows that what the person who is being interrogated has in mind can be discovered by questioning *only if* the object of his thought is a particular instance of a concrete idea. If the object of his thought were truth or goodness, liberty or equality, the method of this game would have little chance of detecting it. The chances would be somewhat greater if the person being interrogated had taken government or democracy, work or wealth, as the object; and greater still if the choice had been a particular instance of one of these ideas.

With the exception of Virtue and Happiness, all the other ideas in Part One can be treated for the most part without reference to the ideas reserved for Part Two. But when we come to the last two ideas in Part Two (Democracy and Citizenship), economic and moral considerations drawn from Part One necessarily come into play.

While we must use words in order to discuss ideas, our concern is with ideas, not words. Sometimes one and the same idea finds expression in two words that are strictly synonymous; for example, the words "liberty" and "freedom" can be used interchangeably for the same idea.

Sometimes, a set of words, such as "work," "labor," and "toil" are loosely used as synonyms for one and the same idea and it becomes necessary to distinguish their nuances in order to clarify our understanding of an idea that involves two different kinds of work.

Sometimes, one and the same word is used with meanings that are quite distinct and even opposed. When the word "state," for example, is used for any society that is larger than the family and the tribal community or village, the imprecision of that usage beclouds our understanding of the idea under consideration.

Sometimes, as in the case of the word "democracy," the word has been used in one sense for many centuries, going back to Greek antiquity, and in a completely different sense since the middle of the nineteenth century.

Of all the ideas treated in this book, only Democracy can be regarded as a brand-new idea. Calling attention to this fact leads me to make another point that is essential to understanding what follows.

We are here primarily concerned with these ideas in their significance for us today, not with their history, or with the history of the words used to express them. It may be necessary to comment on historical conditions and developments, but only to provide background. The center of the stage is occupied by the idea itself and with the light it throws on the world in which we live.

I have reserved for the final chapter a consideration of the contemporary conditions under which these ideas are influentially operative, together with a consideration of past conditions, under which they were not adequately understood. Most important of all is our vision of future conditions under which we may come to a better, because fuller, understanding than the one we have today.

This concern with conditions past, present, and future as affecting our understanding of these ideas indicates one further difference between them and ideas such as Truth, Goodness, and Beauty and Liberty, Equality, and Justice.

Our understanding of those ideas was much less affected by historical conditions, if at all. The contributions made to our understanding of them by the thought of the last two hundred years, with the possible exception of Equality, do not add up to very much as compared with the accumulated wisdom of the centuries prior. That is why we have so little reason to expect any substantial additions in the future.

It will soon enough become apparent to the reader that our understanding of the ideas treated in this book is affected by historical conditions. The view we take of them today, with the possible exception of Virtue and Happiness, differs remarkably from the view taken in antiquity, in the Middle Ages, and even in the centuries of the modern era preceding our own.

Projecting our minds into a future that will differ in so many important respects from the present (in its scientific conclusions, in its technological advances, in its economic arrangements, in its global affairs), we have every reason to anticipate an enlarged and enhanced understanding of these ideas in the centuries ahead; and, with that, the vision of a better future.

Precisely because the ideas discussed here are more down to earth, they are, like all earthly things, more subject to change and development with the passage of time. They are ideas that look forward to a better world in which the inseparable ideals of a good life and a good society will be more fully realized for the human race as a whole.

PART ONE
A BETTER LIFE

CHAPTER 2 Work and Leisure

THE BIBLICAL STORY of an earthly paradise in the Garden of Eden presents a picture of human life devoid of the necessity of labor or toil. Expulsion from the Garden of Eden as punishment for Adam's sin of disobedience carried with it the dire penalty of toil. The Lord God said to man: "Cursed is the ground for thy sake; in toil shalt thou eat of it all the days of thy life. . . . In the sweat of thy face shalt thou eat bread, till thou return into the ground."

There are secular myths, both ancient and modern, that also picture a golden age in the past when everything needed for the support of life existed in profusion and the human race could nourish and enjoy itself without the pain of toil. In all these accounts, toil is regarded as an affliction, as stultifying drudgery, as a crushing burden that deforms human life.

If there is no distinction between toil and work, we are led to ask: How would human beings spend their time if their lives were exempt from toil? Doing no work of any kind, what would they do with the time of their lives?

One answer will occur to everyone immediately. At least some portion of their time they would have to spend in sleep. But sleep is a recourse to inactivity for the purpose of refreshing the energies needed to engage in activities of one sort or another. In addition to sleeping, what else would human beings have to spend time on? Activities that serve the same purpose that the inactivity of slumbering does. Eating and drinking refuel the body's energies as sleep refreshes them. Cleansing the body, eliminating its wastes, and exercising its muscles all serve the same biological purposes—health, vitality, and vigor.

There is no single word in our vocabulary that is customarily used to name all these biologically necessary activities together with the equally necessary inactivity of sleep. How, then, shall we refer to them as the set of things we must do repetitively, day in and day out, if we are to preserve our health, vitality, and vigor?

I have in the past grouped them under the one word "sleep," using that word with a broader connotation than attaches to the word "slumbering," in order to cover all the things we are compelled to do repetitively for our health's sake. This goes against the grain of ordinary usage, but it is an expedient that I hope readers will permit me to adopt in order to avoid more cumbersome terminology. From time to time, I will remind the reader that sleeping comprises all the biologically necessary inactivities and activities that we are compelled to engage in for some portion of our daily life.

Assuming that sleeping occupies a third of our life's time, what fills the rest of it—the sixteen hours, more or less, that remain each day? To answer this question, and to discover what activities are available to fill the time of our lives, let us consider all the time-occupying parts of life, including in the enumeration both sleep and toil.

The Six Parts of Life

The first distinction to be made in categorizing or classifying all the parts of life divides those that are compulsory from those that are optional.

The compulsory can then be further subdivided into two groups. We have already considered the first of these under the heading of sleep—the absolutely necessary things we must do if life itself is to be preserved and bodily health, vigor, and vitality are to be enhanced. It is, of course, possible for persons to commit suicide by fasting and to ruin their health in other ways, for purposes that we can dismiss as abnormal. Apart from such purposes, the normal conduct of life acknowledges the absolute necessity of sleep in that broader sense of the term which includes more than slumbering—everything that is biologically necessary.

The second group consists of activities that are also compulsory but only under certain conditions. If some form of work is necessary to obtain the means of subsistence—the food, drink, clothing, and shelter that, like sleep, are also biologically necessary for the sake of bodily vitality and vigor—then we are compelled to engage in it for the wealth that supports life and health. Let us use the words "toil" or "labor" for that form of work.

To recognize that the necessity of this second set of compulsory activities is conditional, we need not think only of an earthly paradise, such as the Garden of Eden, or of some mythical golden age that has been a recurrent dream of mankind. Today, as in all the historical realities with which we are acquainted, some individuals possess, in one way or another, sufficient wealth to be exempt from toil. They can sustain life and enjoy whatever they need for their health's sake without having to engage in toil or labor to procure a livelihood.

Today, as in the historic past, such individuals form a class that comprises the few rather than the many. They have been incorrectly referred to as members of "the leisure class." I say incorrectly because the reference involves an egregious misuse of the word "leisure" to mean time that is free from labor or toil. The title of a famous book should not have been *The Theory of the Leisure Class*, but rather *The Life of the Idle Rich*.

Those who have enough wealth to exempt them from toiling for the means of subsistence do, of course, have much more free time than those who have to obtain their livelihood by engaging in labor or toil that uses up a considerable portion of the time that is left unoccupied by sleep. Whatever time is left over should not be called leisure time but free time—meaning time that can be filled with activities that are optional rather than compulsory or necessary. The

miscalled leisure class comprises those who have much more time
for activities that are optional.

Before I go on to name the range of these optional activities in
which individuals can engage (whether they have more free time
because they need not toil or less free time because they must do
so), let me call attention to a point of grammar in the naming of all
the parts of life. This grammatical digression will help us to clarify
the ideas with which we are here concerned.

The grammatical distinction between nouns and verbs divides
words that name things, on the one hand, and their activities or
operations, on the other hand. The nouns "body," "animal," and
"man" name perceptible things; the nouns "health" and "vigor"
name attributes or properties of a body. "Eating" and "drinking,"
the participle forms of the verbs "to eat" and "to drink," name activities in which we engage; so do "sleeping" or "slumbering,"
"eliminating," and "exercising."

Unfortunately, some words that name activities are used by us
both as nouns and verbs. For example, we use "sleep" and "work,"
"toil," and "labor" in both ways. When we say that an individual
obtains work, meaning that he or she has obtained employment and
thereby will engage in working, our use of the word "work" as a
noun may lead us to forget that it is primarily a verb, naming an
activity, and only derivatively a noun. The word "drink" has a similar double usage, but not the word "eat," unless we indulge in the
colloquial jargon of calling food "eats."

The misuse of the word "leisure" as an adjective modifying time
in order to refer to time that is open to optional activities is not the
only mistake we must avoid. We must also avoid the mistake that
results from the grammatical accident that, in almost everyone's vocabulary, the word "leisure" is used either as an adjective or as a
noun, not as a verb. We speak adjectivally of leisure time and of a
leisure class, or we speak substantively of leisure as if it were something we possess or lack, something of which we may have more or
less.

If asked how we make use of our free time, we would think it strange to say that we occupy part of it by leisuring. We would not think it strange to say that we opt for slumbering, playing, amusing ourselves, idling, or even resting. As a result of this inveterate, universal habit of speech, we identify leisure with the way we use free time by playing, amusing ourselves, or just idling, and we fail to identify an activity that we engage in when we use our free time for something other than playing, amusing ourselves, or idling.

To name that distinct activity, which comprises all the pursuits of leisure properly understood, we must use the word "leisure" primarily as a verb, not derivatively as a noun, just as we use the words "sleep," "toil," and "work" primarily as verbs, not nouns. Thus used, we are able to say that one way in which we can occupy our free time is to leisure or to engage in leisuring. There are, of course, other ways to occupy our free time—by playing or amusing ourselves, by idling, by resting, or by resorting to pastimes which, as that word indicates, consist of the things we do to kill time.

I have now named all six parts of life, all the activities that can fill the time of our lives, including under sleeping everything that is biologically necessary. They are:

1. *Sleep:* slumbering, eating, drinking, eliminating, cleansing, exercising, etc.
2. *Toil or labor:* toiling or laboring, which can *also* be called working to earn one's livelihood
3. *Leisure:* leisuring, which can *also* be called working for some purpose other than earning a living
4. *Play or amusement:* playing or amusing one's self
5. *Idling,* but not idleness
6. *Rest:* resting

Readers are put on notice that, in what follows, I may sometimes use the noun and sometimes the participle to refer to the activity under consideration, but I will always be referring to an activity, for the most accurate designation of which the participle of a verb should be used.

The one word that does not appear in the above listing of the six

parts of life is the word "work" or "working," even though it is
the word that names the idea to which this chapter is devoted. The
reason for its omission is that two of the six parts of life—toil and
leisure—are both forms of work. Each is working, but working for
a different purpose.

Our undertaking to clarify the idea of work requires us, therefore, to distinguish work that is toil from work that is leisure, and
to distinguish both forms of work from sleep, on the one hand, and
from play or amusement, on the other.

I will for the moment postpone the consideration of the remaining two parts of life—idling and resting. While they are in themselves matters of great interest, we do not need to consider them in
an effort to understand work—both toiling and leisuring.

Categorizing Human Activities

To define the four main categories under which the activities that
fill most of our life's time can be classified, it is necessary to answer
four questions, as follows:

First, is the activity compulsory or optional? Here we must consider two subordinate questions. If compulsory, is its necessity absolute (unconditional) or relative (conditional)? If optional, is it also
morally obligatory for the purpose of leading a good life or living
well, even though it is not biologically necessary for the preservation of life and health, and not economically necessary for earning
a livelihood—the means of subsistence? If optional and not morally
obligatory, is it nevertheless morally permissible because it does not
frustrate our efforts to lead a decent human life?

Second, what purpose does the activity serve? Why do we engage
in it? What goods or values do we achieve by doing it, either for
ourselves or for the society in which we live?

Third, how is the result we achieve by the activity related to the
activity by which we achieve the result, and also how is it related
to the agent performing the activity? On the one hand, the result—
the good or value aimed at by the activity—may be extrinsic to the
activity. It may be a consequence of the activity, one that follows

from it and lies beyond it. On the other hand, it may be inherent in or intrinsic to the activity itself. When the activity has no consequences as part of its purpose or aim, it is strictly nonutilitarian. When it is utilitarian, it may, on the one hand, result in some perfection or improvement of the agent performing the activity; on the other hand, it may improve something other than the performing agent. The result may also be only a good or value for the individual performing the activity, or it may also be a good or value for the society in which the performing agent lives.

Fourth, what sort of activity is it? Is the activity physical, mental, or both in different measures: more or less physical, more or less mental?

The full importance of these questions will become clearer as we now use them to characterize the four main categories under which activities can be grouped or classified.

SLEEP OR SLEEPING

It is compulsory, not optional; and its necessity is unconditional, not conditional. Its purpose is the preservation of life and the enhancement of bodily health and vigor. The values aimed at are primarily goods for each human individual, though these goods are also matters of importance for the community in which the individual lives. The results achieved are extrinsic to and consequent upon the activities rather than inherent in them. Finally, the character of the activities is primarily physical; or, more properly speaking, they are physiological activities.

WORK OR WORKING THAT IS TOIL OR LABOR

For the great multitude of human beings—excepting only the few who, at any time, are exempt from toil because they are otherwise provided with the means of subsistence and the comforts or conveniences of life—toiling, or working to earn a living, is compulsory, not optional.

However, if we consider the whole of humankind at any time, that statement must be qualified by saying that toil is never uncon-

ditionally necessary, since it is always possible for some individuals
to be exempt from it by the privileged condition that their possession of sufficient wealth confers upon them. It is not possible to
stay alive and healthy without using some portion of one's time for
the biologically necessary activities; but it is possible to stay alive
and healthy, and even to live well, *in the fullest sense of that term,*
without engaging in the form of work that is toil.

There is nothing intrinsically good about toil, neither in itself nor
as a means to a good human life. However, this is mitigated by two
extrinsic considerations, which cast some measure of favorable light
upon toil. Toiling is a more honorable way of obtaining a needed
livelihood than stealing. It is also a more dignified way to take care
of one's economic needs or the needs of one's family than receiving
a welfare handout. To this extent the person compelled to engage
in toil preserves his self-respect by doing so.

WORK OR WORKING THAT IS LEISURING RATHER THAN TOILING

It is always optional, never necessary, either biologically or economically. One can stay alive and healthy without leisuring. One
can possess the means of subsistence and enjoy the comforts and
conveniences of life without leisuring. But if we pass from *just living* to *living well,* living a morally good human life, then it must be
said that leisuring is the only form of work that is morally obligatory. In other words, one can live well without toiling, but one cannot live well without leisuring.

Before I pass on to playing or amusing one's self (the last of the
four main categories under which our activities can be classified),
let me summarize all the points we must bear in mind about the
two distinct forms of work, toiling and leisuring. I feel compelled
to do so because most people think of leisure as the very antithesis
of work. The fact that most people think of work as working for a
living prevents their understanding the different kinds of work.

The form of work that is toiling aims at obtaining wealth, the
means of subsistence and, beyond the necessities of a bare liveli-

hood, the amenities as well—the comforts and conveniences of a decent human life.

In sharp contrast, the form of work that is pure leisuring does not aim at wealth, neither the necessities of a livelihood nor the amenities of a decent life, but aims rather at living well, a morally good human life. Leisuring is, therefore, morally obligatory, even though it is neither biologically nor economically necessary. The goods or values that leisuring aims at and achieves are goods that perfect the human person individually and also contribute to the welfare of the society in which the individual lives.

Both labor and leisure contribute to the social welfare, but in different ways. The results of labor enrich the wealth of the community as well as obtain wealth for the individual who toils. The results of leisure improve the community as well as perfecting the individual person, by enriching it not by wealth but by all the goods of civilization or culture—all the arts and sciences.

The results achieved by both labor and leisure are extrinsic to or consequent upon the activities that constitute both forms of work. The result achieved by leisuring always perfects the performing individual in mind or character. It may also be an improvement in something else; for example, some art, science, or other body of knowledge, or some social institution. In sharp contrast, the result achieved by labor may sometimes be solely an improvement of the materials on which the laborer worked. The performing agent, the worker who toils, may be in no way perfected as a human being by the work done. That is never the case when the worker leisures instead of toils.

However, it is also true that work may involve a mixture of toiling and leisuring. Its results may involve both some perfection of the worker and also some improvement of the materials worked on. I shall return to such mixtures of toiling and leisuring when I come presently to a delineation of the spectrum of work, which ranges from work that is purely toil at one extreme to work that is purely leisure at the other extreme, with all degrees of admixture in between.

Work that is toil may, at one extreme, be mainly physical in character with little or no mental activity involved. This is what we call unskilled labor. At the other extreme, it may be work that is mainly or exclusively mental rather than physical in character. When that is the case, the leisure component in the mixed character of the work done predominates. Some knowledge is acquired, some skill is developed, that perfects the individual as well as the materials on which he or she works.

This is especially true if the mental activity involved is to any degree creative, rather than the performance by rote memory of a repetitive routine. To the extent that anything is learned by doing the work, it must be leisure-work that is mental rather than physical. When the work done is purely leisure-work, without any admixture of labor or toil, it always has a mental component, even though strenuous and prolonged physical effort may be involved in doing it.

Before we turn to play or amusement, one more point must be mentioned in our consideration of work in both of its forms, toiling and leisuring.

The production of wealth being the purpose of toil, the results of such work are always possessions, either things possessed by the worker or things possessed by the company or corporation that employs the worker or by the community in which the worker lives. In contrast, the result of work that is leisuring always confers intrinsic perfections of mind or character upon the worker even when, in addition, the work produces external goods, either economic goods or the cultural goods that perfect the community in which he or she lives.

PLAYING OR AMUSING ONE'S SELF

There can be no question that it is optional rather than biologically or economically necessary. But there is some question about whether it is morally obligatory.

To answer that question, we must move on to the result at which play or amusement aims. The purpose of play being pleasure and pleasure being one of the real goods that enrich a human life and contribute to happiness, it would appear to follow that we are under some obligation to play and amuse ourselves in our pursuit of happiness or in our effort to make a good human life for ourselves.

That statement must be immediately qualified by a consideration of the limited value of pleasure as one of life's real goods. Some real goods are goods without limit. We cannot, for example, have too much knowledge or too much skill. Other real goods, such as liberty, wealth, and pleasure are limited goods, of which we can have too much, more than is good for us to have or good for our fellow human beings in the community in which we live. Overindulgence in play or amusement is, therefore, not morally permissible, even if some enjoyment of the pleasure derived from play is morally obligatory for the sake of leading a good human life.

Two further questions remain, one about the pleasure that results from play and the other about the character of that activity.

Of the four main categories under which our activities can be classified, only play produces a result that is entirely intrinsic to the activity itself. When the activity is purely and simply play, no extrinsic consequence then follows upon doing it. We are playing or amusing ourselves purely and solely for the pleasure that is inherent in the activity performed.

To whatever extent a given activity has some extrinsic result as its consequence, whether that be health, wealth, or the perfection of our minds and character, the activity ceases to be pure play and takes on another aspect. Just as work may involve in varying degrees an admixture of labor and leisure, so an activity that is in one respect play may also in another repect fall under some other category. It then becomes utilitarian play.

Is playing or amusing ourselves ever purely physical or ever purely mental? Clearly, there are some forms of play that are purely mental or are for the most part so, involving little or no physical effort. On the other hand, it is doubtful whether any form of play can be purely physical, since playing usually involves some skill or know-how, which is a mental trait.

One fundamental problem in the classification of our activities under the four main categories has emerged in the preceding discussion.

We have noted admixtures of toil and leisure in some kinds of work. We have observed that a given activity may be play in one aspect and something else in another. It is also the case that a given activity may, at different times, serve all the purposes so far mentioned: It may aim at enhancing our health, at increasing our possessions, at improving or perfecting ourselves, and at giving us pleasure. It may even achieve two or more of these results at one and the same time.

How, then, shall we characterize the diverse particular activities in which we engage to fill the time of our lives? Some may fall wholly under one of the four main categories. Some may fall under two or more of them, varying in the degree to which the differing aspects of the activity constitute an admixture of different categories.

Is a Particular Activity Sleep, Toil, Leisure, Play, or Some Mixture of These?

A particular activity may fall solely under one of these categories; for example, ditch-digging or feeding an assembly line is sheer toil. It may fall primarily under one of these categories, but have an additional aspect that is subordinate to its primary character; for example, a person employed gainfully as a gardener may, in addition to earning his living by that activity, enjoy the work he does as much as he would any other form of play.

Sometimes, however, an activity of one kind is transformed into a different kind of activity. For example, at one time, tennis was entirely a sport of amateurs. It subsequently became a professional sport. Engaged in by amateurs, it was once entirely play. When it is engaged in by professionals whose exclusive interest in the game is the money or the reputation they make, it becomes toil. For some professionals, it can, of course, be a mixture of toil and play.

There is still one more alternative. A particular activity may fall under two or more categories where neither aspect of the activity is primary or subordinate. The individual engaged in the activity would continue doing it if either one of its two aspects were absent. The individual may be equally motivated in either direction.

Professional musicians who earn their living by the performance of their art are workers whose work involves an admixture of toil and leisure. They would continue to exercise their skill and try to improve it even if they were no longer employed in an orchestra or no longer had to earn a living by such employment. If that is not the case, then working in an orchestra is simply toil for them.

Another example of double motivation is to be found in any activity that aims at both health and pleasure. A physician may recommend to a patient that for his health's sake he swim a certain amount of time each day. The patient who follows that recommendation may be one who enjoys swimming as a playful exercise, but now engages in it with the regularity prescribed for therapeutic purposes.

Swimming thus becomes for the patient both sleep and play. By calling the patient's swimming therapeutic or utilitarian play, we indicate its double motivation. If an exercise prescribed by a physician were performed by a patient who abhorred that activity, it would be purely sleep for that person, though for some other individual who engaged in that activity solely for pleasure and not for the sake of health, it would be pure play.

Consider the case of the professional athlete—in football, baseball, tennis, or basketball—who performs without pleasure, who does not need to perform for the sake of his health, and who has reached the point where no increment of skill is likely to occur. He may even have lost interest in the game and continue to play it only for the money earned by doing so.

Then it is sheer toil for him, but it need not be so. It is quite possible for athletes to enjoy what they are doing for its own sake as well as do it to earn a living, and at the same time also strive to improve their performance by increments of skill. Under such triple motivation, the activity becomes an admixture of toil, play, and leisure.

Eating and drinking, activities which for many individuals are

nothing but biological refueling, and so fall entirely under the category of sleep, can be for other individuals who take sensuous de-
light in fine foods and excellent wines a playful indulgence as well.
They eat and drink not only to refuel their energies but, whenever
they can, they do so also for the pleasure inherent in the process.
For a rare few, entitled to be regarded as gourmets, eating and
drinking beyond the calls of hunger and thirst are purely playful
activities. Just as we called an exercise prescribed by a physician,
one that is also enjoyable to the patient, therapeutic or utilitarian
play, so we might call a gourmet's eating and drinking playful or
sensuously delightful sleep.

I have so far called attention to activities that have double or triple motivations, requiring us to classify them under two or three of
the main categories. I turn now to activities that at first blush appear to be pure instances of leisuring. I have in mind such activities
as teaching, producing any work of art, giving lectures, writing
books, engaging in political life, or for that matter practicing any
of the learned professions that serve the well-being of others and
the welfare of society.

All of these would appear to be prime examples of pure leisuring,
especially if their performance involves some learning—some increment of knowledge or skill—on the part of the performer and some
contribution to society as well. They remain pure leisuring *if* the
performing agent has no other motivation than self-improvement or
the social benefits conferred, or both.

However, that "if" italicized in the preceding statement introduces a supposition that is usually contrary to fact. Many practitioners in the learned professions and many creative artists work for
some extrinsic compensation as well as for the rewards of leisuring.
For them, the activity in which they engage is work that can be
called compensated leisure. We dare not overlook the fact that for
many others (one dares not say how many), the extrinsic compensation, the money they earn, is their only motivation. Then it is toil
for them, not compensated leisure.

By their very nature, the aforementioned activities are such that one can learn and benefit others. They should, therefore, have the aspect of leisure, even if they are activities that earn a living.

What for some individuals is pure leisuring and for others compensated leisuring can become for still others work that is toil without a scintilla of leisuring in it.

Monetary gain is their only interest. They would turn to something else if they could earn more money by doing it. If self-perfection and social service are no part of their aim, we are entitled to ask whether they have not violated the ethics of their profession. Can they be regarded as true practitioners of a learned profession or of one of the fine arts if the work they do is nothing but toil for them? It makes no difference whether the compensation received is large or small.

A large part of our population today consists of employees of government, from the president, justices of the Supreme Court, members of the cabinet, and senators and congressmen down to the clerks in government bureaus, police officers, and so on. Let us call all of them citizens who are also office-holders, whether elected or appointed. The rest of us are citizens not in public office.

Non-office-holding citizens who perform their duties as citizens by engaging in political action of one sort or another do so as forms of leisuring. How about the others—the citizens who are also office-holders?

We know that the work they do for compensation is in that respect highly or slightly compensated toil for them. But does it also have the aspect of leisuring, as it should *for them as well as for ordinary citizens?* I need not pause to comment on what a negative answer means for the general welfare of the state, for the integrity of government, and for the prospects of a democratic form of government.

Work that is sheer toil seldom has any playful aspect. By those who have to earn a living, it is done solely for that purpose. Work that is pure leisuring or leisuring in part may be just as devoid of any inherent pleasure as the drudgery of sheer toil is.

When we understand that leisuring as well as toiling is work in the full sense of that term and when we understand that leisuring is never to be confused with play, we should not be surprised by the statement that leisure activities or activities that have a leisuring component may be just as painful and as fatiguing as work that is toil.

It follows that both forms of work, whether in separation or in combination, may require us to resort to play for its relaxing and recreational effects—removing the strains and tensions of work and refreshing our energies. The playing we do for this purpose then becomes therapeutic or utilitarian play.

Nevertheless, it is also possible for leisure-work, or work that has an aspect of leisuring in it, to have an aspect of playfulness, because the worker genuinely enjoys the work while doing it. This is not true of what I have called sheer toil and may also be called, for that reason, drudgery.

No housewife, as contrasted with women employed in other occupations, would fail to recognize that she also is engaged in work. Domestic work, the doing of household chores, is certainly work, not play. Much of it is sheer toil, as much for the housewife who does not receive an hourly or weekly payment for it as it is for the domestic servant or hired hand who engages in such work to earn a living.

The tasks performed, whether by the housewife or by a hired hand, consist of repetitive chores, from the doing of which almost nothing is learned and in the doing of which little pleasure is found. The work is for the most part manual rather than mental; its repetitiveness makes it stultifying; having nothing creative about it, it yields no self-improvement. The drudgery of the toil is alleviated only if an element of leisuring enters into the work for the housewife because she does it as an act of love and for the good of the family. Then it differs from the same work performed by a domestic servant solely for the money to be earned.

In contrast to such domestic work, which is largely manual rather than mental and repetitive rather than creative, such activities as gardening, carpentry, repairing plumbing or electrical gadgets, and the use of other skills to improve the household, are work that is leisuring rather than toiling. They can also be play to whatever extent the doing of them is enjoyed.

I have left to the last the most interesting example of an activity that can fall under all four of our main categories, either entirely under one or another, or involve some admixture of several at the same time. Consider sexual activity. If its motivation is purely biological, it belongs in the category of sleep. If it has no other motivation than financial gain, then it is toil. If it is indulged in solely for the inherent pleasure in the process, it is sheer play.

Is it ever leisuring? Does it ever have an aspect of leisuring combined with some other aspect? Yes, if the sexual union of two persons is an act of benevolent love on their part, an act that confers mutual benefits. We know that the sexual act may be performed by one of the partners without pleasure. Then, if it is an act of love, it is leisure-work without any aspect of play. When it is performed with pleasure, it is erotic love as distinguished from other forms of benevolent love that do not involve any sexuality whatsoever.

When the sexual act is performed without love, it may be sleep, toil, or play, but there is nothing leisurely about it.

The Spectrum of Work, Compensated and Uncompensated

Work is either toil or leisure or some combination or mixture of both. If it is sheer toil, it must be extrinsically compensated, since no one would voluntarily engage in it unless motivated by the dire necessity of having to earn a living.

When work is pure leisure, it may or may not be compensated. It is the kind of work we should be willing to do without extrinsic compensation if we had no need to earn a living. When it is compensated leisuring, it is usually work that produces marketable goods or services. The same holds true for work that involves some combination of both toil and leisure.

There are three pure forms of work: (1) sheer toil that is compensated and thereby earns a living for the worker; (2) pure leisure that is also compensated; and (3) all forms of leisuring that can occupy time that is not taken up by sleep, play, and one or another form of compensated work.

In addition to the three pure forms of work, there are various admixtures of toiling and leisuring. At one extreme of the spectrum of compensated work there is sheer toil; at the other, there is pure leisuring. In between, there are admixtures of toiling and leisuring, in which either the component of toil predominates (and then such work is at the lower end of the spectrum) or in which the component of leisuring predominates (and then such work is at the upper end of the spectrum).

Work that is pure toil, done solely for the sake of the money it earns, is also sheer drudgery because it is stultifying rather than self-improving. It improves only the materials on which the worker works, but not the worker himself or herself. It may be either manual work or mental work, but in neither case is it creative. In either case, it usually has deleterious effects upon the worker—upon his body if the work is mainly manual; upon his mind if it is mainly mental. Far from resulting in any self-perfection, it results in the very opposite—self-deterioration.

The tasks performed by such work are, for the most part, tasks that can be much more efficiently performed by machines or robots precisely because they are in essence mechanical rather than creative operations.

More than a century ago Karl Marx and, even earlier, Alexis de Tocqueville were right in describing such work as an activity that enhances or improves the materials worked on, but which at the same time degrades or deteriorates, both in body and mind, the condition of the worker. Neither of them could have anticipated the technological progress that has now eliminated many of those tasks from the sphere of human work. That progress promises a future in which machines will further emancipate human beings from the drudgery that a large part of the human race has until recent times suffered, under the dire necessity of suffering it or starving.

At the opposite and upper extreme of the spectrum of compensated work are the tasks or undertakings that persons would discharge or take on even if they did not have to work for a living. Included here are all forms of productive artistry, all forms of scientific research or philosophical thought, political activity that involves compensated employment by government, employment by religious and other social institutions, and all forms of truly professional activity, such as teaching, healing, nursing, engineering, military service, practicing law, and so on.

What characterizes all these forms of compensated leisure-work that makes it possible for us to think of a person doing such work even if he or she did not have to earn a living by doing so?

In the first place, such work is always self-rewarding and self-perfecting, in the sense that the worker learns or grows, improves as a human being, by doing it.

In the second place, it is always to some extent creative work, involving intellectual innovations that are not routinized and repetitive. It is in this respect the very opposite of mechanical operations. It may involve some chores that are repetitive, but these are a minor part of such work.

In the third place, like other forms of work that involve little or no leisuring, such work is productive of goods valuable to others and, therefore, marketable, or goods gratuitously conferred upon society. Like other forms of compensated work, which impose certain obligations to be performed for the compensation earned, such work, even though it is leisuring rather than toiling, can be just as tiring or fatiguing as sheer toil. But unlike those for whom work is sheer toil, those for whom work is compensated leisure may find some pleasure in the performance of their tasks. This makes the work they do play as well as leisure.

The larger the creative input of the work, the more it is self-perfecting, the better it is as work for a human being to do. The more the work involves stultifying chores and repetitive mechanical operations that machines can perform more rapidly and efficiently than human beings, the less is it desirable work for human beings to do. It has less human dignity as work because it is self-deteriorating rather than self-perfecting, even though it produces marketable economic goods or services, or results in other social values. It is more like the kind of work one hopes technological progress will alleviate or eliminate entirely by producing machines that will perform such tasks.

The degree of compensation for the work done does not always match the place it occupies in the spectrum of work. Work that lies at the lower end of the scale usually earns less than work that lies at the upper end of the scale, but that is not always the case.

Nor is it always the case that individuals who have some options with regard to employment exercise their options by choosing work that is more highly compensated. They may, for very good reasons indeed, reasons that express sound moral judgments on their part, choose work that lies at the upper end of the scale, but is not as highly compensated as work that has less of a leisure component and offers them less opportunity for the enjoyment that is provided by doing work that also has the aspect of play.

A well-paid job is not necessarily a good job, humanly speaking. It may be well paid for reasons having nothing to do with the character of the work or the quality of life it confers on the worker. The reverse is equally true. A good job, humanly speaking, may be poorly paid in terms of the marketable value of the products turned out by the work.

The foregoing delineation of the spectrum of compensated work does not exhaust the whole range of activities that are leisuring. What kind of activities constitute uncompensated leisuring?

Before I attempt to answer the question, let me call attention to the etymology of the English word "leisure" and the words in the Greek and Latin languages that our English word translates.

The English word "leisure" derives through the French word *"loisir"* from the Latin word *"licere,"* which means the permissible rather than the compulsory. This confirms one connotation that we have attached to the word "leisure"; namely, that it is an optional activity rather than compulsory. Regarding leisuring as permissible rather than compulsory leaves open the question whether, in addition to being permissible, it is also obligatory for ethical reasons.

The Greek word that our English word translates is *"skole,"* the

Latin equivalent of which is *"schola"* and the English equivalent "school." The connotation hereby given to the word "leisure" is that it always involves learning, some increment of mental, moral, or spiritual growth, and hence some measure of self-perfection.

These two connotations of leisuring—(1) an optional use of free time, (2) for personal growth or self-perfection—leave only one further connotation to be mentioned: In addition to producing self-improvement, leisuring may also confer benefits upon other individuals or upon the organized community as a whole.

With this before us, we should be able to see why certain activities that human beings engage in without any thought of financial or economic compensation are leisuring in exactly the same sense as the activities we have called compensated leisuring.

These include all acts of benevolent love and friendship, among which are the acts of conjugal love and the rearing of children.

They include the political activities of citizens who are not holders of public office and who are not paid for the performance of their duties, as office-holders are.

They include travel and other experiences through which individuals learn, such as serious conversation or the discussion of serious subjects.

They include sustained thinking and intellectual activity that enlarges one's understanding, amplifies one's knowledge, or improves one's skills.

Every use of one's mind in study, inquiry, or investigation, in reading, writing, speaking, and listening, in calculating and estimating—all these, when the work involved is purely for personal profit, are instances of uncompensated leisure.

Idling and Rest

We have already considered two kinds of activity by which we can fill our free time—uncompensated leisuring and play solely for the sake of pleasure. Two more were mentioned earlier in the listing of the six categories of human activity, but I have not discussed them so far. They are idling and rest.

I use the participle "idling" rather than the noun "idleness" because the connotation of the latter is one of emptiness or vacancy, a vacuum that is filled by mere pastimes or time-killing diversions.

When, in the past, the owners of factories or their managers resisted the demands of labor for reduced hours of work, they gave as one reason the deleterious or corrupting effects upon the workers of the idleness that would result. It did not occur to them that they themselves had ample free time to dispose of, which they did not regard as an occasion for idleness, but rather as an opportunity to engage in the pursuits of leisure.

The Latin word "*vacatio*" was the antonym for the Latin word "*negotio*," which means business—an economically or socially useful employment of one's time. From the Latin word, we get the English word "vacation," which many take as signifying an opportunity for idleness. The Latin word like its English translation gives idleness the connotation of emptiness or vacancy when free time is devoid of anything but time-killing or time-wasting pastimes.

I mean something other than that by my use of the word "idling." I give it a meaning that borrows from the meaning of the same word when applied to an engine that is idling. The engine is turning over, but the gears are not engaged, and so the automobile is not moving. It is not going anywhere. The engine is not serving the purpose for which it was designed and placed in the chassis of the car.

I think of human idling as a use of free time in which we are awake, not asleep, and in which we are not engaged in any purposeful line of thought. Our minds are turning over but are not moving in any intended or purposeful direction. All kinds of thoughts are likely to occur to us when we use free time to engage in idling, especially if the idling occurs toward the end of a day in which we have been engaged in work that is either pure leisuring, whether or not compensated, or has some leisure component in it.

Those who insist upon being busy all through their waking hours by engaging in some purposeful activity, whether that be some form of play or leisure, deprive themselves of the benefits of idling. Their lives are the poorer for it. The spontaneous creativity of their minds is seriously diminished or may even be totally suppressed.

"Rest," like "idling," is a word that calls for a brief explication. Many individuals use that word as a synonym for slumber. "Take a rest" means for them lying down and going to sleep. When they say "Take a rest from what you are doing," they are recommending that you relax by ceasing work.

They have forgotten the meaning of the word "rest" when in the Bible it said that God, having finished the work of creation in six days, rested on the seventh when He contemplated the created universe. In that context, the word could not possibly have signified either sleep or relaxation.

They have also forgotten the meaning of the word when the Sabbath is called a "day of rest"—a day in which one does not work, nor does one play or leisure.

Still further, they may not know what theologians have in mind when they speak of souls in the presence of God as enjoying "heavenly rest."

For Orthodox Jews in mediaeval ghettoes, or alive in the world today, the Sabbath or day of rest was a sacred day, devoid of the secular activities that filled the time of other days. It had the same character for the Puritans. Strict observance of the Sabbath prohibited not only work of any kind but also play of any kind. How, then, was the time of the Sabbath occupied—the time left free from all but biological necessities? The answer is prayer and other forms of religious contemplation.

Orthodox Jews, especially in the mediaeval ghettoes, did not need the day of rest to recoup the energies exhausted by six long days of unremitting toil. Sufficient slumber would serve that purpose. The Sabbath served another purpose for them. It expanded their lives beyond confinement to sleep and toil. It took them out of one world into another. It refreshed their spirits, not their bodies.

Rest, in the sense of contemplation, is the very opposite of the activities subsumed under all the other categories. All of them have some practical purpose in this life. Rest lifts us above and out of the exigencies of practical involvement of every kind.

Is there any rest for those who are not religious—who do not devote time to prayer and the contemplation of God? There is, if the contemplation of works of art and the beauties of nature has the same effect for them. It has that effect when the enjoyment of beauties contemplated involves a degree of ecstasy, which takes us out of ourselves and lifts us above all the practical entanglements of our daily lives.

The Orthodox Jew and the Benedictine monk fill much of their free time with rest. They lead three-part lives, constituted by sleep, work, and rest. The motto of the Benedictine Order is *ora et labora* (prayer and work). Chattel-slaves in antiquity and in modern times, serfs in the feudal system, and wage-slaves, as Marx called them in the early years of the industrial revolution, led two-part lives—of sleep and toil—with little or no play because they had little or no free time. They worked seven days a week and often as much as fourteen hours a day. The feudal serfs and nineteenth-century factory workers led three-part lives only to the extent that some time was allowed on the Sabbath for religious observances.

The Options Open to Us for the Use of Our Free Time

For many years, in lecturing about work and leisure and in conducting discussions of these subjects, I have put the following question to my audiences.

On the supposition that you were under no compulsion to earn a living, for whatever reason, what would you do with all the free time at your disposal? The amount of free time at your disposal would be at least two-thirds of every day since only one-third or less would be taken up by biologically necessary activities.

The supposition is real for those who have independent means and have no need to work for a living. It is also real for all who, while engaged in work at present, can look forward to a future in which their retirement from compensated work puts the same amount of free time at their disposal.

Even those for whom the supposition is not real now or who do not see it as a reality for their future should face the question as a way of considering the quality of their lives; for under present conditions of increasingly shortened hours in the work week, they too have enough free time at their disposal to think about the options they can exercise in filling it.

Idling, properly resorted to, cannot take up too much of anyone's free time. It should be done only occasionally and then only for brief periods. Nor can rest occupy a large portion of anyone's time, except for religious persons who enter strict monastic orders the members of which are withdrawn from all worldly cares, or for others like them whose religious devotions occupy a large part of their waking life.

After the time consumed by necessary biological activities and after what little time is devoted to rest and idling is subtracted from the day's twenty-four hours and the time of the week's seven days, there is still a considerable portion of free time available to those whose good fortune it is not to have to work for a living. *Suppose that were you. What options would you exercise to fill it?*

Let me tell you how I would judge, on ethical grounds, the answers you might give.

Were you to say that you would use up the free time at your disposal in one or another form of play, my judgment would condemn you as a childish playboy, a profligate, overindulging your lust for pleasure. While pleasure is a real good that enriches a human life, it is, as noted before, a limited good—good only in a certain measure—and so it should be pursued with moderation.

Were you to respond by saying that you would stay in bed slumbering many more hours than workers can allow themselves, and that you would kill the rest of your free time with pastimes or empty idleness, I would condemn you as a sluggard, choosing for yourself a contracted life, one devoid of the qualities that make it a decent and honorable human life. One does not have to be an orthodox Christian acquainted with the seven deadly sins to know that sloth is one of them. Its seriousness consists in its being an utter waste of one's talents and of one's human resources.

Quite apart from these moral judgments, I would also be obliged to warn the sluggards, the slothful, the profligate, the playboys and playgirls, that they are doomed to suffer boredom and ennui by this use of free time. To escape from it, they are likely to resort to ways of killing time that may turn out to be irreparably injurious to their health—to alcoholism, to drug addiction, to sexual excesses and depravities, or to other forms of human corruption.

What, then, is the ethically right answer to the question?

The major portion of the free time at one's disposal, on the supposition of no need to spend any of it working for a living, should be devoted to doing things that fall within the range of the widely diverse activities that constitute uncompensated leisuring. A reasonable modicum of play should be added, not only for its own sake but also to relieve the tensions of serious and intense leisure-work and to refresh the energies exhausted by it. That would still leave time for idling and rest, sacred or secular, to be enjoyed by those who are wise enough to make them parts of their expanded lives.

As compared with the contracted two-part life of the chattel-slave, and the three-part life of the feudal serf or nineteenth-century industrial wage-slave, the person who adopts the answer I have set forth above has chosen for himself or herself an expanded four- or five-part life.

In such an expanded life, one part is, of course, sleep (the hours devoted to the biological necessities). This part is common to all human lives. Beyond it, for the person not engaged in any form of compensated work, a five-part life would consist mainly of (2) leisure activities, embellished by (3) a modicum of play, and enriched by (4) a little idling, and (5) some measure of rest. The only part of life here omitted is toil. If, in addition, either idling or rest is omitted, it becomes a four-part life. In any case, a four- or five-part life is the ethical ideal—the kind of human life the morally virtuous man would choose to live.

While it must be reiterated that the omission of any semblance of toil from life in no way diminishes its excellence, we may still ask whether it will be included in the four- or five-part life just described, and whether a six-part life is possible.

To answer that question, consider the individual whose work to earn a living consists entirely of compensated leisure. That leisure-work has an aspect that resembles toil to the extent that the receipt of compensation imposes certain obligations upon the worker as to the use of his time, the punctuality of his performance, and so on. The worker whose work is compensated leisuring is under certain compulsions. The work done having mainly the aspect of leisure and, only in a minor respect being like toil, the person so engaged would be able to use the rest of his free time for play, for idling, for rest, and especially for additional leisure activities that are un-compensated.

This brings us, finally, to two further questions that have been implicit in the original question I posed.

What about the person whose work involves both toil that is drudgery and also leisure that is compensated? If you were that person, what would you do if, suddenly, you came into a large fortune that exempted you from the need to work for a living? Would you continue the same job, doing the same work, or would you seek a change?

The answer, of course, depends upon the extent of the repetitive chores and the drudgery involved in the job. If that were large enough to be disagreeable or even insufferable, you would most probably seek to quit work. If, on the other hand, the leisure component in the job were very large, and the chores and drudgery slight and in-frequent, you might choose to continue doing the work, because you enjoyed doing it, because you personally profited from doing it, or because you regarded yourself as performing a useful public service. Whether or not you continued to take compensation for the work you did would make no difference to the quality of your life.

The last question I am going to ask is the easiest to answer. The supposition is still the same. You have just learned that you no longer need to work for a living. The work you have been doing to earn your livelihood is purely a leisure activity. Would you continue to do it, more or less in the same way, with the compensation for doing it relinquished because unneeded?

If your answer is that you would not continue, that you would stop doing any work, and devote most of your greatly enlarged free time to amusing yourself and to killing with pastimes the remaining hours that would hang heavy on your hands, my response would be, as before, a moral condemnation of you as slothful and immoderately playful. It would also carry a warning about boredom and ennui.

The ethically right answer should be immediately obvious. You should continue doing the work you have for so long been doing, with nothing changed except the removal of any aspect of toil and the foregoing of any compensation.

All of the questions considered, together with the answers indicated as ethically sound, apply to all workers who have the good fortune of being able to look forward to a long and healthy life after retirement from compensated work, regardless of how much drudgery and how much leisuring was involved in it.

To retire from compensated work without prior planning for the uncompensated leisure-work that should take its place is to face the disaster of a life that has become contracted and emptied of its most meaningful content—a prolonged vacation that is not only boring but also disabling, both mentally and physically.

QUOTATIONS WITHOUT COMMENT

With Regard to Toil and Other Kinds of Work

. . . If every instrument could accomplish its own work, obeying or anticipating the will of others . . . if, in like manner, the shuttle would weave and the plectrum touch the lyre without a hand to guide them, chief workmen would not want servants, nor masters slaves.

> Aristotle, *Politics*, Bk. I, Ch. 4, (4th cent. B.C.)

★　★　★

In the morning when thou risest unwillingly . . . let this thought be present—I am rising to the work of a human being. Why, then, am I dissatisfied if I am going to do the things for which I exist and for which I was brought into the world? Or have I been made for this, to lie in the bed-clothes and keep myself warm? But this is more pleasant. Dost thou exist, then, to take thy pleasure, and not at all for action and exertion?

> Marcus Aurelius, *Meditations*, Bk. V, Ch. 1 (c. 175 A.D.)

★　★　★

There is one sort of labour which adds to the value of the subject upon which it is bestowed: there is another which has no such effect. The former, as it produces a value, may be called productive; the latter, unproductive labour. Thus the labour of a manufacturer adds, generally, to the value of the materials which he works upon, that of his own maintenance, and of his master's profit. The labour of a menial servant, on the contrary, adds to the value of nothing. . . . The labour of the latter, however, has its value, and deserves its reward as well as that of the former. But the labour of the manufacturer fixes and realizes itself in some particular subject or vendible commodity, which lasts for some time at least after that labour

is past. It is, as it were, a certain quantity of labour stocked
and stored up to be employed, if necessary, upon some other
occasion. . . .

The labour of some of the most respectable orders in the society
is, like that of menial servants, unproductive of any value, and does
not fix or realize itself in any permanent subject; or vendible commodity, which endures after that labour is past, and for which an
equal quantity of labour could afterwards be procured. The sovereign, for example, with all the officers both of justice and war who
serve under him, the whole army and navy, are unproductive labourers. They are the servants of the public, and are maintained by
a part of the annual produce of the industry of other people. Their
service, how honourable, how useful, or how necessary soever, produces nothing for which an equal quantity of service can afterwards
be procured. The protection, security, and defence of the commonwealth, the effect of their labour this year will not purchase its protection, security, and defence for the year to come. In the same class
must be ranked, some both of the gravest and most important, and
some of the most frivolous professions: churchmen, lawyers, phy-
sicians, men of letters of all kinds; players, buffoons, musicians,
opera-singers, opera-dancers, etc. The labour of the meanest of these
has a certain value, regulated by the very same principles which
regulate that of every other sort of labour; and that of the noblest
and most useful, produces nothing which could afterwards purchase or procure an equal quantity of labour. Like the declamation
of the actor, the harangue of the orator, or the tune of the musi-
cian, the work of all of them perishes in the very instant of its
production.

Both productive and unproductive labourers, and those who do
not labour at all, are all equally maintained by the annual produce
of the land and labour of the country. This produce, how great
soever, can never be infinite, but must have certain limits. According, therefore, as a smaller or greater proportion of it is in any one
year employed in maintaining unproductive hands, the more in the
one case and the less in the other will remain for the productive,

and the next year's produce will be greater or smaller accordingly; the whole annual produce, if we except the spontaneous productions of the earth, being the effect of productive labour.

Adam Smith, *Wealth of Nations*, Bk. II, Ch. 3 (1776)

* * *

When a workman is unceasingly and exclusively engaged in the fabrication of one thing, he ultimately does his work with singular dexterity; but, at the same time, he loses the general faculty of applying his mind to the direction of the work. He every day becomes more adroit and less industrious; so that it may be said of him that, in proportion as the workman improves, the man is degraded. What can be expected of a man who has spent twenty years of his life in making heads for pins? And to what can that mighty human intelligence, which has so often stirred the world, be applied in him, except it be to investigate the best method of making pins' heads? When a workman has spent a considerable portion of his existence in this manner, his thoughts are forever set upon the object of his daily toil; his body has contracted certain fixed habits, which it can never shake off: in a word, he no longer belongs to himself but to the calling which he has chosen. It is in vain that laws and manners have been at pains to level all the barriers round such a man and to open to him on every side a thousand different paths to fortune; a theory of manufactures more powerful than manners and laws binds him to a craft, and frequently to a spot, which he cannot leave. It assigns to him a certain place in society, beyond which he cannot go; in the midst of universal movement, it has rendered him stationary.

In proportion as the principle of the division of labor is more extensively applied, the workman becomes more weak, more narrow-minded, and more dependent. The art advances; the artisan recedes. On the other hand, in proportion as it becomes more manifest that the productions of manufactures are by so much the cheaper and better as the manufacture is larger, and the amount of capital employed more considerable, wealthy and educated men come for-

ward to embark in manufactures, which were heretofore abandoned
to poor or ignorant handicraftsmen. The magnitude of the efforts
required, and the importance of the results to be obtained, attract
them. Thus, at the very time at which the science of manufactures
lowers the class of workmen, it raises the class of masters. . . .

The master and the workman have then here no similarity, and
their differences increase every day. They are only connected as the
two rings at the extremities of a long chain. Each of them fills the
station which is made for him and which he does not leave; the one
is continually, closely, and necessarily dependent upon the other and
seems as much born to obey as that other is to command. . . .

Not only are the rich not compactly united amongst themselves
but there is no real bond between them and the poor. Their relative
position is not a permanent one; they are constantly drawn together
or separated by their interests. The workman is generally dependent on the master, but not on any particular master. These two
men meet in the factory but know not each other elsewhere; and,
whilst they come into contact on one point, they stand very wide
apart on all others. The manufacturer asks nothing of the workman
but his labor; the workman expects nothing from him but his wages.
The one contracts no obligation to protect, nor the other to defend;
and they are not permanently connected either by habit or duty.

                  Alexis de Tocqueville, *Democracy in America*, Vol. II,
                                        Bk. II, Ch. 20 (1835–40)

                              ★   ★   ★

Hitherto it is questionable if all the mechanical inventions yet made
have lightened the day's toil of any human being. They have enabled a greater population to live the same life of drudgery and imprisonment, and an increased number of manufacturers and others
to make fortunes. They have increased the comforts of the middle
classes. But they have not yet begun to effect those great changes
in human destiny, which it is in their nature and in their futurity
to accomplish. Only when, in addition to just institutions, the increase of mankind shall be under the deliberate guidance of judi-

cious foresight, can the conquests made from the powers of nature by the intellect and energy of scientific discoverers, become the common property of the species, and the means of improving and elevating the universal lot.

John Stuart Mill, *Principles of Political Economy*, Bk. IV,
Ch. VI, Sec. 2 (1848)

With Regard to Leisure and Play

. . . We provide plenty of means for the mind to refresh itself from business. We celebrate games and sacrifices all the year round, and the elegance of our private establishments forms a daily source of pleasure and helps to banish the spleen; while the magnitude of our city draws the produce of the world into our harbour, so that to the Athenian the fruits of other countries are as familiar a luxury as those of his own.

Speech of Pericles, the Athenian leader, in Thucydides, *The
Peloponnesian War*, Bk. II, Ch. VI (5th cent. B.C.)

★ ★ ★

Happiness, therefore, does not lie in amusement; it would, indeed, be strange if the end were amusement, and one were to take trouble and suffer hardship all one's life in order to amuse oneself. For, in a word, everything that we choose we choose for the sake of something else—except happiness, which is an end. Now to exert oneself and work for the sake of amusement seems silly and utterly childish. But to amuse oneself in order that one may exert oneself . . . seems right; for amusement is a sort of relaxation, and we need relaxation because we cannot work continuously. Relaxation, then, is not an end; for it is taken for the sake of activity.

Aristotle, *Nichomachean Ethics*, Bk. X, Ch. 6 (4th cent. B.C.)

★ ★ ★

. . . Those who are in a position which places them above toil
have stewards who attend to their households while they occupy
themselves with philosophy or with politics.

Aristotle, *Politics*, Bk. I, Ch. 7 (4th cent. B.C.)

⋆   ⋆   ⋆

. . . We should be able, not only to work well, but to use leisure
well; for, as I must repeat once again, the first principle of all action is leisure. Both are required, but leisure is better than occupation and is its end; and therefore the question must be asked,
what ought we to do when at leisure? Clearly we ought not to be
amusing ourselves, for then amusement would be the end of life.
But if this is inconceivable, and amusement is needed more amid
serious occupations than at other times (for he who is hard at work
has need of relaxation, and amusement gives relaxation, whereas
occupation is always accompanied with exertion and effort), we
should introduce amusements only at suitable times, and they should
be our medicines, for the emotion which they create in the soul is
a relaxation, and from the pleasure we obtain rest. But leisure of
itself gives pleasure and happiness and enjoyment of life, which are
experienced, not by the busy man, but by those who have leisure.

Aristotle, *Politics*, Bk. VIII, Ch. 3 (4th cent. B.C.)

⋆   ⋆   ⋆

Great labour, either of mind or body, continued for several days
together, is in most men naturally followed by a great desire of relaxation, which, if not restrained by force or by some strong necessity, is almost irresistible. It is the call of nature, which requires to
be relieved by some indulgence, sometimes of ease only, but sometimes, too, of dissipation and diversion.

Adam Smith, *Wealth of Nations*, Bk. I, Ch. 8 (1776)

⋆   ⋆   ⋆

Leisure, though the propertied classes give its name to their own
idleness, is not idleness. It is not even a luxury: it is a necessity,
and a necessity of the first importance. Some of the most valuable

work done in the world has been done at leisure, and never paid for in cash or kind. Leisure may be described as free activity, labor as compulsory activity. Leisure does what it likes: labor does what it must, the compulsion being that of Nature, which in these latitudes leaves men no choice between labor and starvation.

George Bernard Shaw, *Socialism and Culture* (1889)

CHAPTER 3 Wealth and Property

WEALTH IS TOO IMPORTANT a subject to be left exclusively in the hands of economists. Centuries before the modern science of economics was born, wealth was a critical term in moral philosophy, in both ethics and politics. Many of us are likely to forget that the first great classic in the field of economic science, *The Wealth of Nations*, published in 1776, was written by a professor of moral philosophy at the University of Edinburgh.

The consideration to be given here to the idea of wealth, and the related idea of property, will necessarily be philosophical. We are concerned with ideas, not with the phenomena investigated and analyzed by scientific economists. The philosophical consideration of wealth stands in the same relation to economic science as the philosophy of nature does to physical science. It throws light on the whole domain under investigation by the scientist and sees that area of human affairs in the perspectives of a wider context.

Let me state at once what that wider context is. It is the pursuit of happiness for the individual and the general economic welfare of the state that a government seeks to promote.

The idea of wealth covers one important group of external goods that a human being can possess, as the idea of virtue covers the most important group of personal perfections—those of mind and character. These two terms—possessions and perfections—cover the gamut of goods that are the ingredients of happiness, when that is ethically, not psychologically, conceived as a whole human life well lived because it has, in the course of its days, accumulated all the things that are really good for humans to have or become.

Viewed in this broad perspective, the idea of wealth has critical significance for the ideas discussed in the preceding chapter. There the distinction between work that is sheer toil and work that is pure leisure, as well as the distinction between compensated and uncompensated leisure, turns on the dominant purpose for which the work is done—to obtain wealth, acquire the means of subsistence, earn a livelihood, as contrasted with some other purpose that involves no interest at all in such external goods.

When we regard wealth as compensation for work done, whether in the form of wages and salaries or in the form of consumable goods, we are equating it with external goods that are purchasable, on which a price can be put when they are bought and sold.

External goods other than wealth are not marketable, yet they, too, are possessions. For example, the friends one has are possessions that are good for a human being to have. So, too, is the peace of the community in which the individual lives, and also the freedom of action that the society in which individuals live allows them to exercise.

To regard freedom of action in society and the peace of that society as external goods is to see them as somehow dependent on the external conditions under which an individual lives. The achievement of personal perfections is always entirely within the power of the individual; not so an individual's possessions. That is why we must regard them as external goods—external because they do not fall wholly within the power of the individual.

Even if a human being earns his daily bread by dint of his own labor, with no apparent dependence on the efforts or cooperation of anyone else, it is still the case that the wealth he thus obtains can be taken away from him by theft, natural disaster, or other misfortunes. If he has acquired moral virtue or knowledge, no external force or circumstance can deprive him of it, short of mind-affecting drugs.

In what follows, we shall be concerned with the group of external goods that constitute wealth, but I will always remind readers, when necessary, that other external goods are also ingredients of happiness.

As we have seen in the preceding chapter, not all human work produces wealth. The kind of human work that is pure, uncompensated leisure results solely in personal perfections or in social values that no one pays for. In the spectrum of compensated work, the kind that has an aspect of leisure to some degree similarly results in personal perfections while also producing wealth. To keep these matters clear, I will in this chapter use the word "labor" for the kind of work that is paid for because it produces the kind of wealth that is marketable.

As we have seen, not all work produces wealth. It is also true that wealth is seldom produced by human labor alone. Another factor enters into the production of most wealth—the raw materials that nature provides and, in addition, usually but not always, the beasts of burden, the hand tools, and the power-driven machinery with which the laborer works.

Though wealth is produced and earned by labor, it is possible for an individual to earn wealth without doing a stroke of labor. Let us consider an individual who owns raw materials, beasts of burden, and tools or simple machines. Let us not ask for the moment how he comes to own them. If that individual puts these possessions of his into the productive process and employs others to put them to use productively, but does no work himself, not even that of supervision, does he not earn a portion of the wealth produced—the portion that remains after the hired hands are paid off? I shall return to this question presently.

Wealth is always regarded by the moral philosopher as a means rather than an end. Some means are also desirable for their own sake and, in that respect, are ends. Not wealth, which is always a mere means, never desirable for its own sake but only desirable for the sake of other goods. It is nonetheless a real good and an ingredient in happiness.

Wealth is also regarded as a limited good, good only to the degree that it is needed and useful as a means. The moral strictures concerning wealth-getting turn on these two points: that wealth is always to be sought as a means not as an end in itself; and it is always to be sought and accumulated with moderation, not without limit.

Herein lies the reason why economics should be subordinated to moral philosophy. When it is not thus subordinated, it tends to view wealth as an end to be sought for its own sake and to be sought without limit. The more wealth, the better, regardless of how it is used.

Most of us know and have quoted the statement by St. Paul that "the love of money is the root of all evil." Why? Because the pursuit of wealth without limit, as an end in itself and not as a means, is the archetype of almost every moral iniquity and mistake. It is ethically perverse to turn that which should be regarded as a means with limited value into an end worthy of limitless pursuit.

The root of all evil? Not quite, for there is one other form of moral iniquity which consists in treating as a mere means that which should be treated as an end, worthy of respect. Owning human beings as chattel-slaves and treating them as mere means is the prime example of this fault. I will return to this point later in connection with the idea of property. The one thing that a human being can *never* rightly make his or her property is another human being.

The Forms of Wealth and Other External Goods

We have seen that wealth consists of goods that are external possessions, not inner perfections. Other goods are also possessions, not perfections, and therefore must be classed as external goods. What are they and how is wealth related to them?

One other group of external goods consists in the goods of human association, such as friendships, family relationships, and being loved, respected, and honored by others. Still another consists in political goods, such as civil peace; political liberty; as much freedom of action in society as justice allows; the equalities and inequalities of condition that justice requires; security of life and limb through the enforcement of just laws; and the protection of individual freedom by the prevention of violence, aggression, coercion, and intimidation.

Before we consider the diverse forms of wealth, let us ask how all the goods lumped under that head stand in relation to the other two sets of external goods mentioned above.

I would say that the goods of human association are the least dependent upon external circumstances. They are largely within the power of the individual to obtain, even though external circumstances—accidental good fortune or misfortune—may affect an individual's attainment of them.

The second set, political goods, are dependent on favorable or unfavorable external circumstances to a much greater extent. This is not to say that what persons are able or unable to do, or what they do or fail to do, has no effect upon their attainment; but they are never wholly, and seldom largely, within an individual's own power to possess.

The economic goods of wealth are the most dependent upon external circumstances. That is not the only difference between economic goods and the other types of external goods. Some of them, unlike wealth, are not mere means. We think of political liberty and freedom of action as goods desirable for their own sake as well as for their use as means to happiness. The same can be said of having friends, having the love and respect of one's fellows, and being honored by others or by society.

In order to see why economic goods are, of all external goods, the most dependent upon external circumstances and what makes them so dependent, it is necessary now to examine the diverse forms of wealth. This group of goods can be subdivided in a number of ways.

First of all, we must observe that economic goods can be possessed either by solitary individuals, or by families, corporations, and society as a whole. Some are never or seldom individual possessions, but belong only to organized groups. Let us begin by considering the forms of wealth that are individual possessions.

When we speak of goods and services, we distinguish between

consumable commodities and otherwise useful services. Food, drink, clothing, and housing are consumable commodities. Having one's food cooked, one's house painted, and one's clothing repaired by a tailor are useful services; so, too, are having one's hair cut by a barber or having one's shoes shined. While individuals can do these things for themselves, they can also have them done by others who are paid to do them.

A third form of personal wealth consists in an individual's possession of the means of producing wealth for himself. If individuals cook their own food, make or repair their own clothing, build their own housing, cut their own hair, and shine their own shoes, they must have the relatively simple tools for doing these things. They must also, in the case of food, clothing, and shelter somehow come into the possession of the raw materials on which they work with the tools in their possession.

Does this exhaust the forms of wealth that are individual possessions? Not quite, for there are the economic goods which go beyond those necessary for bare subsistence and are necessary for a decent human life. Such desirable means include living and working conditions conducive to health, medical care, legal services, and beyond these, opportunities of many sorts—opportunity for access to the pleasures of sense and the enjoyment of beauty; opportunity for access to the benefits of travel; opportunity for access to educational facilities that support and promote an individual's pursuit of skill, knowledge, and understanding; and, last but not least important, enough free time to enable individuals to take full advantage of all these opportunities.

What is immediately puzzling about the economic goods in the foregoing inventory is that, while some of them appear to be purchasable goods, not all of them appear to have the character of goods that can be bought in the marketplace, as consumable commodities and useful services can be.

A moment's reflection will help anyone to see that all of them can be procured by the few who have enough wealth at their disposal to buy them for themselves. How are they procured by the many who do not have sufficient purchasing power?

Consider living conditions conducive to health. That now requires environmental protection, though this may not always have been true in the remote industrial past. Environmental protection, in turn, requires the intervention of government. If the pollution of air, water, and earth continues unabated, no one may be able in the future, no matter how rich, to use their wealth to procure for themselves locations that are relatively free from dangerous contamination. That is still possible for the few, but the rest must depend on governmental intervention for the enjoyment of a benefit that is purchasable by the very rich.

The same can be said, with one exception, of all the other benefits named above. Medical care, legal services, and educational facilities are provided for those who cannot afford to buy them by the welfare programs instituted by governments, by social agencies, and by public schools. Access to the pleasures of sense and to the enjoyment of beauty are provided by public parks and other recreational facilities and by public museums.

The one exception would appear to be having enough time free from compensated work to take full advantage of the opportunities mentioned. While free time cannot be purchased in the marketplace, the rich possess it because their purchasing power enables them to obtain all the necessities and amenities of life, and even its luxuries, without using any of their time for compensated work.

How do others come into possession of sufficient free time, the benefit that I have classified as an important economic good or form of wealth? The members of the laboring class could seldom get it in the past, when they worked six or even seven full days a week and twelve to fourteen hours a day. But they can get it now as a result of negotiation by organized labor, which bargains not only for increased wages, but also for reduced hours of work.

Has the foregoing enumeration of economic goods—commodities, services, instruments of production, and benefits—exhausted all the forms of wealth that an individual can possess? No, for it omits the mention of money.

Contemporary economists may be concerned with mystiques that puzzle them about the operation of money, but moral philosophers, from the beginning of thought about the subject, offer us a few simple insights about it.

First of all, they point out that money is artificial, not real, wealth. By this they do not mean that money is the only man-made form of wealth; all other forms of wealth, except the resources that nature provides, are also man-made artifacts. They mean rather that money is not real wealth because, in and of itself, it is not a real good. It cannot be consumed, as Midas learned to his dismay when, being able to turn everything he touched into gold, he starved to death.*

Money is useful only in two ways: as a means of exchange in the marketplace and for its purchasing power. Even when owners of money lend it out to others in order to gain interest in return, the lending of money to get more money produces no real wealth, but only increases purchasing power whereby real wealth can be obtained.

Instead of calling money artificial wealth, the denial that it is real wealth can, perhaps, be better expressed by calling it, because of its purchasing power, the economic equivalent of real wealth. It can be converted into one or another form of real wealth. Failing to recognize that gold is only an economic equivalent of wealth, Midas came to grief.

With money treated as the economic equivalent of wealth, do we now have an exhaustive enumeration of the forms of wealth? The answer is a qualified yes and no, because the two things omitted differ from all the enumerated economic goods in significant respects.

One of the things omitted consists of all government services. They are performed by persons who are paid to perform them, but they are not, for the most part, goods that individuals can purchase, no matter how much money they have. One exception is to be found in private enterprises that deliver mail and packages. Such service can be purchased by individuals and firms to replace the benefits

---

*Machines and other instruments of production are, of course, real wealth even though not consumable. All real wealth is divided into consumables and instruments of production.

now so poorly conferred by the government's inefficient postal service. There are others, such as personal security, private transportation, fire protection, and so on.

The other thing omitted consists of all the instruments of warfare and the military establishments that governments purchase or pay for in the interests of national defense, and sometimes for less worthy purposes. National security may be regarded as a government service that the members of society possess as a personal benefit. Apart from this, it must be acknowledged that we do not have here a form of real wealth—neither consumable goods nor instruments for their production.

On the contrary, the use of these things involves the destruction of wealth and the payments made for them out of a country's available funds renders the country and its people poorer by the channeling of those funds into instruments of destruction, even if they are never used.

Money that could have been used, singly or collectively, to purchase consumable goods and useful services, or to pay for instruments of production, the use of which increases wealth, has been taken from the citizenry by taxation to pay for instruments of destruction. Money that could have been used by government to pay for the services that confer a wide variety of benefits upon the members of society, especially medical care and educational facilities, has been reduced substantially by being channeled instead into payment for the one benefit that is national security.

How Is Wealth Produced?

To state the question more precisely: How are the goods, services, and benefits that constitute wealth produced?

I indicated earlier the two principal factors in the production of wealth. One is human labor. The other is everything else. This conglomerate of other things subdivides into beasts of burden, hand tools, man-powered machines, power-driven tools and machinery, automatons such as robots, the raw materials that nature provides in mineral and agricultural lands, the land that is improved by farming or by buildings constructed on it, and other materials that are refinements of the raw stuff that nature provides or are synthetic products of one sort or another.

The word "capital" is sometimes used in the narrowest sense for the physical instruments used in the production of wealth, both inanimate and animate. That connotation of "capital" is sometimes extended to include money, then called financial capital in contradistinction to physical capital. Calling money financial capital means that its purchasing power makes it the equivalent of physical capital. By its purchasing power, it can be converted into physical capital.

The most extensive use of the word "capital" includes all the resources that enter into the production of wealth—all the human resources (which are then called human capital) and all the physical resources, whether natural or man-made artifacts. This, it seems to me, is too broad a use of the term and one that tends to obliterate the important distinction between labor and capital.

I trust the reader will follow me in adopting another use of the word "capital" which is broader than the first use mentioned above, but narrower than the second. I wish to use it for everything involved in the production of wealth except labor.

I mentioned domesticated animals used as beasts of burden, either for their strength, as in the case of oxen or for their skill as well as strength, as in the case of elephants. I did not mention chattel-slaves, whose strength is less than that of elephants but whose skill may be greater, because they are rational, not brute, animals.

Looked at one way slaves are part of the human labor force. Looked at another way, they are like domesticated animals that someone owns as items of property and uses to produce wealth. Fortunately, one does not have to solve the problem of whether chattel-slaves are capital or labor. The problem ceases to exist for us once we acknowledge that human beings cannot be rightly owned, as beasts of burden can be.

Human beings are persons. They must be respected as ends to be served. All other animals are things, just as inanimate physical instruments of production are. They can be used as means within humane limits. To reduce human beings to the status of things violates their dignity as persons, which animals do not have.

The labor factor in the production of wealth comes in a variety of forms that differ in the degree of skill they represent, from unskilled and semiskilled labor at one extreme, to the most highly skilled labor at the other. At the latter extreme, we find the labor involved in the supervision of work, the labor of inventors and innovators who increase the efficiency of the work done by others, and the labor of the managers who operate productive enterprises.

Still another way of differentiating types of labor turns on differences among the physical instruments of production that the laborer uses or cooperates with.

In a few instances, which are the exception rather than the rule, labor is the sole factor in production.

One individual can provide the service of transportation by carrying another on his back. Pulling him in a rickshaw would be easier, but that introduces a tool. Laborers can move heavy objects by their muscle power, or with tools or devices of the simplest sort. The Great Wall of China and the Egyptian pyramids were built by the muscle power of organized labor, assisted only by ropes and other simple contrivances. Teachers receive pay for their labor in giving private lessons; so do nannies for their services in helping to rear children.

Ditches were once dug by laborers without tools, or with the most rudimentary devices, but the work done involved the raw materials nature provided. That is probably true of all other commodities that labor can produce, while not true of services produced by labor.

Apart from this one type of labor that functions without the use of any physical capital in the form of tools (but may not be able to function without some materials provided by nature), all other types of labor differ according to the physical capital they employ, as follows: (a) labor the individual productivity of which is enhanced by hand tools or beasts of burden or both; (b) labor that performs services by using hand tools of the simplest sort, such as barbers and manicurists; (c) labor working at home by operating humanly powered machinery, such as the spinning wheel and the sewing machine; (d) an organized labor force that operates much more complicated machinery in factories and other industrial plants; and (e) highly skilled labor that works with automated machinery and robots.

With all this in mind, let us examine the relation of all sorts of labor to capital of all sorts in the production of wealth.

Whenever capital and labor cooperate in the production of wealth, labor is the independent factor and capital the dependent factor. This is indicated by the fact that some wealth can be produced by labor alone, but no wealth can be produced by capital alone.

Among the commodities or services produced by the cooperation of labor and capital, some can be produced both by individuals using relatively simple hand tools and also by an organized labor force tending power-driven machinery. Shoes and furniture provide examples of this.

However, some wealth which cannot be produced without labor, cannot be produced by labor alone, as shoes and furniture can be. In the domain of commodities, petroleum is a case in point. It can be produced by labor only in cooperation with the highly intense capital of an oil refinery. The same is true of high speed transportation in the domain of services. The rickshaw and the horse and buggy will not do. What labor must work with here is highly intense capital in the shape of automobiles, railroad trains, steamships, and airplanes.

The examples of labor working with capital as well as without capital in the production of wealth reveal two things, not one. They show us not only that labor is the independent and capital the dependent factor, but also that labor and capital are quite distinct and separate factors.

The dream of a completely automated factory, in which wealth is produced by computers programmed to operate robots, without any human intervention or cooperation once the computers have been programmed and the robots have been installed, has not yet become a reality and possibly never will. Nevertheless, the technological progress with which we are acquainted and the prediction of mechanical wizardry that still belongs in the realm of science fiction indicate the increasingly augmented role of capital and the increasingly diminished role of labor in the cooperation of men and machines to produce wealth.

That the production of wealth is becoming more and more capital-intensive, less and less labor-intensive, should not surprise us. It has been that way from primitive times onward. The reason why this has been so and will continue to be so lies in the simple fact that man power (considered for the moment apart from any degree of human skill) is a relatively constant unit, just as horsepower and candlepower are. So far as any measure of brute strength is concerned, the man power now employed in the production of wealth has diminished considerably since the beginning of the industrial era. Most of the burdensome work done by human and animal muscle, aided only by the simplest tools or machines, has been taken over by power-driven tools and machinery.

In sharp contrast to the constancy of man power, the productive force of power-driven tools and machines is ever on the increase and would appear to be multipliable without foreseeable limits. Technological advances in capital do more than shift the burden of applying power from men and animals to machines. They also, in many cases, replace human skills by a more rapid and more efficient performance of the same function; as, for example, in bookkeeping. The only human skills that are on the increase are the truly creative, innovative, and judgmental ones.

Apart from these, the differences between unskilled, semiskilled, and slightly skilled labor do not alter the point that the average unit of man power (including both strength and skill) is a relatively constant unit. Hence, taking it as a whole, the labor force is a diminishing factor in the production of wealth as compared with capital. Capital tends more and more to become the major and labor the minor factor in the production of wealth.

This remains true even with the shift of labor that is now taking place from the production of industrial and agricultural products to the performance of services. To see that this is so, we need only think of dentistry, medical diagnosis, accounting, and legal services, all of which employ technological devices that make them more and more capital-intensive.

There is only one unique contribution to the production of wealth that machines will never replace human beings in making—outside of science fiction that will always remain fiction. It derives from man's creative intelligence. No machine that man can construct will ever have anything like it. Its innovative and judgmental powers are manifested not only in the invention of machines and other useful devices, not only in planning and controlling the most efficient ways to operate them, but also in the management of the productive enterprise as a whole.

Property: Its Rightful Possession

Everyone understands what property is. The difficult question is not what constitutes property, but rather by what right does anyone possess it.

We all use the words "mine" and "thine," or "yours" and "ours." By their functioning as possessive pronouns, they signify property—what belongs to me or to you, to us or to them. What, however, is the word in our vocabulary to signify the opposite of property—that which no one possesses? It is a word we use frequently for other purposes, but seldom to signify the opposite of property. Yet any student of our colonial history will remember something called the Boston Common; in fact, the park that is now there is still called that.

The original Boston Common was land and everything on it that belonged to no one. It was not the property of any individual, any group of individuals, or even the whole society. When man first came upon this earth, the whole surface of this globe was like the Boston Common. Then, as the Englishman John Locke said at the end of the seventeenth century, "all the world was America." That would have been true were it not for the resident Indian tribes who had much earlier staked out their territories on the newly discovered continent.

Some people think of property too narrowly, as that which belongs either to individuals, to families, or to associations of individuals organized as companies or corporations. They identify property with private property. When they do so, they think of land that belongs to the state, land said to be held in eminent domain, as not property at all. But whatever *belongs* is not *common*. By belonging it is property, in this case public property, collective property, or state-owned property.

Speaking only of the land itself, no common remains in America today, in contrast to the way John Locke thought of it in his day. All of it is divided up into private and public property—land in the possession of individuals or groups of individuals and land controlled and administered by the government's Department of the Interior.

What is true of land applies, with one striking exception, to other forms of wealth. Certain consumable goods constitute the exception.

The food I eat and the clothing I wear must be mine as I consume or use them. The house I live in may be public property, and so too the tools or machines I work with and the raw materials I work on. This also holds for services such as transportation, health care, and educational and amusement facilities—all these and many others may be state-owned, controlled, and operated.

With the one exception noted, the distinction between private and public property applies to all forms of wealth. Does anything on this globe still remain the common for all mankind? Yes, the waters of the ocean beyond the territorial limit and the air we breathe.

In the sphere of private ownership, one further distinction remains to be made. In the past, private property consisted of wealth that belonged wholly to one individual or wholly to an association of individuals comprising the family unit. In either case, it was wholly, not partly, owned. With the emergence in very recent time, first, of joint-stock companies and, then, of business corporations, it became possible for individuals or families to be part-owners of wealth that is private property rather than being the sole or whole owners of it. What they own are shares of it, or equities in it. The property owned by a corporation is in fact property that is divided into shares owned by individuals, groups of individuals, and even by other corporations.

Just as all of us who are accustomed to using possessive pronouns understand what property is and to whom it belongs, so all of us who use such words as "theft" and "stealing" or "stolen property" recognize the existence of property that is wrongfully, not rightfully, owned. The thief has appropriated for himself what rightfully belongs to someone else. But how did the individual from whom property has been stolen rightfully come into possession of it in the first place? If all appropriations of property are not theft, how are they to be justified as rightful possession?

The first philosopher to ponder this question, John Locke, employed his distinction between property and the common to expound what has come to be called the labor theory of property rights (which must never be confused with what later came to be called the labor theory value, as developed by Karl Marx). To explain his theory, Locke resorted to very simple models that call upon us to consider the first private appropriations when the earth and everything on it belonged to no one, and man entered the scene under the dire necessity of having to make some use of the common in order to survive.

Before he employed his mind and muscles to make use of the common that he found all around him, did he own any property at all? Yes, Locke tells us, he owned himself. His mind and body, and all their powers, were his and his alone by natural right. They were his *natural* property. All else that might become his by the use of his powers then became his *acquired* property. By what right did he acquire it?

Locke's answer is at first simple and only becomes complicated when certain other considerations enter the picture. The simple answer is as follows.

Whatever the individual takes out of the common by mixing his own labor with it becomes his private possession. This rightful acquisition or appropriation of it rested on the fact that he mixed what was his (his labor power) with what was not his and did not belong to anyone else (the common).

Thus, the fruit that he gathered in the field, the horse that he captured in the wild to tame, the land that he fenced, the crude tools that he fashioned out of materials he picked up, all these became rightfully his by dint of the work that he did, using nothing but his own labor power in the first instance. It makes no difference whether this was done by a solitary individual or by a number of individuals associated as members of a single family.

The picture becomes complicated under the following circumstances. Let us imagine a situation in which an individual has acquired fenced-in land, horses or other beasts of burden, and relatively simple tools that he fashioned with his own hands. All these means of production, or capital wealth, being rightfully his, he can use this capital to produce consumable goods that are the means of subsistence for himself or his family.

Now let us suppose that he wishes to retire from toiling for a livelihood in order to engage purely in leisure-work—to study for the sake of improving his mind or to create something for the enjoyment of it rather than for use. How can he do so?

Standing at the fence that encloses his land, he meets with another individual walking by, an individual who has not yet appropriated anything for himself but the berries and other wild foods he has picked up to satisfy his daily needs. Our landowner and owner of other forms of capital wealth offers him work on his estate, using his horse and tools to produce consumable goods, a portion of which he is willing to give the passerby as compensation for his labor.

Let us suppose that the latter accepts the offered wage-payment as fair and enters voluntarily into a contract with the capitalist (the owner of capital wealth) to work for him in recompense for the payment offered him in the form of consumable goods. Money not yet being in existence, the exchange in this primeval marketplace is barter.

In the week after this transaction has taken place, the capitalist sits in the house built with his own hands and engages in the leisure-work that his hiring of a workman or laborer enables him to devote all his free time to. He toils not for a single hour. All the labor involved in producing the needed consumable goods are the work of another. His contribution to the wealth produced comes solely from the capital that, being his, he puts into the productive process instead of allowing it to lie idle.

At the end of the week, he gives the laborer his share of the total wealth that results from the productive power of labor and capital together—the wage-payment the capitalist and the laborer agreed upon at the start. Everything that went into that process is owned by the capitalist except the laborer and his labor power. The latter being a free laborer, not a chattel-slave, he owns himself and also his labor power. The capitalist does not own that labor power. He has merely rented it for a time and paid for it by the wages given the laborer.

Does the capitalist rightfully own all the wealth produced that week except for the portion of it paid out in wages to the laborer? The affirmative answer that Locke gives, and which I think should be accepted, means that wealth can rightly be acquired as private property by an individual who does no work for it. He can rightfully appropriate it because he rightfully owns the capital that he is willing to put to productive use by hiring a laborer to make use of it.

In this more complicated case, his rightful acquisition of wealth does not involve mixing his own labor with the raw materials to be found in the common. Instead, it involves mixing with the rented labor power of another person the capital that he has previously appropriated rightfully by his own labor power.

Let me postpone until later the complications that arise when the capital does not consist solely of agricultural land, beasts of burden, and simple hand tools, and when the capital involved is not privately possessed by the capitalist as a result of his own labor. A number of important points remain to be considered first. They emerge from the simpler model that we have just examined.

One is the distinction between two kinds of property—property in the form of wealth to be consumed and property that is used to produce wealth. The same piece of property may be either. The house that an individual owns is consumable wealth if lived in by its owner. It is income-producing property if rented or sold to another. Only some forms of property can be used either for consumption or to produce income. Most forms of capital are exclusively income producing.

A second point follows close on the first. Just as a given piece of property may be only consumable wealth or only income-producing capital, or may be used by different persons or at different times by the same person as one or the other, so an individual may engage in the production of wealth solely as a laborer or solely as a capitalist, and may at the same time or at different times be both a capitalist and laborer. Which an individual is depends upon the source from which his income is derived—from the use of his labor power alone, from the productive use of his capital, or from both at the same time or at different times.

Still another point reflects back on matters already considered. The fact that wealth can be earned and become the property of the capitalist who does no work as well as by the laborer who does shows, as clearly as one might wish, that labor and capital are quite distinct and separate factors in the production of wealth. If that were not the case, they could not be separately owned by the capitalist who does no work but puts his capital to work and by the laborer who works by using the labor power that is his.

Anyone who does not accept Locke's answer to the question about the capitalist's appropriation of all the wealth left from the week's productive efforts, after the laborer has been paid the wages agreed upon, must defend the opposite answer—that the capitalist's appropriation, being unearned, is theft.

I cannot pass on without venturing to say that the distinction between earned and unearned income under our present income tax law would appear to identify earned income entirely with the wages of labor and unearned income with the profits accruing to capital. As we saw earlier, Locke thought that the nonworking capitalist who put his capital to work earned income from doing so.

Still another point deserves our attention. The simple model presented by Locke pictured a barter transaction between the capitalist and the laborer in which the wage-payment to the laborer took the form of consumable goods. After that wage-payment to the laborer, the rest of the wealth produced became the income of the capitalist, also in the form of consumable goods. Money as an instrument of exchange has not yet entered the picture.

When money enters the picture, many things change. First of all, money facilitates the exchange of commodities and other forms of wealth. Second, the wages paid to labor and the income derived by the capitalist from the productive use of his capital cease to be in some form of real wealth and take the form of its economic equivalent—money. This economic equivalent can also be regarded as property, as an earned possession.

The money people place in banks, in boxes, or under the bed is their private property as much as the food they eat or the physical capital they own. When the money they have in banks earns interest for them, it is income-producing property, just as the physical capital they own outright or own shares of is income-producing property. The financial capital they own is not income producing if they keep it in boxes or put it under the bed.

The introduction of money also changes Locke's simple picture when we face the question whether there are any limits to the rightful acquisition of private property, appropriated by the productive use of labor power, of capital, or both.

Staying within the confines of his primeval models, Locke sets three limits to the rightful acquisition of property.

One is that no more wealth should be acquired than can be consumed or used for daily needs. A second is that if more than what is needed on a day to day basis is accumulated and stored away for future consumption, it should be limited to an amount that does not spoil or perish before it is put to use. Locke's third limitation required the appropriator to consider the needs of others. What an individual takes out of the common should leave enough untouched for others to appropriate for their needs.

All three of these limitations are set aside by the introduction of money, either coined metal or its paper equivalent. Not being con-

sumable wealth, the accumulation of it cannot be limited by reference to need for the means of subsistence. Nor can it be limited by
reference to wastage and spoilage. And since money can be multi-
plied beyond a fixed limit, as the natural resources to be found in
the common cannot be, Locke's third limitation does not appear to
apply to money as it does to natural resources, even with an ever-
increasing population on earth.

Aristotle before Locke had distinguished natural wealth-getting,
which acquires consumable goods and other forms of real wealth,
from artificial wealth-getting, which acquires only the monetary
equivalent of real wealth.

When individuals or families engage in natural wealth-getting, their
acquisition cannot avoid being subject to the limitations of need and
spoilage or waste. In a barter economy, no one would produce shoes
in excess of need except to exchange them for other goods that are
in short supply.

But when anyone engages in artificial wealth-getting, there is no
such limitation on the amount of money he can try to accumulate.
He can lend the money he has, in excess of what he must use to
purchase things he needs, to make more money in the form of interest on the money loaned. He can use his excess money to buy
commodities and other forms of wealth in order to make more money
by selling them at a profit.

Aristotle and Marx disagree about the criteria that determine a
fair exchange in the marketplace. Marx's labor theory of value
maintains that a fair exchange is one in which commodities of equal
value are exchanged, their respective values being determined solely
by the amount of labor that went into their production. It makes
no difference whether the exchange occurs through bartering or
through the use of money.

Aristotle, on the other hand, in a passage that Marx confesses to
having read, first formulates the principle of fair exchange as involving an exchange of equal values determined by the amount of
labor employed in the production of the things exchanged. He then
dismisses this principle as untenable. He substitutes for it the op-

eration of supply and demand in the exchange of goods under the conditions of a free market.

Having mentioned Marx in this context, I cannot refrain from calling attention to his disagreement with Locke as well as with Aristotle. Locke's position leads to the view that the private ownership of capital, of the instruments of production, can be justified, either by the labor of the individuals who appropriated them, by the purchase of them in the marketplace, or by inheritance from those who have acquired them by labor or purchase. Marx maintains that this view holds true only of hand tools, relatively small parcels of land cultivated by an individual or a family, and a few domesticated animals similarly employed.

In his view, the power-driven machinery of modern industrial capital differs in two significant respects. Hand tools can be made by individuals and used by them to produce wealth; therefore, they can be rightfully owned by the individuals who make and use them, and so can the wealth produced by their use. But, according to Marx, modern industrial capital is socially produced and socially used. The whole of human society, both past and present, has contributed to its production. An organized labor force must be employed to put it to use.

Therefore, it must be socially or collectively owned—owned by the state. It cannot rightfully be owned as the private property of individuals, families, and other associations that are private not public enterprises.

Whether Marx is right or wrong about this ultimately turns on one critical point. The contributions made by society as a whole to the production of modern industrial machinery consist in all of mankind's inventions or discoveries from the wheel and pulley and other simple devices in antiquity down to the intricate devices that result from scientific discoveries and their applications in technology.

Let it be granted that none of these contributions is paid for by a modern industrial capitalist. He only pays the inventor who makes use of them in projecting the technological innovation he contracts to sell for a fee, a royalty, or both. Can the purchaser of this new capital instrument rightfully own it without having paid for everything that went into its production? Is there some measure of unearned ownership or stolen property here?

The answer turns on the limited time within which inventions or innovations can be patented or copyrighted. When patents and copyrights run out, the things that they protect return to the public domain and can be appropriated by anyone with the enterprise to do so. The public domain, like the common, is open to such rightful appropriation by anyone. The point just made applies to discoveries, inventions, and innovations that were made before any individual paid for them or could patent them. They are all in the public domain, just as are the paid for and patented inventions when the patent runs out.

The matters we have so far considered are not the only matters that raise questions of economic justice with regard to the production, exchange, distribution, and ownership of wealth. The matters we shall next consider raise further questions of the same sort.

The Wealth of Societies: Different Economies Compared

The first distinction that must be made between different economies is one that turns on the way in which they produce wealth for the society in which the economy operates, whether the society is a tribe or village, a city-state or a nation-state.

To begin with, we have an economy that is labor-intensive. The amount of wealth it is able to produce depends largely on the number of individuals employed in labor, and only slightly on all the other, or capital, factors put to use.

Let us consider two labor-intensive economies, calling one Economy Alpha and the other Economy Beta. In Economy Alpha, the labor force is double the quantity of the labor force in Economy Beta. All other things being equal, Economy Alpha will produce more wealth for its society than Economy Beta.

While both are still labor-intensive economies, Economy Alpha may depend almost wholly on its labor force, while Economy Beta may employ a labor force that uses efficient hand tools and is also aided by powerful beasts of burden, neither of which are present in Economy Alpha. Now, if their labor forces are equal in number, Economy Beta will be more productive; and this may also be the case even if Economy Beta employs a smaller labor force than Economy Alpha.

Economy Alpha can, however, overcome the superiority of Economy Beta by doubling or tripling its work force. With much more labor at work, Economy Alpha can produce as much wealth as Economy Beta, even though it lacks the better hand tools used in Economy Beta and also the domesticated animals.

Economy Alpha remains a labor-intensive economy and Economy Beta becomes a capital-intensive economy under the following conditions. Economy Alpha produces all its wealth by the work of its labor force, augmented by the effectiveness of its hand tools and labor's skill in using them, as well as by the work done by domesticated animals. In sharp contrast, Economy Beta produces most of its wealth by power-driven machinery, tended by a labor force that has less skill than those still engaged in the use of hand tools.

Because the major portion of its wealth is produced by industrial capital in the form of power-driven machinery in factories and by the power-driven machinery of mechanized agriculture, Economy Beta is a capital-intensive economy. It can produce more wealth than Economy Alpha even if the labor force of the latter is many times larger.

In fact, the difference in productiveness between labor-intensive Alpha and capital-intensive Beta can become so great (with technological advances and innovations) that no feasible increase in the labor force of Alpha and no augmentation of it by hand tools, increase of skill, or the use of animals as powerful and skillful as elephants, will be able to overcome the difference between them.

Comparing economies in this way raises an important question that I wish to submit to readers for their consideration, without trying to answer it myself. Here it is: Does the employment of capital in any form by an economy only increase the productiveness of its labor force, or does it increase the productiveness of the economy as a whole without increasing the productiveness of its labor force, or does it do both? If the latter, in what proportion does it do each?

Whatever answer one gives to this question determines the share of the wealth produced by the economy that should rightfully go to the owners of labor power who work to produce wealth and to the owners of capital who put it to use in the production of wealth. The underlying principle here can be stated as follows: Each of the two factors in the production of wealth should receive a share of the wealth produced equal to the degree of its contribution to the production of the society's wealth. If capital contributes nothing, it should receive nothing; if capital contributes more than labor, it should receive more in the aggregate than labor; if less, less.

Let us now consider only capital-intensive economies. The economies of all technologically advanced, industrialized societies with mechanized agriculture are capital-intensive. In that respect, considering only how wealth is produced, not how the capital instruments are owned and operated, all such economies can be called forms of capitalism.

That name applies to socialist and even communist economies as well as to the most extreme form of free-enterprise, private ownership, laissez-faire economy. The differentiation among all forms of capitalism, so-called because they are all capital-intensive economies, is to be made in terms of how the capital instruments are owned and how they are controlled and operated.

Without regard to the ownership and operation of the capital involved, capital-intensive economies can be differentiated in another respect. As a result of the extraordinary technological advances made in this century, a capital-intensive economy may be one in which the system of production is highly flexible and, therefore, easily changeable; and also one that involves high degrees of skill in its work force, with its efficiency augmented by the planned cooperation of all its members from the top management down. Or it may be a capital-intensive economy of an older type, developed in the era prior to recent technological innovations. It will then be a high-volume, standardized system of production of the assembly line va-

riety, with much less skill in its work force, and little or no cooperation among its members from the top management down.

There would appear to be four quite different forms of capitalism
(capital-intensive economies) to which names have been applied that
instantly indicate their character.

Of these four forms, the first predominated exclusively throughout the nineteenth century, persisted in existence in the first decades of this century, and is now rapidly disappearing. It has become
nonexistent in all the technologically advanced industrial and post-
industrial economies, and remains only in relatively undeveloped or
slowly developing economies.

What Marx called bourgeois capitalism, and can just as readily
be called nineteenth-century capitalism, is the form that antedates
the three other forms of capital-intensive economies. In this form
of capitalism a relatively small portion of the population, less than
one-tenth, privately owns all its capital, operates it for the sake of
maximizing profits, and is able to do so because its operations are
an extreme form of unregulated free enterprise.

In such an economy, a chasm separates the few very rich, who
are the capitalists, and the many very poor who are the proletariat.
Their only income consists in the wages of labor which, prior to the
emergence of labor unions, the laborers must sell in the labor market at whatever price the capitalists are willing to pay. The capitalists cannot, of course, pay less than bare subsistence wages, enough
for laborers just to stay alive and replenish the labor force by re-
production. They are seldom compelled to pay more, except by un-
usual circumstances of short supply and great demand.

From bourgeois capitalism emerged two other forms of capitalism in the twentieth century. Both innovations were motivated by
the misery of the laboring class under bourgeois capitalism and by
a correct sense of the economic injustice done—the serious deprivations suffered by the working class, unable to earn by their work
what anyone needs to live a decent human life.

These two new forms of capitalism appeared more or less simul-
taneously in the second and third decades of this century. The one

that emerged in England and the dominions of the British Commonwealth, in the United States, and in the Scandinavian countries and the Netherlands, to name only some outstanding examples of one of these two new forms, can be called mixed economies, because they have both a private and a public sector so far as the ownership and operation of capital is concerned.

This new form can also be called socialized capitalism, because free enterprise is so regulated that labor is paid a living wage, more than what is needed for bare subsistence. These increased wages go part way toward providing the conditions for a decent human life. They are augmented by a wide variety of welfare payments and by government intervention in the fields of education, health care, recreation, and so on.

The other emergent form of capitalism first saw the light of day with the communist revolution in tsarist Russia and then spread far and wide to the satellites, wards, and progeny of the Soviet Union.

Communist economies are all capital-intensive. It is extremely difficult for a labor-intensive economy to adopt communism or to do so without making every effort to change into a capital-intensive economy as rapidly as possible.

That, in fact, was what had to happen in Russia's transition to a communist economy. Tsarist Russia was neither technologically advanced nor highly industrialized. Communism has prospered in the Soviet Union only to the extent it has succeeded in becoming more and more a capital-intensive economy with more and more mechanized agriculture. The same holds true for communist China.

To call a communist economy a form of capitalism because it is or must become capital-intensive amounts to calling it state capitalism. All of the major forms of capital are owned and operated by the state. The private ownership of capital is negligible. No private corporations or associations exist, not even labor unions. The economy is state controlled. There is little or no free enterprise in its operation. The unequal distribution of the wealth thus produced is determined entirely by government.

State capitalism is also a form of socialism. Like the mixed economies that are forms of socialized capitalism, state capitalism seeks, in principle at least, to see that all individuals and families participate in the general economic welfare. It has not so far achieved for its people a standard of living that compares favorably with the standards of living achieved by the mixed economies. In both types of economy, the standard of living enjoyed by the people is affected by the conflict between guns and butter—by the size of government expenditures for destructive military establishments, relative to the amount that is left for the economic welfare of the people.

When I call communist economies and mixed economies forms of socialism, I have in mind the distinction between socialism and communism. An economy is socialist if it has the economic welfare of all its people as its end, regardless of the means it adopts to achieve that end. The mixed economy is socialist in aim without abolishing the private ownership and operation of capital and by retaining free enterprise under more or less government regulation. The means it employs thus differ from the means employed by communism, which abolishes the private ownership and operation of capital, transferring both to the state.

The fourth and last form of capitalism, more recently emergent and not yet fully in existence, is also socialist in aim, but it is not communist because it employs means that include the private ownership of capital, private corporations, and free enterprise regulated to a certain extent.

It also differs from the mixed economy by seeking to enlarge the private sector of the economy and reduce the public sector as far as possible. While in this respect it resembles bourgeois capitalism, it differs radically from it. The private ownership of capital under bourgeois capitalism was in the hands of the very few. In contradistinction, universal capitalism, as its name implies, seeks to achieve the aims of socialism by approaching, as a limit, the private ownership of capital by all members of the population. Most of them would derive their income from the wages of labor and from the profits of capital. Comparatively few, at either extreme, would support themselves solely by the wages of labor or solely by the returns from income-producing property.

Some slight approach to universal capitalism now exists in the

United States, to the extent that a larger and larger number of individuals or families derive their income from two sources: (1) the wages or salaries of employed labor and (2) the returns received from the profits made by the capital in which they own equity shares, together with the interest they receive on money saved in bank accounts, and the returns from the pension trusts in which they participate.

Whether universal capitalism can be enlarged in scope and can flourish as an economy remains to be seen. There are those who think not only that it can, but also that it must, in order for the production of wealth to be increased and for it to be earned and distributed in as just a manner as possible.

All three of the capital-intensive economies that I have classed together as being socialist in their aims (of which only one is communist with regard to means) try to embody two principles of economic justice.

All three, in varying degrees, try to secure the basic economic rights of every individual by seeing that they possess, through the incomes they earn and the goods or benefits they receive through social welfare, the wealth that any human being needs to lead a decent human life. So far as that minimum amount of wealth is concerned, these three capitalist economies try to establish an equality of economic conditions.

Beyond that, however, all three distribute wealth unequally according to the principle *to each according to his contribution,* waiving for the moment the question of how the degree of contribution is determined and by whom.

The principle just mentioned is subordinate to the principle already stated, which was *to all according to their common human needs,* the basic minimum of wealth that anyone and everyone needs to lead a decent human life, to which all human beings have a natural right.

These two principles of justice, operating together, bring into existence a nonegalitarian socialism—a society that has established an equality of economic conditions according to the first principle, and an inequality of incomes according to the second.

Only the earliest form of capitalism was nonsocialistic. There a wide gulf of unequal conditions separated the few capital-owning rich from the vast multitude of the laboring class. There neither of the two principles of justice were in operation for most human beings.

For the substantial and serious injustices it inflicted, that early form of capitalism deserved the extinction it suffered, when economic reforms transformed it into one or another of the other three types of capitalism.

QUOTATIONS WITHOUT COMMENT

With Regard to Wealth and Other External Goods

He who possesses great store of riches is no nearer happiness than he who has what suffices for his daily needs, unless it so hap that luck attend upon him, and so he continue in the enjoyment of all his good things to the end of life.

> Solon, the Greek wise man, as quoted in Herodotus,
> *History*, Bk. I, Sec. 32 (5th cent. B.C.)

★ ★ ★

Riches are for the sake of the body, as the body is for the sake of the soul. The latter are good, and wealth is intended by nature to be for the sake of them, and is therefore inferior to them both, and third in the order of excellence.

> Plato, *Laws*, Bk. IX (5th cent. B.C.)

★ ★ ★

. . . All men think that the happy life is pleasant and weave pleasure into their ideal of happiness—and reasonably too; for no activity is perfect when it is impeded, and happiness is a perfect thing; this is why the happy man needs the goods of the body and external goods, i.e. those of fortune, viz. in order that he may not be impeded in these ways.

> Aristotle, *Nichomachean Ethics*, Bk. VII, Ch. 13
> (4th cent. B.C.)

★ ★ ★

Men seek after a better notion of riches and of the art of getting wealth than the mere acquisition of coin, and they are right. For natural riches and the natural art of wealth-getting are a different thing; in their true form they are part of the management of a household; whereas retail trade is the art of producing wealth, not in every way, but by exchange. And it is thought to be concerned with coin; for coin is the unit of exchange and the measure or limit of it. And there is no bound to the riches which spring from this art of wealth-getting. . . . The art of wealth-getting which consists in household management, on the other hand, has a limit; the unlimited acquisition of wealth is not its business. And, therefore, in one point of view, all riches must have a limit; nevertheless, as a matter of fact, we find the opposite to be the case; for all getters of wealth increase their hoard of coin without limit. The source of the confusion is the near connexion between the two kinds of wealth-getting; in either, the instrument is the same, although the use is different, and so they pass into one another; for each is a use of the same property, but with a difference: accumulation is the end in the one case, but there is a further end in the other. Hence some persons are led to believe that getting wealth is the object of household management, and the whole idea of their lives is that they ought either to increase their money without limit, or at any rate not to lose it. The origin of this disposition in men is that they are intent upon living only, and not upon living well; and, as their desires are unlimited, they also desire that the means of gratifying them should be without limit.

Aristotle, *Politics*, Bk. I, Ch. 9 (4th cent. B.C.)

*   *   *

It is not the man who has too little who is poor, but the one who hankers after more. What difference does it make how much there is laid away in a man's safe or in his barns, how many head of stock he grazes or how much capital he puts out at interest, if he is always after what is another's and only counts what he has yet to get, never what he has already. You ask what is the proper limit to a person's wealth? First, having what is essential, and second, having what is enough.

Lucius Annacus Seneca, *Letters to Lucilius*, 2 (63–65 A.D.)

*   *   *

. . . It is impossible for man's happiness to consist in wealth. For wealth is two-fold . . . natural and artificial. Natural wealth is that which serves man as a remedy for his natural wants, such as food, drink, clothing, conveyances, dwellings, and things of this kind, while artificial wealth is that which is not a direct help to nature, as money, but is invented by the art of man for the convenience of exchange and as a measure of things saleable.

Now it is evident that man's happiness cannot consist in natural wealth. For wealth of this kind is sought as a support of human nature; consequently it cannot be man's last end, but rather is ordered to man as to its end. Therefore in the order of nature, all such things are below man, and made for him. . . .

And as to artificial wealth, it is not sought save for the sake of natural wealth, since man would not seek it except that by its means he procures for himself the necessaries of life. Consequently much less does it have the character of the last end. Therefore it is impossible for happiness, which is the last end of man, to consist in wealth.

Thomas Aquinas, *Summa Theologica*, Pt. I–II, Q. 2, A. 1
(c. 1265)

★ ★ ★

Since it is plainly contrary to the law of nature . . . that the privileged few should gorge themselves with superfluities while the starving multitude are in want of the bare necessities of life . . . [it is] one of the most important functions of government to prevent extreme inequalities of fortunes; not by taking away wealth from its possessors, but by depriving all men of means to accumulate it: not by building asylums for the poor, but by securing the citizens from becoming poor.

Jean-Jacques Rousseau, *Political Economy* (1755)

★ ★ ★

I am indeed rich, since my income is superior to my expense, and my expense is equal to my wishes.

Edward Gibbon, *Autobiography* (c. 1789)

*   *   *

The World is Too Much With Us

The World is too much with us; late and soon,
Getting and spending, we lay waste our powers;
Little we see in Nature that is ours;
We have given our hearts away, a sordid boon!
This Sea that bares her bosom to the moon,
The winds that will be howling at all hours
And are up-gather'd now like sleeping flowers,
For this, for every thing, we are out of tune;
It moves us not.—Great God! I'd rather be
A Pagan suckled in a creed outworn,—
So might I, standing on this pleasant lea,
Have glimpses that would make me less forlorn;
Have sight of Proteus rising from the sea;
Or hear old Triton blow his wreathéd horn.

William Wordsworth, *Poems in Two Volumes*
(1807)

*   *   *

It is essential to the idea of wealth to be susceptible of accumulation: things which cannot, after being produced, be kept for some time before being used, are never, I think, regarded as wealth, since however much of them may be produced and enjoyed, the person benefited by them is no richer, is nowise improved in circumstances.

John Stuart Mill, *Principles of Political Economy*, Bk. I,
Ch. III, Sec. 3 (1848)

*   *   *

It is difficult, if not impossible, to define the limits which reason should impose on the desire for wealth; for there is no absolute or definite amount of wealth which will satisfy a man. The amount is always relative, that is to say, just so much as will maintain the proportion between what he wants and what he gets; for to measure a man's happiness only by what he gets, and not also by what he expects to get, is as futile as to try to express a fraction which shall have a numerator but no denominator. A man never feels the loss of things which it never occurs to him to ask for; he is just as happy without them; whilst another, who may have a hundred times as much, feels miserable because he has not got the one thing he wants. In fact, here too, every man has a horizon of his own, and he will expect as much as he thinks it is possible for him to get.

Arthur Schopenhauer, *Essays: Property* (c. 1851)

With Regard to Property

Though the earth and all inferior creatures be common to all men, yet every man has a "property" in his own "person." This nobody has any right to but himself. The "labour" of his body and the "work" of his hands, we may say, are properly his. Whatsoever, then, he removes out of the state that Nature hath provided and left it in, he hath mixed his labour with it, and joined to it something that is his own, and thereby makes it his property. It being by him removed from the common state Nature placed it in, it hath by this labour something annexed to it that excludes the common right of other men. For this "labour" being the unquestionable property of the labourer, no man but he can have a right to what that is once joined to, at least where there is enough, and as good left in common for others.

He that is nourished by the acorns he picked up under an oak, or the apples he gathered from the trees in the wood, has certainly appropriated them to himself. Nobody can deny but the nourishment is his. I ask, then, when did they begin to be his? when he digested? or when he ate? or when he boiled? or when he brought them home? or when he picked them up? And it is plain, if the first gathering made them not his, nothing else could. That labour put a distinction between them and common. That added something to them more than Nature, the common mother of all, had done, and so they became his private right. And will anyone say he had no right to those acorns or apples he thus appropriated because he had not the consent of all mankind to make them his? Was it a robbery thus to assume to himself what belonged to all in common? If such a consent as that was necessary, man had starved, notwithstanding the plenty God had given him. We see in commons, which remain so by compact, that it is the taking any part of what is common, and removing it out of the state Nature leaves it in, which begins the property, without which the common is of no use. And the taking of this or that part does not depend on the express consent of all the commoners. Thus, the grass my horse has bit, the turfs my servant has cut, and the ore I have digged in any place, where I have a right to them in common with others, become my property without the assignation or consent of anybody. The labour that was mine, removing them out of that common state they were in, hath fixed my property in them.

John Locke, *Second Essay on Civil Government*, Ch. V, Secs. 26–27 (1690)

★   ★   ★

The measure of property Nature well set, by the extent of men's labour and the conveniency of life. No man's labour could subdue or appropriate all, nor could his enjoyment consume more than a small part; so that it was impossible for any man, this way, to entrench upon the right of another or acquire to himself a property to the prejudice of his neighbour, who would still have room for as good and as large a possession (after the other had taken out his) as before it was appropriated. Which measure did confine every man's possession to a very moderate proportion, and such as he might appropriate to himself without injury to anybody in the first ages of the world, when men were more in danger to be lost, by wandering from their company, in the then vast wilderness of the earth than to be straitened for want of room to plant in.

John Locke, *Second Essay on Civil Government*, Ch. V, Sec. 35 (1690)

★   ★   ★

This I dare boldly affirm . . . every man should have as much as he could make use of, would hold still in the world, without straitening anybody, since there is land enough in the world to suffice double the inhabitants, had not the invention of money, and the tacit agreement of men to put a value on it, introduced (by consent) larger possessions and a right to them.

John Locke, *Second Essay on Civil Government*, Ch. V, Sec. 36 (1690)

★   ★   ★

Nothing is implied in property but the right of each to his (or her) own faculties, to what he can produce by them, and to whatever he can get for them in a fair market; together with his right to give this to any other person if he chooses, and the right of that other to receive and enjoy it.

John Stuart Mill, *Principles of Political Economy*, Bk. II, Ch. II, Sec. 3 (1848)

With Regard to Money

All things that are exchanged must be somehow comparable. It is for this end that money has been introduced, and it becomes in a sense an intermediate; for it measures all things.

Aristotle, *Nichomachean Ethics*, Bk. V, Ch. 5 (4th cent. B.C.)

★   ★   ★

Money is not, properly speaking, one of the subjects of commerce; but only the instrument which men have agreed upon to facilitate the exchange of one commodity for another. It is none of the wheels of trade: It is the oil which renders the motion of the wheels more smooth and easy.

David Hume, *Essays Moral, Political, and Literary: Of Money*
(1741–42)

★   ★   ★

. . . In the beginning, all the world was America, and more so than that is now; for no such thing as money was anywhere known. Find out something that hath the use and value of money amongst his neighbours, you shall see the same man will begin presently to enlarge his possessions.

John Locke, *Second Essay on Civil Government*, Ch. V,
Sec. 49 (1690)

★   ★   ★

. . . Since gold and silver, being little useful to the life of man, in proportion to food, raiment, and carriage, has its value only from the consent of men—whereof labour yet makes in great part the measure—it is plain that the consent of men have agreed to a disproportionate and unequal possession of the earth—I mean out of the bounds of society and compact; for in governments the laws regulate it; they having, by consent, found out and agreed in a way how a man may, rightfully and without injury, possess more than he himself can make use of by receiving gold and silver, which may continue long in a man's possession without decaying for the overplus, and agreeing those metals should have a value.

John Locke, *Second Essay on Civil Government*, Ch. V,
Sec. 50 (1690)

★   ★   ★

Wealth does not consist in money, or in gold or silver; but what money purchases, and is valuable only for purchasing. . . . Goods can serve many other purposes besides purchasing money, but money can serve no other purpose besides purchasing goods. Money, therefore, necessarily runs after goods, but goods do not always or necessarily run after money. The man who buys does not always mean to sell again, but frequently to use or consume; whereas he who sells always means to buy again. . . . [That] wealth consists in money, or in gold and silver, is a popular notion which naturally arises from the double function of money, as the instrument of commerce, and as the measure of value.

Adam Smith, *The Wealth of Nations*, Bk. IV, Ch. 1 (1776)

* * *

In exchanging the complete manufacture either for money, for labor, or for other goods, over and above what may be sufficient to pay the price of the materials, and the wages of the workmen, something must be given for the profits of the undertaker of the work who hazards his stock in this adventure. The value which the workmen add to the materials, therefore, resolves itself in this case into two parts, of which the one pays their wages, the other the profits of their employer upon the whole stock of materials and wages which he advanced. He could have no interest to employ them, unless he expected from the sale of their work something more than what was sufficient to replace his stock to him; and he could have no interest to employ a great stock rather than a small one, unless his profits were to bear some proportion to the extent of his stock.

Adam Smith, *The Wealth of Nations*, Bk. I, Ch. 6 (1776)

* * *

There cannot . . . be intrinsically a more insignificant thing, in the economy of society, than money; except in the character of a contrivance for sparing time and labour. It is a machine for doing quickly and commodiously, what would be done, though less quickly and commodiously, without it: and like many other kinds of machinery, it only exerts a distinct and independent influence of its own when it gets out of order.

John Stuart Mill, *Principles of Political Economy*, Bk. III, Ch. VII, Sec. 3 (1848)

* * *

. . . The value of money, other things being the same, varies inversely as its quantity; every increase of quantity lowering the value, and every diminution raising it, in a ratio exactly equivalent. This, it must be observed, is a property peculiar to money.

John Stuart Mill, *Principles of Political Economy*, Bk. III, Ch. VIII, Sec. 2 (1848)

With Regard to Labor and Capital

That the annual produce of the land and labor of a country can only be increased in two ways—by some improvement in the productive powers of the useful labor which actually exists within it, or by some increase in the quantity of such labor. That, with regard to the first, the labor of artificers being capable of greater subdivision and simplicity of operation than that of cultivators, it is susceptible, in a proportionably greater degree, of improvement in its productive powers, whether to be derived from an accession of skill or from the application of ingenious machinery: in which particular, therefore, the labor employed in the culture of land can pretend to no advantage over that engaged in manufactures. That, with regard to an augmentation of the quantity of useful labor, this, excluding adventitious circumstances, must depend essentially upon an increase of capital, which again must depend upon the savings made out of the revenues of those who furnish or manage that which is at any time employed, whether in agriculture or in manufactures, or in any other way. . . .

The employment of machinery forms an item of great importance in the general mass of national industry. It is an artificial force brought in aid of the natural force of man; and, to all the purposes of labor, is an increase of hands—an accession of strength, unencumbered, too, by the expense of maintaining the laborer. May it not, therefore, be fairly inferred that those occupations which give greatest scope to the use of this auxiliary contribute most to the general stock of industrious effort and, in consequence, to the general product of industry? . . .

The cotton mill, invented in England within the last twenty years, is a signal illustration of the general proposition which has just been advanced. In consequence of it, all the different processes for spinning cotton are performed by means of machines which are put in motion by water, and attended chiefly by women and children; and by a smaller number of persons, in the whole, than are requisite in the ordinary mode of spinning. And it is an advantage of great moment that the operations of this mill continue, with convenience, during the night as well as through the day. The prodigious effect of such a machine is easily conceived. To this invention is to be attributed, essentially, the immense progress which has been so suddenly made in Great Britain in the various fabrics of cotton. . . .

Besides this advantage of occasional employment to classes having different occupations, there is another, of a nature allied to it, and of a similar tendency. This is the employment of persons who would otherwise be idle and, in many cases, a burden on the community, either from the bias of temper, habit, infirmity of body, or some other cause, indisposing or disqualifying them for the toils of the country. It is worthy of particular remark that, in general, women and children are rendered more useful, and the latter more early useful, by manufacturing establishments, than they would otherwise be. Of the number of persons employed in the cotton manufactories of Great Britain, it is computed that four-sevenths, nearly, are women and children; of whom the greatest proportion are children, and many of them of a tender age.

Alexander Hamilton, *Reports of the Secretary of the Treasury of the United States: On Manufactures* (Dec. 1791)

★   ★   ★

We, the journeymen mechanics of the city and county of Philadelphia, conscious that our condition in society is lower than justice demands it should be, and feeling our inability, individually, to ward off from ourselves and families those numerous evils which result from an unequal and very excessive accumulation of wealth and power into the hands of a few, are desirous of forming an association which shall avert as much as possible those evils which poverty and incessant toil have already inflicted, and which threaten ultimately to overwhelm and destroy us. . . .

If unceasing toils were actually requisite to supply us with a bare, and in many instances wretched, subsistence; if the products of our industry, or an equitable proportion of them, were appropriated to our actual wants and comfort, then would we yield without a murmur to the stern and irrevocable decree of necessity. But this is infinitely wide of the fact. We appeal to the most intelligent of every community and ask—Do not you, and all society, depend solely for subsistence on the products of human industry? Do not those who labor, while acquiring to themselves thereby only a scanty and penurious support, likewise maintain in affluence and luxury the rich who never labor?

Do not all the streams of wealth which flow in every direction and are emptied into and absorbed by the coffers of the unproductive, exclusively take their rise in the bones, marrow, and muscles of the industrious classes? In return for which, exclusive of a bare subsistence (which likewise is the product of their own industry), they receive—not anything!

Is it just? Is it equitable that we should waste the energies of our minds and bodies, and be placed in a situation of such unceasing exertion and servility as must necessarily, in time, render the benefits of our liberal institutions to us inaccessible and useless, in order that the products of our labor may be accumulated by a few into vast pernicious masses, calculated to prepare the minds of the possessors for the exercise of lawless rule and despotism, to overawe the meager multitude, and fright away that shadow of freedom which still lingers among us? Are we who confer almost every blessing on society never to be treated as freemen and equals and never be accounted worthy of an equivalent, in return for the products of our industry? . . . No! at the present period, when wealth is so easily and abundantly created that the markets of the world are overflowing with it, and when, in consequence thereof, and of the

continual development and increase of scientific power, the demand
for human labor is gradually and inevitably diminishing, it cannot
be necessary that we, or any portion of society, should be subjected
to perpetual slavery. . . .

No greater error exists in the world than the notion that society
will be benefited by deprecating [sic] the value of human labor. Let
this principle (as at this day in England) be carried towards its full
extent, and it is in vain that scientific power shall pour forth its
inexhaustible treasures of wealth upon the world. Its products will
all be amassed to glut the overflowing storehouses and useless hoards
of its insatiable monopolizers, while the mechanic and productive
classes, who constitute the great mass of the population, and who
have wielded the power and labored in the production of this immense abundance, having no other resource for subsistence than what
they derive from the miserable pittance, which they are compelled
by competition to receive in exchange for their inestimable labor,
must first begin to pine, languish, and suffer under its destructive
and withering influence.

Preamble of the Mechanics' Union of Trade Associations (1827)

★   ★   ★

The distinguishing feature of Communism is not the abolition of
property generally, but the abolition of bourgeois property [own-
ership of the means of production]. But modern bourgeois private
property is the final and most complete expression of the system of
producing and appropriating products that is based on class antag-
onisms, on the exploitation of the many by the few.

In this sense the theory of the Communists may be summed up
in the single sentence: abolition of private property.

We Communists have been reproached with the desire of abolishing the right of personally acquiring property as the fruit of a
man's own labour, which property is alleged to be the groundwork
of all personal freedom, activity and independence.

Hard-won, self-acquired, self-earned property! Do you mean the
property of the petty artisan and of the small peasant, a form of
property that preceded the bourgeois form? There is no need to

abolish that; the development of industry has to a great extent already destroyed it and is still destroying it daily. . . .

You are horrified at our intending to do away with private property [i.e., private ownership of the means of production]. But in your existing society private property is already done away with for nine-tenths of the population; its existence for the few is solely due to its non-existence in the hands of those nine-tenths. You reproach us, therefore, with intending to do away with a form of property, the necessary condition for whose existence is the non-existence of any property for the immense majority of society.

In a word, you reproach us with intending to do away with your property. Precisely so; that is just what we intend.

Karl Marx and Friedrich Engels, *The Communist Manifesto*
Ch. II (1848)

* * *

At first the rights of property seemed to us to be based on a man's own labour. At least, some such assumption was necessary since only commodity owners with equal rights confronted each other, and the sole means by which a man could become possessed of the commodities of others was by alienating his own commodities; and these could be replaced by labour alone. Now, however, property turns out to be the right, on the part of the capitalist, to appropriate the unpaid labour of others or its product, and to be the impossibility, on the part of the labourer, of appropriating his own product. The separation of property from labour has become the necessary consequence of a law that apparently originated in their identity.

Karl Marx, *Das Kapital*, Vol. I, Ch. VII, 24 (1867)

* * *

Labor is prior to, and independent of, capital. Capital is only the fruit of labor, and could never have existed if labor had not first existed. Labor is the superior of capital, and deserves much the higher consideration. Capital has its rights, which are as worthy of protection as any other rights. Nor is it denied that there is, and probably always will be, a relation between labor and capital, producing mutual benefits. The error is in assuming that the whole labor of a community exists within that relation. A few men own capital, and that few avoid labor themselves, and, with their capital, hire or buy another few to labor for them. A large majority belong to neither class—neither work for others, nor have others working for them.

> Abraham Lincoln, *Annual Message* (Dec. 3, 1861)

★ ★ ★

It is impossible that the man with capital and the man without capital should be equal. To affirm that they are equal would be to say that a man who has no tool can get as much food out of the ground as the man who has a spade or a plough; or that the man who has no weapon can defend himself as well against hostile beasts or hostile men as the man who has a weapon. If that were so, none of us would work any more. We work and deny ourselves to get capital just because, other things being equal, the man who has it is superior, for attaining all the ends of life, to the man who has it not. . . .

It follows from what we have observed that it is the utmost folly to denounce capital. To do so is to undermine civilization, for capital is the first requisite of every social gain, educational, ecclesiastical, political, aesthetic, or other. . . .

The newest socialism is, in its method, political. The essential feature of its latest phases is the attempt to use the power of the state to realize its plans and to secure its objects. These objects are to do away with poverty and misery, and there are no socialistic schemes yet proposed, of any sort, which do not, upon analysis, turn out to be projects for curing poverty and misery by making those who have share with those who have not. . . .

It is a matter of course that a reactionary party should arise to declare that universal suffrage, popular education, machinery, free trade, and all the other innovations of the last hundred years are all a mistake. . . .

All the institutions which we have inherited were invented to guard liberty against the encroachments of a powerful monarch or aristocracy, when these classes possessed land and the possession of land was the greatest social power. Institutions must now be devised to guard civil liberty against popular majorities, and this necessity arises first in regard to the protection of property, the first and greatest function of government and element in civil liberty.

William Graham Sumner, *The Challenge of Facts and Other Essays* (1914)

CHAPTER 4 Virtue and Happiness

THE IDEAS OF WORK AND OF WEALTH belong to other disciplines as well as being objects of philosophical thought. Many think of wealth as exclusively the subject of economic science. But, as we have seen, philosophy has important things to say about it, things that deserve consideration prior to dealing with the phenomena and matters subject to scientific investigation by economists. Work is studied and discussed in schools of business and in connection with business administration as a profession. But, as we have seen, the philosophical clarification of kinds of work, especially in relation to leisure and the other parts of life, deals with more fundamental matters.

The idea of virtue and the conjoined idea of happiness are exclusively the concern of philosophy. Here, as in the case of work and wealth, the relevant branch of philosophy is moral philosophy.

Under the overarching idea of work, we dealt with all human activities and all the parts of life that use up the time of our lives. Under the overarching idea of wealth, we dealt with all the external goods that constitute human possessions and forms of property.

What important aspect of human life, its welfare and well-being, remains untouched? Virtue and the virtues, together with other human perfections, not only in themselves, but also in relation to human activities and human possessions.

We are faced with having to choose between one activity and another, with having to order and arrange the parts of life, with having to make judgments about which external goods or possessions should be pursued with moderation and within limits and which may be sought without limit. That is where virtue, especially moral virtue, comes into the picture. The role that virtue plays in relation to the making of such choices and judgments determines—in part at least—our success or failure in the pursuit of happiness, our effort to make good human lives for ourselves.

The distinction between perfections of all sorts (of body, of character, and of mind) and possessions of all sorts (economic goods, political goods, and the goods of human association) carries with it a distinction between goods that are wholly within our power to obtain and goods that may be partly within our power but never completely so. The latter in varying degrees depend on external circumstances, either favorable or unfavorable to our possessing them.

However, not all goods that are personal perfections fall entirely within our power. Like external goods, some of them are affected by external conditions.

For example, the way we manage our lives affects our being healthy and vigorous, but our being so is also critically affected by our having a healthy environment, having adequate access to medical care, and by other external conditions and opportunities. So, too, our being knowledgeable and skillful in a wide variety of ways depends upon our own efforts to think, learn, and inquire, but it also depends in varying degrees on our access to educational facilities in youth, to opportunities for continued learning after all schooling is finished, and especially on our having enough free time at our disposal to engage in leisure activities that involve learning of one sort or another.

The only personal perfection that would appear not to depend upon any external circumstances is moral virtue. Whether or not we are morally virtuous, persons of good character, would appear to be wholly within our power—a result of exercising our freedom of choice. But even here it may be true that having free time for leisure activities has some effect on our moral and spiritual growth as well as upon our mental improvement. Only in a capital-intensive economy can enough free time become open for the many as well as for the few.

The idea of happiness, which is conjoined with virtue, embraces all the other ideas considered in Part One of this book. Here it is necessary to remind readers that I am using the word "happiness" in its ethical meaning, not its psychological meaning.

When most people use the word, they have the latter meaning in mind. The word then connotes a mental state of satisfaction or contentment that consists simply in getting whatever one wants. Sometimes we *feel* happy because our wants at that moment are satisfied; sometimes we *feel* unhappy because our wants at that moment are frustrated or unfulfilled. Accordingly, we change from feeling happy to feeling unhappy from day to day, week to week, or year to year. In that meaning of the word "happiness," as the word "feel" that I have italicized above indicates, happiness and unhappiness are psychological phenomena of which we can be conscious and have experience.

Not so, when the word is used in its ethical significance. Then the word connotes something that we are never conscious of and cannot experience at all. It also connotes something that never exists at any one moment of our lives, and does not change from time to time.

In its ethical meaning, the word "happiness" stands for a whole human life well lived, a life enriched by all real goods—all the possessions a human being should have, all the perfections that a human being should attain. What makes them real, as opposed to merely apparent goods, is that they fulfill our inherent human needs, not just our individual, acquired wants. We ought to want them, whether in fact we do or not. Here again is where virtue comes into the picture, now in relation to our seeking or failing to seek the things that are really good for us.

A good life is a temporal whole. It does not exist at any one moment. It occurs with the passage of time and over a span of time. In this respect, it is like any game that human beings play.

In the middle of a football game, one should not say that it is a good game, but rather that it is becoming a good game. If it is as well played in the second half as in the first half, it will have been a good game when it is over.

The same applies to a human life. In the course of its coming to be, it can be described as on the way to becoming a good life or the opposite. Only when it is all over, can we say that it was a good life, that the individual who lived it achieved happiness.

In our consideration of the parts of life, in connection with work and leisure, we learned that a human life may be a contracted or an expanded life—a two- or three-part life, on the one hand, a four- or five-part life on the other, with the sixth part, involving necessary biological activities, common to both. Obviously the more expanded life is better than the more contracted one.

In our effort to live better rather than worse lives, the economic conditions under which we live certainly have an effect upon what types of activity we *must* and what types of activity we *can* engage in, and what opportunities we have for living expanded rather than contracted lives. But external circumstances are not the only determining factor. The other, equally important, factor is moral virtue, controlling the choices we make or do not make.

This brings us, finally, to the question whether being morally virtuous is not only necessary, but also sufficient, for the achievement of a good life. If that achievement also depends on the good fortune of living under favorable external circumstances, then the answer must be that moral virtue is only a necessary, not sufficient, condition and that the other necessary but not sufficient condition is good fortune.

That answer, given by Aristotle and by almost no other moral philosopher, is one I am compelled to adopt in the light of all the foregoing considerations. I hope my readers are also persuaded to adopt it. Adopting it leads us to see that moral virtue may make a man good, but without the addition of the external goods conferred by benign circumstances, it cannot make a life good, an expanded or happy life.

St. Augustine, in a little tract entitled *The Happy Life*, summed up matters by saying, "Happy is the man who, in the course of a complete life, attains everything he desires, *provided he desire nothing amiss.*" I have emphasized the proviso in order to point out that that is where virtue comes into the picture. Being virtuous prevents us from desiring anything amiss.

Wonderful summary that it is, it is nevertheless incomplete. Augustine should have added another proviso. He should have said, "and also provided that he has the good fortune that bestows upon him other goods which are not entirely within the power of his own free choice."

Habits, Good and Bad

Looked at one way, all habits are perfections, whether good or bad. They are improvements of the nature we come into this world with. A carpenter improves the raw materials he works with when he fashions a table out of them, even if, being a poor workman, the table he produces is an inferior one. The improvement consists in the carpenter's realizing the wood's potentialities for being shaped into the form of a table.

The human infant at birth is a cornucopia of potentialities, of diverse abilities needing development. The infant at birth cannot walk, speak, feed itself, wash itself, stand up, sit up, not to mention all the other things it cannot do then, which two to five years later it does: read, write, add, question and answer, judge, think. It may not do these very well—in fact, it may do them poorly—but actually being able to do them at all is an improvement on the raw material of undeveloped potentialities that constitute the baby at birth.

The development of a human potentiality is habit formation. Like the potentiality that it develops, the habit is also an ability. At any given moment, we have countless habits that we are not exercising by acting in one way or another. The unexercised habit is *formed* ability to act in a certain way. In contrast, the original, innate potentiality, before developed by habit formation, is an *unformed* ability to act in that way.

It is precisely this difference between two states of the same ability—the unformed state and the formed state—that explains why it can be correctly said that all habits are improvements, even perfections, whether good or bad.

Human beings are endowed at birth with the ability to speak any language, but then they can actually speak none. By early habit formation, they acquire the formed ability to speak the language of their parents and, subsequently, they may acquire the formed ability to speak another language. Two things should be noted about this. In the first place, their native linguistic ability has been improved by such habit formation, whether they have developed good or bad habits of speech. Second, the habits they have formed are still only abilities, which the habituated persons may or may not be exercising at any given moment.

Attention to these two points enables us to understand the significance of the profound truth that habit is second nature. Habits consist of potentialities for action just as original nature does; but these are acquired, not innate, potentialities; that is why they are second nature.

Of all the actions that we perform every day of our lives, most of them issue from the habits we have formed. Very few of them are acts that exercise a totally unformed native ability. Some of these are the reflex reactions with which we are born, but even these may be conditioned and altered. Some may be spontaneous acts, done for the first time, and as such they do not reflect prior habit formation. Only if the spontaneous act is subsequently repeated again and again does habit formation ensue.

It should be obvious at once that without habit formation, we would be as helpless as the infant in the cradle. Without habit formation, we would have to act spontaneously on every occasion, or deliberately think out what we are about to do and decide each time on how to do it. Think of dressing and undressing every day without habits of doing so; think of doing any sort of work, engaging in any sort of play, driving a car, cooking a meal, and so on, without habits of doing so.

We recoil from the thought with horror, and rightly so. Human life without habit formation would be a nightmare. All the powers inherent in our human nature at birth would be as naught unless and until they are overlaid by habit and become our second nature.

How do we form habits? Let me answer that question by first considering all our bodily habits, all of which are acquired skills in the use of our bodily powers. Every habit of bodily performance is an acquired skill, from simple skills, such as the one that determines how we walk or how we position our body in one posture or another, to much more complex skills, such as those that determine how we play any athletic game, engage in any sport, or perform any artistic act—sing, play a musical instrument, write a letter.

By mentioning these more complex bodily skills along with the much simpler ones, I am calling attention to the fact that all skills acquired by habit have a mental as well as a physical aspect. There are some purely mental skills, but all those mentioned above are skills of both body and mind. The simpler ones have a larger bodily aspect; the more complex ones, a larger mental aspect. All of them have both in varying degrees.

Regardless of where they fall in the spectrum of skills, the habits by which we acquire them are formed by the repetition of actions. By doing it over and over again, we learn how to walk in a certain way. By standing up straight every time we have to stand, instead of slouching, we form that habit of posture instead of the opposite. By repeating again and again the actions prescribed by our tennis coach, our athletic trainer, our piano or violin teacher, we form the habit that consitutes the skill aimed at by our coach, trainer, or teacher.

In the course of such training, our preceptor may stop us and say, "Don't do it that way, do it this way," or just, "Stop doing it that way; now try doing it again the right way." Only if we follow instructions will we form the habit—the skill—that is the object of the exercise.

Habit formation is like the programming of computers, but with a difference. The reflex reactions with which we are born comprise our innate programming—something that nature provides, for which we have no responsibility. All the habits we form ourselves are acquired programming. Whereas computers are always programmed by others, whether human beings or other computers, our voluntary habit formation consists in self-programming, even when it is under the direction of coaches, trainers, or teachers. We can always choose to follow their directions or not. All habits are, in this sense, voluntarily formed by the persons who acquire them. They result from free choices on their part.

A habit, once formed, can be broken in just the same way that it was formed—by repeated acts on our part, only now acts of an opposite sort. Instead of taking another cigarette or another strong drink, we refuse it, and substitute some other act for it. Similarly, in breaking the bad habit of stroking a tennis ball with our eyes somewhere else, we keep our eyes on the ball time and time again. Bad habits, in short, are broken in the same way that good habits are formed.

What, then, is the difference between good habits and bad? If both are perfections in the basic sense that they are developments of our innate abilities and improvements on the raw nature with which we are born, why are good habits perfections in another sense, while bad habits are corruptions rather than perfections?

The only answer to this question should be obvious at once. Habits are good, and therefore perfections, if they develop us in the right direction, the direction we ought to follow. They are bad, and therefore corruptions, if they develop us in the wrong direction, the direction we ought to avoid. But what is the direction we ought to follow and the direction we ought to avoid?

The direction we ought to follow in our habit formation is one that accords with the rules for acting well. The truth of this is easiest to see in the case of any skill or art. I will postpone for a moment the types of habit formation which do not result in skills, concerning which it is more difficult to explain the criteria that divide right from wrong directions and good from bad habits.

In the case of any skill, technique, or art (the three words just used are all synonyms), the rules of the skill or art prescribe the right actions to be performed. The rules for driving an automobile, the rules for baking a cake, the rules for hemming a dress, the rules for making a bed, to take the simplest examples, all prescribe the right way of doing these things. By following such rules, and also by avoiding actions that the rules proscribe or prohibit, we form good habits. What is true of these rules is equally true of the rules of grammar, rhetoric, and logic, or the rules set forth in tennis manuals and other "how to" books that deal with sports and games.

I have written such books, concerned with reading, speaking, listening, and thinking, and I know that laying down the rules does not produce the desired good habits. Nor does learning the rules, being able to recite them in an orderly fashion, or even understanding them well. I have taught logic to students who could pass an examination that tested whether or not they knew and understood the rules. Those same students, put to another test, plainly revealed that they could not think logically and avoid logical errors.

Why? Because knowing and understanding rules of any sort that prescribe the right acts and proscribe the wrong ones do not form habits. Habits are formed by acting repeatedly in accordance with the rules, and in no other way. What I have just said is as true of moral habits as the habits of any art or skill. Knowing and understanding moral rules or ethical precepts does not produce a person of good moral character. One can pass an examination in moral philosophy and still be a scoundrel, knave, or villain

A moral philosophy or a code of ethics that relies solely on obedience to the rules it sets forth for the result it aims at is totally unpragmatic. It is likely to be worse—unsound and dogmatic. Only a moral philosophy that prescribes the formation of good habits of conduct is undogmatic, sound, and truly practical. Extraordinary as this may seem, the only two moral philosophers who make habit formation, not obedience to rules, the center of their teaching are John Dewey in our own day and Aristotle in antiquity.

Though rules that direct acts to be done or avoided underlie habit formation, in the case of moral conduct as well as in the case of skilled performances of all sorts, once persons form the right habits, they not only can forget the rules, they also usually do forget them. They certainly become unconscious of them in the execution of the habits they have formed.

Habits of Mind and of Character

I have so far mentioned two kinds of habits: habits which are skills or arts, and moral habits—habits of conduct.

With respect to the first of these I have said that they always have a mental as well as a bodily aspect, but not all have a bodily as well as a mental aspect; for example, the skill of thinking logically as compared with the skill of any sport or the skill of higher arts, such as singing, playing a musical instrument, painting a picture, or photographing a scene.

With respect to moral habits, as contrasted with skills or arts, I have said that it is more difficult to explain how good habits are to be distinguished from bad. I postponed doing that until a little later.

With respect to all the types of habit so far mentioned, I have said that all of them are formed by the repetition of acts. I must now point out that this does not hold true of every type of habit, but only of those so far mentioned. Some habits can be formed by a single act. They are habits of mind, and they are especially habits of mind that have no bodily aspect, unlike most of the habits that are skills or arts.

When these are good habits of mind, we call them intellectual virtues. The three that I wish first to consider are habits of insight or understanding, habits of knowing, and habits of sound judgment about ultimate matters, usually called wisdom. The Greek words for these three intellectual virtues are *"nous," "episteme,"* and *"sophia."*

When, in the course of study or learning, I come to understand something or gain some insight by intuition rather than by reasoning, that understanding or insight is mine without having to repeat it over and over again. This is equally true of understanding or insight that results from a process of thinking. It is also true of knowledge that I acquire by learning or study. Once I have learned it, it is mine. I do not need to repeat the acts by which I learned it.

The only qualification to be added here concerns the liveliness or vitality of the habit. While a single act may be all that is necessary to form the habit, exercising it may be necessary to keep it alive. We do not lose these habits by failure to exercise them, but lapses in their exercise may result in their becoming weaker, so that we have to take action to revive them. Things that I once understood well may become less clear for me when I have paid no attention to the matter in question for a long time. I must then do something to reactivate my understanding and restore it to the clarity it once had. Everything alive tends to atrophy without exercise.

The three intellectual virtues named above do not exhaust all good habits of mind. There are two others. One kind we have already treated sufficiently—all the arts or skills, whether purely mental or both mental and bodily. The first three intellectual virtues can all be described as habits of knowing—either knowing *that* something is the case or knowing *why* it is so. The fourth group—the arts or skills—can be described as knowing *how* rather than as knowing *that* or *why*. Every art and skill is knowing how to perform a certain activity well or how to produce something that turns out to be well-made.

The fifth and last of the intellectual virtues can also be described as knowing *how*, but the know-how here concerns how to judge well and make good decisions with regard to our conduct. This virtue is called prudence. It is sometimes called practical wisdom to distinguish it from the philosophical or speculative wisdom that consists in knowing *why* about the most ultimate matters.

Like the arts or skills, prudence is a habit formed by repeated acts of deliberating well in order to reach sound judgments or decisions. Unlike the arts and the other intellectual virtues, prudence and prudence alone is concerned with the conduct of our lives. It alone of the intellectual virtues cannot be separated from the moral virtues.

As we shall see, it is impossible to be morally virtuous without being prudent, or prudent without being morally virtuous. That is not true of any of the other intellectual virtues. Illustrious examples abound of great artists and excellent performers in athletic contests who, by their conduct, cannot be judged morally virtuous. The same applies to great scientists and philosophers.

It should be clear from everything that has been said so far that the meaning of the word "virtue" is completely expressed in the phrase "good habit." The Latin word from which the English word "virtue" is derived gives it a slightly different connotation, introducing the notes of virility and strength. The Greek word *"arete,"* which means excellence, is much nearer the mark. Every acquired excellence, of either mind or character, is a virtue. All habits are perfections in the sense of developments of the nature, but only the good habits that we call virtues are perfections in the sense of being developments that achieve excellence.

Turning now to the moral virtues, and associating the one intellectual virtue of prudence with them because it is inseparable from them, we must ask what they are good habits of doing. The answer is that they are good habits of desiring, as contrasted with good habits of knowing.

Desiring has for its objects (1) the goods we aim at—the ends or goals we seek, and (2) the means we choose in order to attain those ends or goals. Our desiring may also consist in (1) acts of will on our part, or (2) emotional impulses or drives. It may combine both at the same time. When it does, both mind and body are involved.

Since desire is the ultimate root and spring of all action, as understanding, knowing, or thinking by themselves are not, the moral virtues, as good habits of desiring, give rise to morally good conduct. The moral vices, as bad habits of desiring, result in morally bad conduct.

Moral virtues, and also vices, are like the arts or skills. They are habits formed by repeated acts, morally good acts or morally bad acts. A single good or bad action does not give an individual a morally good or bad character, does not make him or her a virtuous or vicious person. Not even a few such acts do so. Only many repeated acts, all aiming in the same direction and carried out in the same way, will have that effect.

A person who performs a single virtuous act may not be a virtuous human being. Nor does the performance of a single, unjust, intemperate, or cowardly act, or even a few of them, deprive human beings of their moral virtue. To call a particular act virtuous is one thing; to call the individual who performs that act virtuous is quite another. Virtuous individuals can act unvirtuously and vicious individuals can act virtuously, under certain conditions. This brings us finally to the difficult questions I have so far postponed answering.

Question: What direction must the repeated acts take in order to form the good habits that are the moral virtues? *Answer:* They must be directed to the right ultimate end or goal.

Question: What is that? *Answer:* Happiness, ethically conceived as a good human life, an expanded life, a life enriched by all the things that are really good for a human being to be or have.

Question: How should this intended goal or end be achieved? *Answer:* By choosing the right means for attaining it, means that are not only effective for this purpose, but that do not tend in the opposite direction.

In the light of these questions and answers, we can now see that the moral virtues, together with the inseparable intellectual virtue of prudence, are habits of desiring that consist in aiming at or intending the right end and choosing the right means for attaining it.

Virtue and the Virtues: One or Many?

There is no question that there are many virtues if we consider both the intellectual and the moral virtues. Not only are these two kinds of virtues analytically distinct, but they are also existentially separable. We have recognized that a morally vicious person can have the intellectual virtues of art or science, or even of philosophical wisdom. It is equally clear that a person can be a scientist without being philosophically wise, a scientist without being an artist, or the reverse. Hence these different virtues can exist in complete separation from one another.

Is this true of the moral virtues when we differentiate the three principal or cardinal moral virtues as temperance, courage, and justice, and associate prudence with them? That they are analytically distinct from one another can be made as clear in their case as in the case of the intellectual virtues. But are they existentially separable in the way that intellectual virtues are from one another and from the moral virtues?

Before I try to answer this question, let me be sure that readers fully understand the difference between analytical distinction and existential separation. When bread and butter lie on separate plates they are existentially separate as well as analytically distinct. We recognize their analytical distinction by how they taste and other perceptible properties. Their existential separation is made manifest by the separate plates on which they lie. Now butter the bread and eat it. The bread and butter remain as analytically distinct as before, both to our eyes and to our palates. But when the bread is buttered, the two become existentially inseparable. We cannot take them apart any longer, no matter how we try.

To the question about the unity or plurality of virtue in the moral sphere (whether there are three existentially separate moral virtues, which are also existentially separate from prudence, or four analytically distinct virtues, none of which is existentially separate from the others) the answer given, both by the popular mind and in philosophical treatises dealing with the subject, almost universally favors the plurality of virtue. There are many virtues, existentially separate as well as analytically distinct.

It is well nigh impossible to remove this view from daily speech. We cannot resist thinking of this particular virtue as contrasted with that particular one. We find ourselves saying that an individual has certain moral virtues, but lacks others.

All of our inveterate habits of thought and speech adopt the notion that there are many moral virtues which exist in separation from one another and from prudence. This is as true of the philosophers who write about virtue as it is true of the rest of us—with one exception, Aristotle. Even Thomas Aquinas, a faithful student and follower of Aristotle, when he comes to this question and states the two opposite answers to it, adopts as the right answer the one that Aristotle rejects as wrong.

I reject it also and will try to explain why I think Aristotle was right. Before I do, let me make sure that there is no doubt about the clear analytical distinction of temperance, courage, justice, and prudence. All involve tending toward the right end and choosing the right means for attaining it. That is what is common to all of them as analytically distinct aspects of moral virtue.

Temperance is analytically distinct from the others by reason of its being concerned with pleasure in relation to other goods, either resisting the seductions of pleasure when yielding to them stands in the way of achieving other real goods we need or moderating our emotional desire for pleasure by recognizing that pleasure is a limited, not an unlimited good—good only in a certain measure.

Courage is analytically distinct from the others by reason of its being concerned with pain in relation to other goods, suffering pain for the sake of other real goods we need, which cannot otherwise be attained. Courage may also involve a habitual disposition to overcome our emotional reluctance to suffer any degree of pain or other hardships.

Justice is analytically distinct from the others by reason of its being concerned with the good of others and the good or welfare of the community, not our own good. Yet it also involves the recognition that our own good may depend upon not injuring the community in which we live or our fellow human beings.

All three, as analytically distinct aspects of moral virtue, constitute the good habit of intending the right end. Without a will that habitually aims at or intends the right end, we would not be habitually disposed to resist the temptations of pleasure or moderate our pursuit of it; we would not be habitually disposed to suffer pains and hardships; we would not habitually refrain from injuring other individuals or the community in which we live.

Prudence is analytically distinct from the other three by reason of being a habitual disposition to judge aright concerning the means for attaining the right end, intended or aimed at by the other three. Being a habitual disposition to judge, it is formed by intellectual acts. Being habitual dispositions with respect to pleasure and pain, temperance and courage are formed by acts of will and reason resisting, moderating, or otherwise controlling our passions, our sensuous inclinations, our animal impulses and drives. Being a habitual disposition to act for the good of others, justice may consist entirely in acts of will and reason, though such acts may also involve our passions, our sensuous inclinations, and our animal drives.

All of the points so far made show clearly the respects in which the four habitual dispositions named by the words, "temperance," "courage," "justice," and "prudence" are analytically distinct. But none of them provides any grounds whatsoever for asserting their existential separation.

On the contrary, when these points are carefully considered, it will, I think, be seen that the four habitual dispositions cannot exist in separation from one another.

Prudence cannot exist in separation from the other three because one cannot judge the right means for attaining the right end unless one intends or aims at that end.

Temperance, courage, and justice cannot exist in separation from prudence because one cannot be habitually disposed toward acting for the right end without judging aright the means for attaining it.

At one and the same time, an individual cannot be habitually disposed to aim at and act for the right end and also be habitually disposed to aim at and act for its opposite—one or another wrong end. Therefore, we cannot be temperate without being also courageous and just, courageous without also being just and temperate, or just without being also temperate and courageous.

The existential inseparability of aiming at the right end and selecting the right means for attaining it rests on the insight that the means *are* the end in the process of becoming. We move in the direction of any end, right or wrong, only to the extent that we resort to means effective for attaining it. The morally right end requires us to choose morally sound means for attaining it. No other means would be effective. Only in the case of morally wrong goals, or goals that are morally indifferent, does the end justify any means that are expedient, whether they are in themselves morally good or bad.

The existential impossibility of aiming at or intending the one right end and other wrong ends at the same time establishes the existential inseparability of temperance, courage, and justice.

The Aristotelian position with regard to the unity of moral virtue and its inseparability from prudence still permits us to refer to temperance, courage, justice, and prudence as four analytically distinct aspects of moral virtue. We can, therefore, persist in our inveterate habit of using the words that name these four aspects as if they named four existentially separate as well as analytically distinct virtues.

When we do so, we are, for good reason, under the obligation to remember that such verbal habits of speech violate what should be a sound habit of thought; namely, that temperance, courage, justice, and prudence constitute a unity that cannot be broken up into existentially separable parts, each able to exist in separation from the others.

What are the good reasons that impose this obligation on us? I have already stated all the points about these four aspects of virtue that oblige us to acknowledge their existential inseparability. But there is one additional consideration that I must now mention.

Aristotle's position is the only one that provides an adequate and tenable solution of Plato's problem: Why should anyone be just to others—avoid injuring them or the community?

The oft-repeated golden rule fails completely as an answer. Why *not* do unto others what you wish no one would do unto you? Kant's categorical imperative, together with all the duties that he deduces from it, is merely a high-sounding and more elaborate statement of the golden rule. It is not much better. Nor is an appeal to conscience and the wish to avoid the pangs of remorse and guilt feelings.

The only categorical imperative that is a self-evident truth, which Kant's formulation is not, can be stated as follows: *One ought to seek everything that is really good for one's self and nothing else.* Since that categorical imperative imposes the obligation to pursue one's own happiness as the sum of all real goods, it heightens the point of the problem posed by Plato. It does not solve it.

Plato's problem once again: What reason is there for not being unjust to others if you can gain substantially by so doing, on condition, of course, that you can get away with it and go unpunished?

If we consider the difference between justice, on the one hand, and temperance or courage, on the other hand, it is easy to explain why we should be temperate and courageous. To be habitually intemperate or uncourageous is to ruin or seriously blemish our own lives. We injure ourselves by these vices. We cannot achieve happiness or make good lives for ourselves without being habitually temperate and courageous.

But being habitually just toward others serves *their* pursuit of happiness, not our own, just as injuring them may frustrate or impede it. How are we barred from our own ultimate good, our own happiness, by the injustice we do others?

The solution of the problem lies in the unity of moral virtue. If we cannot effectively pursue our own happiness without being temperate and courageous, and if we cannot be temperate and courageous without also being just (because these three are inseparable aspects of integral moral virtue), then it follows inexorably that we must be habitually just for the sake of attaining our own ultimate end as well as for the sake of facilitating others in their pursuit of happiness.

Virtue as an End and as a Means

The intellectual virtues—the goods of the mind—occupy a high rank, if not the highest, in the scale of real goods. Moral virtue, while involving no form of knowledge, has an intellectual aspect, for it manifests the role played by reason and will in the control and moderation of the passions.

Together these virtues represent the greatest human perfections that can be achieved by learning and personal growth. These are the goods of mind and character that the pursuits of leisure aim at. They constitute the ends for which leisuring is the means.

But while they are ends, desirable for their own sake, they are also means to a good life. They are among its most important ingredients or components. A life not enriched by these goods would be greatly deprived, just as a life devoid of leisuring would be a contracted one.

Only happiness itself—a whole good life—is an ultimate end, never a means to be sought for the sake of some other good. Happiness, being the sum of all real goods, leaves no other good to be desired. That is why happiness should never be referred to as the *summum bonum* (the highest good), but rather as the *totum bonum* (the complete good).

The virtues may be the highest of all human goods, but taken all together, they are certainly not the complete good. One can have all the virtues and still lack freedom, friendship, health, and moderate amounts of pleasure and of wealth. A virtuous person deprived of all these things would certainly be prevented from living well or achieving happiness in the course of time.

I have explained how the virtues are both ends, desirable for their own sake, and also means, desirable for the sake of a good life. I must now go further and explain how moral virtue, from which prudence is inseparable, differs from the intellectual virtues as means.

All the real goods are means to a good life in the sense that they are constitutive components of it. But moral virtue is more than that. It is one of the two operative factors—one of the two efficient causes—of our *becoming* happy. The other consists in such good fortune as befalls us and confers on us the real goods we cannot attain through free choice on our part and solely through the voluntary exercise of our powers.

In the light of all these considerations, we must finally face the question: Which is primary—the intellectual virtues or moral virtue? As constitutive components of good life, they are on a par as personal perfections. But if, with a view to *becoming* happy, one had to choose between strengthening one's moral virtue or increasing one's knowledge, one's skills, one's understanding, and even one's philosophical wisdom, there is in my mind little doubt as to what the answer should be.

It is better, in the long run and for the sake of a good life, to have strength of character than to have a richly cultivated mind. It is impossible to live without some knowledge and skill, but without moral virtue it is impossible to live well and to become happy. One can have all the intellectual virtues to the highest degree and for lack of moral virtue fail to lead a good life.

How Can One Individual Help Another to Become Morally Virtuous?

I am tempted to say, "Don't ask," because I am persuaded that no one has ever come up with the answer, and probably no one ever will. The fact that we know how moral virtue is acquired does not mean that we know how one person can help another to acquire it.

Had the question been about the acquisition of the intellectual virtues, all except prudence, the answer would have been by teaching and learning. We acquire knowledge with the aid of didactic teachers; we acquire all our arts or skills with the aid of teachers who function as coaches or trainers; we acquire such understanding and wisdom as we come to have through experience and with the help of teachers who ask questions as Socrates did.

None of these methods of teaching, nor any form of learning that is aided by them, avails when we turn from the intellectual virtues to moral virtue, linked with prudence. Twenty-five centuries ago, Socrates asked, "Can moral virtue be taught?" He argued that it cannot be. To my knowledge, no one has successfully countered the arguments advanced by Socrates in Plato's dialogues.

His reasons boiled down to three things. First, moral virtue is a habit formed by free choice on our part. While it is also true that free choice enters into the formation of the habits that are intellectual virtues, it does so only to the extent that one must be voluntarily disposed to learn and to profit from teaching. In contrast, every action we perform that develops either a virtuous or vicious habit is itself a freely chosen act. Precisely because free choice operates at every stage in the development of moral virtue, no one attempting to inculcate moral virtue by teaching can succeed.

Consider in contrast the teaching and learning of mathematics. Granted that the learner must be motivated to learn, must voluntarily submit to instruction, and must voluntarily make the effort required to succeed. However, given all these prerequisites, free choice does not enter into the actual process of learning mathematics. When presented with the demonstration of a conclusion in geometry, the student is not free to accept or reject the conclusion. The reasoning presented necessitates the assent of his or her mind.

The individual's passions and predilections do not function as obstacles to learning mathematics, as they do, often overwhelmingly, when it comes to an individual's adopting the moral advice or injunctions offered by parents or other elders. Neither the carrot nor the stick can overcome an individual's obstinate resistance to moral instruction, whether that takes the form of wise counsel, eloquent exhortation, praise and blame, or setting forth examples of good conduct and the rewards it reaps.

Please note that I am not saying that ethics cannot be taught or that morality cannot be preached. Of course, they can be. But remember what was said earlier: There is a world of difference between (1) knowing and understanding the principles of ethics and the moral precepts that should be followed and (2) forming the habit of acting in accordance with those principles and precepts. Being able to pass an examination in ethics does not carry with it having moral virtue or a good moral character.

A second point made by Socrates in his attempt to explain why moral virtue cannot be taught concerns the role of prudence as an inseparable aspect of moral virtue.

If moral virtue were identical with knowledge, it could be taught; but it is not identical with knowledge. We are acquainted with instances, in our own life and the lives of others, where individuals know what they ought to do and fail to do it, or do what they know they ought not to do.

However, it may be thought that prudence, like art, is a form of know-how. We certainly acknowledge that arts can be taught, by coaches or trainers. Why, then, cannot prudence be similarly taught?

The answer lies in the distinction between all the skills as forms of know-how and prudence as a very special form of know-how. The arts or skills consist in knowing how to perform something well or to produce something that turns out to be well-made. In every case, there are clearly formulated rules to be followed by an individual in the effort to develop skill.

There would appear to be rules that should be followed in order to develop prudence, which consists in knowing how to form a sound judgment and reach the right decision about the means to be chosen. These rules include taking counsel, deliberating about alternatives and weighing their pros and cons, and being neither precipitate or rash on the one hand, nor obstinately indecisive on the other hand.

But at each step of the way an individual's passions and predilections can intervene to prevent him or her from following these rules, as they do not intervene when one undertakes to acquire a skill. That is why no one can train or coach another person to become prudent, as one can train or coach another person to write well, play tennis well, play the violin well, and so on.

In the third place, Socrates calls our attention to facts of experience with which everyone is acquainted. If moral virtue could be taught, why do virtuous parents, who make every effort they know how to inculcate it in their offspring, succeed with some and fail with others?

Let us suppose, for the moment, that such parents bring their children up in substantially the same way, that they offer the same moral advice, that they mete out the same rewards and punishments, that they tell them what good consequences follow from one course of action and what bad consequences follow from another, that they hold up examples of virtuous persons who succeeded in living well and persons who came to grief, and that they do all this with manifest love and kindness.

Would anyone dare to say that children thus reared in the same way will inevitably turn out in the same way? Only someone who had no experience at all in the rearing of children could be so foolish. The rest of us, giving the opposite answer, have some sense of why we think different children, similarly reared, turn out differently.

The different results, we sense, stem from the differences of the children—differences of temperament, differences in their innate propensities, inner differences in the way they think and feel that no outsider can ever touch, and, most fundamental of all, differences in the way they exercise their free will. The similarity in the way two children are reared, even if all the outer conditions are identical, cannot overcome these innate and inner differences between them.

The free choice that enters at every step into the formation of moral character and does not enter into the development of excellent behavior on the part of domesticated animals is the crux of the matter. That is why we can train horses and dogs to behave well habitually, but not human beings.

To the three reasons offered by Socrates, I would add a fourth. The thinking that enters into the formation of moral virtue as the habit of making sound judgments and right decisions about how one should act here and now involves considering one's life as a whole, taking the long-term view of it, and judging what is for the best in the long run.

This is the very thing that the young simply cannot do. Their thinking tends to consider the immediate moment, the next day, or the next week, but not much beyond that. Most of them are motivated by present or imminent pleasures and pains. Since they are unable to think about what is best in the long run, they are also unable to forego immediate pleasures for the sake of a greater good in the long run, or to suffer immediate pains for the same long-term reason.

Unfortunately, one's moral character gets formed, one way or another, in youth. It can, of course, be changed later, but only by heroic effort and, without that, seldom successfully. Toward the end of our lives, when maturity enables us to take the long-term point of view and think about our lives as a whole, little time is left for judgments about what is best in the long run. The young who have ample time ahead of them, and so should profit from thinking about their life as a whole, are prevented by their immaturity from taking thought for the future.

Parents and elders often tell children about their own experiences. They point out the bad consequences they suffered from acting in a certain way and the good consequences that followed from another course of action. Children listen to such talk, but do not have the experiences that prompt it. They are also unable to profit from the experience of an older generation. To paraphrase a statement by George Santayana, those who cannot profit from the mistakes of others are condemned to repeat them. They are thus destined to find out everything for themselves by trial and error. How this enables some of them to grow up into adults of sound moral character and others to grow up into adults lacking moral virtue, no one knows.

Is there, then, no answer at all to the question of how human beings, especially the young, can be aided in the development of moral virtue? I said at the beginning that there is none. There is one exception, perhaps. Christian doctrine makes the acquisition of moral virtue dependent upon having the supernatural virtues of faith, hope, and charity. It declares that these supernatural virtues are not acquired by human effort, but are a gift of God's grace. This leaves us with a theological mystery. Why does God bestow that gift upon some and not upon others, since all who are born with original sin are in need of it for their moral virtue in this life as well as for their salvation hereafter?

Does my conclusion, that there is no philosophical or scientific solution of the problem of how to rear children so that they become morally virtuous adults, carry with it the corollary that there is little or no point in explaining why moral virtue is so important in human life and how it is to be acquired by the choices individuals make and by their actions? A large part of this chapter has been devoted to just that. To no effect whatsoever? Has it all been a purely academic exercise, with no practical benefit conferred?

I wish I could promise that the elucidations offered in this chapter would definitely produce good effects. But I know this to be far from the truth. I know, as all of us do, individuals who have developed good moral characters without the benefit of being acquainted with and understanding what has been said in the foregoing pages about moral virtue and its development.

I am, therefore, left with the relatively feeble conclusion that those who are acquainted with and understand these matters are thereby just a little better off in regulating their own lives and in influencing the lives of others. Slight as the satisfaction may be that this gives the reader, it is the best I can do.

Is Anyone Ever Perfectly Virtuous or Completely Happy?

Since we are here concerned with a philosophical understanding of virtue and happiness and not with theological doctrines concerning these subjects, I will state the Christian answer to this question only for the sake of its contrast to the philosophical answer.

Christianity teaches that the saints achieve perfect or heroic virtue, but only with God's gift of grace. It also teaches that natural moral virtue cannot exist except in the company of the supernatural virtues of faith, hope, and charity. In addition, it teaches that having these virtues, taken together, assures happiness hereafter, the eternal happiness of the saints in the presence of God.

When happiness is regarded as we have been regarding it (as temporal, not eternal; here on earth, not hereafter in heaven), then loyalty to the vows of chastity, poverty, and obedience and other abstentions from worldly goods result in an earthly life that is voluntarily deprived of many real goods that we have counted as indispensable to an enriched and expanded human life here and now, though such deprivations may be required for eternal happiness in the life to come hereafter.

Perfect moral virtue, philosophically considered, is an ideal always to be aimed at, but seldom if ever to be attained. Our moral characters are blemished by this flaw or that. Individuals who have morally good characters are morally virtuous to a degree that is measured by the frequency with which they commit acts that are not virtuous. That frequency may not be so great that it breaks the habit of virtuous conduct, but it can be great enough to weaken an individual's moral fiber.

The result is a degree of moral virtue that only approximates the ideal aimed at. Accordingly, individuals may have moral virtue in varying degrees, some more, some less, but rarely if ever is the ideal of perfection attained.

Another consequence is the incompleteness of the happiness achieved. The more virtuous a person is, the more that individual has it in his power to make a good life for himself or herself. However, variations in degree of moral virtue are not the only factor in determining how nearly individuals can approximate the ideal of complete happiness in their earthly lives. The other factor consists in the degree of good fortune with which the individual is blessed. Some are more fortunate, some less. The more fortunate a person is, the more he will come into possession of all those real goods that are not wholly within his own power to obtain.

Reference to good fortune and misfortune leads us to another factor that flaws our happiness and renders it incomplete. Almost all of us at one time or another, and even perhaps on several occasions, meet with the misfortune of having to make a tragic choice. Circumstances beyond our control confront us with alternatives that permit us no good choice. Whichever alternative we choose results in our voluntarily taking evil unto ourselves.

This occurs when we must choose between one love and another, between love and duty, between conflicting duties or between conflicting kinds of law to both of which we owe loyalty, and between justice and expediency.

One of our greatest debts to the ancient Greeks is their discovery of human tragedy, so clearly exemplified in two plays by Sophocles, *Antigone* and *Oedipus Rex*. Modern exemplifications of it exist in the classical French tragedies of Racine and Corneille and also in one short story told by Herman Melville, *Billy Budd*. But let no one suppose that tragedy befalls only these fictional heroes and heroines. The rest of us also experience it through tricks of fate, played on us by outrageous fortune.

Tragedy befalls only the morally virtuous who are already on the way toward making good lives for themselves. It does not occur in the lives of fools or knaves, villains or criminals. They have ruined their own lives. There is nothing left for misfortune to ruin.

We could not speak of degrees of moral virtue were it not one and the same personal perfection for all human beings. Nor could we speak of degrees of happiness did not a good human life comprise the same real goods for all human beings. Only in the purely psychological meaning of the word "happiness" does what makes one man happy make another miserable. Only in that meaning of the term are there as many different states of happiness as there are different individuals.

The felt contentment or satisfaction that is called happiness psychologically depends on our individually differing wants as well as on the extent to which they are fulfilled or frustrated. In contrast, the whole good life that is called happiness ethically depends on the fulfillment of our common human needs as well as upon the extent to which they are fulfilled by the attainment of the real goods that we seek.

So far as its enrichment by all real goods is concerned, one person's happiness or good life is the same as another's, differing only in the extent to which their common human needs are fulfilled. However, there may be another source of difference between one person's happiness and another's. While remaining the same with respect to the real goods that everyone needs, it may differ with respect to the apparent goods that individuals want. The things that appear good to one person because he or she wants them will obviously differ from the things that appear good to another person. That individual's wants are different.

Of all such apparent goods, some may also be real goods, needed as well as wanted. Some may be merely apparent goods, not needed but nevertheless innocuous in the sense that wanting and getting them does not interfere with or impede our attaining the real goods all of us need. And some may be noxious rather than innocuous. Wanting these and getting them can defeat our pursuit of happiness.

Apparent goods that are detrimental to the pursuit of happiness cannot, of course, play any part in differentiating one person's happiness from another's. But in addition to being enriched by all the same real goods, in varying degrees, one person's happiness may also differ from another's by the different innocuous apparent goods that still further enrich the happiness of each.

One further question remains concerning the degree to which individuals approximate the ideal of complete happiness on earth. As almost everyone is subject to the occurrence of tragedy in their lives, so almost everyone is also subject to misfortunes, some more dire than others. An early death, enslavement, the agony of poverty carried to the extreme of destitution, imprisonment in solitary confinement, these things can completely frustrate a person's pursuit of happiness. They result in the misery that is the very opposite of happiness. However, misfortunes may not completely frustrate, but merely impede, an individual's effort to make a good life for himself or herself. Under what conditions are we best able to overcome such misfortunes and still save our lives from the wreckage of bad luck?

The stronger our moral virtue, the more likely are we to be able to make good lives for ourselves in spite of these misfortunes. The other side of the same picture is that hard luck and adversity, when the misfortunes do not cause irreparable damage or destructive deprivations, may result in the strengthening of moral virtue.

Being blessed by benign conditions and the affluence of unmitigated good fortune usually has exactly the opposite effect. It is more difficult to develop moral virtue under such conditions than it is under adversity, when that is not crippling or totally destructive.

I wish to end this chapter by returning to one recurrent theme that provides a transition to the second part of this book. Readers probably do not need to be reminded that success in the pursuit of happiness depends on two factors, not one, each necessary, neither sufficient by itself. But they may be interested in examining Aristotle's one sentence definition of happiness. It summarizes the point compactly and succinctly. In reporting it below, I have added in brackets words not in the original, but which make its intent clearer.

> Happiness consists in a complete life [well-lived because it is] lived in accordance with [moral] virtue, and accompanied by a moderate possession of [wealth and other] external goods.

I never tire of reiterating the importance of understanding that moral virtue by itself is not enough to make a life good. Were it sufficient by itself, there would be no point whatsoever in all the political, social, and economic reforms that have brought about progress in the external condition of human life.

If morally virtuous persons can live well and become happy in spite of dire poverty; in spite of being enslaved; in spite of being compelled by circumstances to lead two- or three-part lives, with insufficient time for leisure; in spite of an unhealthy environment; in spite of being disfranchised and treated as nonparticipating subjects of government rather than as citizens with a voice in their own government, then the social, political, and economic reforms that eliminate these conditions and replace them with better ones make no contribution to human happiness.

Precisely because being morally virtuous is not enough for success in the pursuit of happiness, it is better to live in a full-fledged state than in a small village, in a society that has all the advantages peculiar to a political community; better to live under the peace of civil government than under the violence of anarchy; better to live under constitutional government than under despotism, no matter how benevolent; better to live in a democratic republic and in a capital-intensive socialist (but not communist) economy than under a less just political institution and under less favorable economic arrangements.

I trust readers will perceive the ways in which the two foregoing paragraphs connect the pivotal idea of happiness with all the other ideas so far considered and with all the ideas that remain to be considered in the rest of this book.

QUOTATIONS WITHOUT COMMENT

With Regard to Happiness

. . . We call that which is in itself worthy of pursuit more final than that which is worthy of pursuit for the sake of something else, and that which is never desirable for the sake of something else more final than the things that are desirable both in themselves and for the sake of that other thing, and therefore we call final without qualification that which is always desirable in itself and never for the sake of something else.

Now such a thing happiness, above all else, is held to be; for this we choose always for itself and never for the sake of something else, but honour, pleasure, reason, and every virtue we choose indeed for themselves (for if nothing resulted from them we should still choose each of them), but we choose them also for the sake of happiness, judging that by means of them we shall be happy. Happiness, on the other hand, no one chooses for the sake of these, nor, in general, for anything other than itself.

Aristotle, *Nichomachean Ethics*, Bk. I, Ch. 7 (4th cent. B.C.)

★   ★   ★

. . . The final good is thought to be self-sufficient. Now by self-sufficient we do not mean that which is sufficient for a man by himself, for one who lives a solitary life, but also for parents, children, wife, and in general for his friends and fellow citizens, since man is born for citizenship. But some limit must be set to this; for if we extend our requirement to ancestors and descendants and friends' friends we are in for an infinite series. Let us examine this question, however, on another occasion; the self-sufficient we now define as that which when isolated makes life desirable and lacking in nothing; and such we think happiness to be; and further we think it most desirable of all things, without being counted as one good thing among others—if it were so counted it would clearly be made more desirable by the addition of even the least of goods; for that which is added becomes an excess of goods, and of goods the greater is always more desirable. Happiness, then, is something final and self-sufficient, and is the end of action.

Aristotle, *Nichomachean Ethics*, Bk. I, Ch. 7 (4th cent. B.C.)

★   ★   ★

Why then should we not say that he is happy who is active in accordance with complete virtue and is sufficiently equipped with external goods, not for some chance period but throughout a complete life? Or must we add "and who is destined to live thus and die as befits his life?" Certainly the future is obscure to us, while happiness, we claim, is an end and something in every way final. If so, we shall call happy those among living men in whom these conditions are, and are to be, fulfilled—but happy *men*.

Aristotle, *Nichomachean Ethics*, Bk. I, Ch. 10 (4th cent. B.C.)

★   ★   ★

This definition of Happiness given by some—Happy is the man that has all he desires, or, whose every wish is fulfilled—is a good and adequate definition if it be understood in a certain way, but an inadequate definition if understood in another. For if we understand it absolutely of all that man desires by his natural appetite, thus it is true that he who has all that he desires, is happy, since nothing satisfies man's natural desire except the perfect good which is Happiness. But if we understand it of those things that man desires according to the apprehension of the reason, in this way it does not pertain to Happiness to have certain things that man desires; rather does it belong to unhappiness, in so far as the possession of such things hinders man from having all that he desires naturally; just as reason also sometimes accepts as true things that are a hindrance to the knowledge of truth. And it was through taking this into consideration that Augustine added so as to include perfect Happiness—that "he desires nothing amiss," although the first part suffices if rightly understood, that is to say, that "happy is he who has all he desires."

> Thomas Aquinas, *Summa Theologica*, Pt. I–II, Q. 5, A. 8.
> (c. 1265)

* * *

Whatever is desired otherwise than as a means to some end beyond itself, and ultimately to happiness, is desired as itself a part of happiness, and is not desired for itself until it has become so.

> John Stuart Mill, *Utilitarianism*, Ch. 4 (1863)

With Regard to the Moral and Intellectual Virtues and the Unity of Moral Virtue

Virtue, then, is a state of character concerned with choice, lying in a mean, i.e. the mean relative to us, this being determined by a rational principle, and by that principle by which the man of practical wisdom would determine it.

> Aristotle, *Nichomachean Ethics*, Bk. II, Ch. 6 (4th cent. B.C.)

* * *

Virtue, then, being of two kinds, intellectual and moral, intellectual virtue in the main owes both its birth and its growth to teaching (for which reason it requires experience and time), while moral virtue comes about as a result of habit, whence also its name (ἠθική) is one that is formed by a slight variation from the word ἔθος (habit). From this it is also plain that none of the moral virtues arises in us by nature; for nothing that exists by nature can form a habit contrary to its nature. . . . Neither by nature, then, nor contrary to nature do the virtues arise in us; rather we are adapted by nature to receive them, and are made perfect by habit.

> Aristotle, *Nichomachean Ethics*, Bk. II, Ch. 1
> (4th cent. B.C.)

* * *

. . . It is not possible to be good in the strict sense without practical wisdom, nor practically wise without moral virtue. But in this way we may also refute the dialectical argument whereby it might be contended that the virtues exist in separation from each other; the same man, it might be said, is not best equipped by nature for all the virtues, so that he will have already acquired one when he has not yet acquired another. . . . The choice will not be right without practical wisdom any more than without virtue; for the one determines the end and the other makes us do the things that lead to the end.

Aristotle, *Nichomachean Ethics*, Bk. VI, Ch. 13
(4th cent. B.C.)

★   ★   ★

. . . Human virtue is a habit perfecting man in view of his doing good deeds. Now, in man there are but two principles of human actions, namely, the intellect or reason and the appetite. . . . Consequently every human virtue must be a perfection of one of these principles. Accordingly if it perfects man's speculative or practical intellect in order that his deed may be good, it will be an intellectual virtue, but if it perfects his appetite, it will be a moral virtue. It follows therefore that every human virtue is either intellectual or moral.

Thomas Aquinas, *Summa Theologica*, Pt. I–II, Q. 58, A. 3
(c. 1265)

★   ★   ★

. . . Moral virtue can be without some of the intellectual virtues, namely, wisdom, science, and art, but not without understanding and prudence. Moral virtue cannot be without prudence, because moral virtue is a habit of choosing, that is, making us choose well. Now in order that a choice be good, two things are required. First, that the intention be directed to a due end; and this is done by moral virtue, which inclines the appetitive power to the good that is in accord with reason, which is a due end. Secondly, that man take rightly those things which have reference to the end, and he cannot do this unless his reason counsel, judge and command rightly, which is the function of prudence and the virtues joined to it.

Thomas Aquinas, *Summa Theologica*, Pt. I–II, Q. 58, A. 4

(c. 1265)

★   ★   ★

. . . Speaking absolutely, the intellectual virtues, which perfect the reason, are more excellent than the moral virtues, which perfect the appetite.

But if we consider virtue in its relation to act, then moral virtue, which perfects the appetite, whose function it is to move the other powers to act . . . is more excellent. And since virtue is called so from its being a principle of action, for it is the perfection of a power, it follows again that the nature of virtue agrees more with moral than with intellectual virtue.

Thomas Aquinas, *Summa Theologica*, Pt. I–II, Q. 66, A. 3

(c. 1265)

★   ★   ★

. . . These four [cardinal] virtues are understood differently by various writers. For some take them as signifying certain general conditions of the human soul, to be found in all the virtues, so that, namely, prudence is merely a certain rectitude of discernment in any actions or matters whatever; justice, a certain rectitude of the soul by which man does what he ought in any matters; temperance, a disposition of the soul moderating any passions or operations, so as to keep them within bounds; and fortitude, a disposition by which the soul is strengthened for that which is in accord with reason, against any assaults of the passions, or the toil involved by any operations. To distinguish these four virtues in this way does not imply that justice, temperance and fortitude are distinct virtuous habits. For it pertains to every moral virtue, from the fact that it is a habit, that it should be accompanied by a certain firmness so as not to be moved by its contrary, and this, we have said, belongs to fortitude. Moreover, since it is a virtue, it is directed to good which involves the notion of right and due, and this, we have said, belongs to justice. Again, owing to the fact that it is a moral virtue partaking of reason, it observes the mode of reason in all things, and does not exceed its bounds, which has been stated to belong to temperance. It is only in the point of having discernment which we ascribed to prudence, that there seems to be a distinction from the other three, since discernment belongs essentially to reason; but the other three imply a certain participation of reason by way of a kind of application (of reason) to passions or operations. According to the above explanation, then, prudence would be distinct from the other three virtues but these would not be distinct from one another; for it is evident that one and the same virtue is both habit, and virtue, and moral virtue.

Others, however, with better reason, take these four virtues, according as they have their special determinate matter, each its own matter, in which special praise is given to that general condition from which the virtue's name is taken. . . . In this way it is clear that the aforesaid virtues are distinct habits, differentiated in respect of their diverse objects.

Thomas Aquinas, *Summa Theologica*, Pt. I–II, Q. 61, A. 4
(c. 1265)

With Regard to External Goods and the Goods of Fortune

. . . All men think that the happy life is pleasant and weave pleasure into their ideal of happiness—and reasonably too; for no activity is perfect when it is impeded, and happiness is a perfect thing; this is why the happy man needs the goods of the body and external goods, i.e. those of fortune, viz. in order that he may not be impeded in these ways. Those who say that the victim on the rack or the man who falls into great misfortunes is happy if he is good, are, whether they mean to or not, talking nonsense.

Aristotle, *Nichomachean Ethics*, Bk. VII, Ch. 13 (4th cent. B.C.)

★   ★   ★

It is also disputed whether the happy man will need friends or not. It is said that those who are supremely happy and self-sufficient have no need of friends; for they have the things that are good, and therefore being self-sufficient they need nothing further, while a friend, being another self, furnishes what a man cannot provide by his own effort; whence the saying "when fortune is kind, what need of friends?" But it seems strange, when one assigns all good things to the happy man, not to assign friends, who are thought the greatest of external goods.

Aristotle, *Nichomachean Ethics*, Bk. IX, Ch. 9 (4th cent. B.C.)

★　★　★

. . . Herein of necessity lies the difference between good fortune and happiness; for external goods come of themselves, and chance is the author of them, but no one is just or temperate by or through chance.

Aristotle, *Politics*, Bk. VII, Ch. 1 (4th cent. B.C.)

★　★　★

. . . A good life requires a supply of external goods, in a less degree when men are in a good state, in a greater degree when they are in a lower state. Others again, who possess the conditions of happiness, go utterly wrong from the first in the pursuit of it.

Aristotle, *Politics*, Bk. VII, Ch. 13 (4th cent. B.C.)

★　★　★

We do not acquire or preserve virtue by the help of external goods, but external goods by the help of virtue.

Aristotle, *Politics*, Bk. VII, Ch. 1 (4th cent. B.C.)

PART TWO
A BETTER SOCIETY

CHAPTER 5   State and Society

MY FASCINATION WITH IDEAS goes beyond the inner structure of each idea in itself, its many facets, the interplay of its themes. I am equally struck by the relationships that exist among them and by the crisscross patterns that result from their interweaving.

All through the discussion in Part One of work and leisure, wealth and property, virtue and happiness, there were countless references to the community in which human beings live and to the economic institutions of organized society, to the individual activities that benefit society and to the actions of government that benefit individuals.

The movement in Part One was upward. We went from work and leisure and the other kinds of activity which provide a context for them, to the larger picture of the economy in which wealth is produced by labor and capital, resulting in property that is acquired and exchanged. The last step put all these ideas into a still larger setting. The activities with which we were concerned in our consideration of work and leisure, constituting the parts of a human life, and the human possessions with which we were concerned in our consideration of wealth and other external goods, were then seen in relation to the virtues as human perfections. The interconnection of all these ideas came into focus when viewed as causes or constituents of happiness—parts or aspects of a good human life as a whole.

The movement that lies ahead in Part Two will be downward. Instead of ending with the kingpin idea as we did with happiness in Part One, we begin here with the most all-embracing of these ideas, society, and its correlative idea, state. With the consideration of government and constitution, we turn our attention to aspects of the state, and to differences among states according to their forms of government. Still moving downward, the differentiation of forms of government will lead to one particular form of government, democracy; that in turn will require dealing with the role that individuals play as constituents of a constitutional government and as citizens of a democracy.

Looking at all twelve ideas, the six principal ones and their conjoined correlatives, we cannot help being struck by the way in which two ideas tie them all together.

Happiness, we have seen, is the ultimate goal of human striving, for the sake of which everything else should be sought and to the consummation of which everything else should be ordered. It is the complete good, the whole that includes all other goods as its component parts.

However, society and the state are larger wholes than their individual members. The prosperity of society and the welfare and security of the state would also appear to be ultimate goals.

The individual members of society manifest their justice by acting for the good of the society and state in which they live. Serious antisocial conduct is criminal injustice, doing injury or damage to the welfare of the community as well as to other human beings who participate in the community's common good.

Hence the very first question that confronts us is, perhaps, the most fundamental of all the questions we have to face. How are these two ultimate goods to be ordered in relation to one another—the happiness of individual persons who are members of a society and the welfare of the society to which they belong?

A solution of the problem requires us to resolve the contradiction contained in the phrase "two ultimate goods." Two ultimates are impossible; there can be only one. That being so, the problem to be solved is: Which one?

Both are common goods, but they are common in different senses of that term. The happiness of individuals is common in the sense that the essential components of a good human life are the same for *all* human beings, their happiness differing only in accidental respects. The Latin name for this common good is *bonum commune humanis,* the human common good.

The welfare of society and of the state is common in the sense that it is a good in which all the members of the state *participate,* deriving benefits for themselves from that participation. The Latin name for this common good is *bonum commune communitatis,* the social common good.

Each of these two common goods subordinate all individual goods. The essential components of happiness, the real goods that are the same for all human beings, subordinate the accidental components, the apparent goods that differ from individual to individual.

The selfish interests of individuals should be subordinated to the common good that is the welfare of society as a whole and the security of the state. Almost everyone, certainly all virtuous persons, recognize this as soon as the security of the state or the welfare of the community is seriously threatened.

But the pursuit of happiness is not a selfish individual interest. It seeks the attainment of a good that is shared by all human beings because it is the same for all of them. Should the human common good be subordinated to the security of the state and the welfare of the community, even when the social common good is seriously threatened?

For those who hold, as philosophers from Plato to Hegel have held, that man is made for the state, not the state for man, the question is already answered, yet not without residual difficulties.

For those who hold, from Aristotle to John Dewey, that the state is made for man, not the other way around, the question is also answered, again with residual difficulties that are not easy to resolve.

I do not hesitate to say at once that I side with the latter answer. It is true that individual members of a society are parts of a whole. It is also true that the good of a part can be sacrificed for the good of the whole. But it is not true that individual human beings as members of society are parts of that whole in the same way that arms and legs are parts of a human being.

The critical error here consists in converting a metaphor into a literal truth.

When it is said that the society or the state is a living organism or an organic whole, the truth is that it is *like* a living organism or an organic whole because it, too, is organized, as all living organisms are. But its being organized only makes it *appear to be* a living organism.

The *apparent* likeness does not make it *really* a living organism. That it is an organized whole having parts does not subordinate the parts to the whole as the parts of a living organism are subordinated to the organism as a whole.

Residual difficulties remain for anyone who tries to solve this problem simply and neatly.

This becomes manifest to us when we discover that Hegel, who subordinates individual human beings to the state as parts to a whole, also declares that the state serves the happiness of the persons who are its members. So also Aristotle, who says again and again that the happiness of its citizens is the ultimate good to be aimed at by the state, permits himself, in one passage, to compare the individual members of society to the limbs of a living organism. Nor does he avoid the implication that they can be sacrificed, as arms and legs can be sacrificed, for the good of the whole.

Setting such difficulties aside for the moment, I think the most telling point in favor of the position that the state is made for man, not man for the state, lies in our recognition of the fact that participation in the social common good is indispensable to the happiness of human beings. In contrast, the welfare of the community can be achieved and preserved even if all its individual members do not succeed, by lack of moral virtue, in attaining their own personal happiness.

Human beings cannot lead good lives in total isolation from one another. We are social, not solitary, animals. We depend for our happiness upon associating with others, living in society and deriving the benefits that living in society confers upon us, especially the goods that are not wholly within our power to obtain for ourselves.

On the other hand, if the welfare of society depended upon the successful attainment of happiness by all its members, it would follow that the common good of the community could never be achieved. We know that all human beings do not become morally virtuous persons. For that and other reasons, all do not and never will succeed in attaining happiness, even to a slight degree.

The two common goods are, therefore, not both equally ultimate as, of course, they simply cannot be. The social common good is ultimate only to the extent that it is the good aimed at by individuals in their social or public lives. But human beings also lead private lives, of which their social conduct is only an aspect.

Their personal happiness is their ultimate good *without any qualification*. The social common good is ultimate for them *only in so far as they act socially*.

Their action for the common good of the society in which they live does more than serve its welfare. It serves their own happiness, which depends on their deriving benefits from society that are beyond their power as solitary individuals to achieve.

The truth of this is confirmed by the fact that the benefits conferred upon its individual members by society are all external goods and, as such, are possessions that rank lower in the scale of human goods than a human being's personal perfections.

Even when the views just expressed are fully understood and accepted, the fact still remains that the only two entities that human beings have ever acknowledged as their superiors are the state *on earth* and God *in the cosmos*.

We find the English philosopher, Thomas Hobbes, referring to the state as "that great Leviathan, or (to speak more reverently) as that Mortal God, to which we owe under the Immortal God, our peace and defence." We find the German philosopher, Hegel, declaring that "the State is the Divine Idea as it exists on earth."

Those who, in our time, are proponents of the totalitarian state and worship the state in a pseudoreligious fashion, turn it into a secular divinity. They alone acknowledge no residual difficulties when they maintain that man is made to serve the state and that all individual interests are subordinate to the welfare of the state and can be sacrificed for it.

When States Exist, Are They Identical With Society?

The question is introduced by a conditional clause. States did not always exist. In what we regard as the remote past, the only human associations were families or tribes and villages.

To answer the question, it is necessary to spend a moment on the words that crowd in on us when we consider these ideas. We have already used some of these words: "society," "community," "association." These appear to be synonymous. Every form of human association is a type of human society. Every type of human society is a community.

We have already used the word "state." Other words occur in this connection: "political community," "civil society," "body politic," "commonwealth." These words, too, appear to be interchangeable synonyms. Two of them—"civil society" and "political community"—indicate at once that what their synonym, "state," refers to is always only one type of society or community, in contradistinction to still other types of human associations—clubs, fraternities, companies, corporations, labor unions, trade associations, professional associations, and so on.

Still other words remain to be considered, such as "city," "nation," "country," and even "civilization" and "culture." As we shall see presently, two of them enter into hyphenated conjunctions to form such terms as "city-state" and "nation-state." Whether or not the difference between these two kinds of state are important in other connections, they are not important in connection with the problem of how state and society are related.

The word "country" adds little to the connotations of the other words except, perhaps, the indication of a place on earth that is the location of the state. We more often say "my country" than we say, "my state" because it is so obviously the place of our birth or the place we have moved to as an inhabitant.

A Greek and a Latin word add to our understanding of these matters. The Greek word "polis" is translated into English by the word "state" whether that refers to a city-state or a nation-state. Its ancient reference was to a city-state. That persists in modern times when we refer to a large city as a metropolis. The phrases "political community" and "body politic," both of which refer to a state, also derive from that Greek root. When Immanuel Kant held before us what he regarded as the utopian idea of a world state, he called it a "cosmopolitical ideal."

The Latin equivalent of the Greek *"polis,"* the word *"civis,"* comes down to us along another etymological stream, in which what is called a "civil society" is synonymous with what is called a "political community." It also adds a new connotation to the word "state."

From *"civis,"* we derive the English word "civilization." When we distinguish civilization from culture, as we should, we are able to recognize that other forms of society have cultures, but only civil societies or states bring civilizations into existence.

To live in a civil society, to engage in political activity is to lead a civilized life, which means more than what is meant by saying that to live in any society that has a culture enables individuals to become cultured. Becoming acculturated is not the same as becoming civilized.

One concrete example of these concentric spheres should suffice. Take the present population of the United States. It is made up of persons who inhabit the land that stretches from the Atlantic to the Pacific, from the Canadian to the Mexican border, and also the land of Alaska and of the Hawaiian Islands. Viewed another way, that same population is composed of all the members of the society, called by the same name that we give to the land on which they live. Viewed in still another way, they are also citizens or subjects of the state, for which once again the same name is the label; and they are involved in the American economy, or the economy of the United States.

"United States of America" or "Americans," used as an identifying label in all four ways, identifies four different associations or organizations of the same people.

That the four circles in which the same people are related to one another involve them in different relationships and different activities underlies the distinction among the four sciences that investigate those relationships and activities: geography, sociology, political science, and economics.

With these considerations in mind, let us now return to the question posed: When states exist, are they identical with society? The totalitarian answer to this question is affirmative.

Why? Because the totalitarian state is one in which there are no human associations of any sort, including the family, that are not politically controlled or are not creatures of the state. Even the cultural activities of the totalitarian state, its educational institutions and its artistic productions, are all organized by the state, conducted by the state, and controlled by the state. So, too, are its professional enterprises and its economic associations and operations.

Under such conditions, and only under such conditions, the state is identical with society. Nothing that human beings do is left out. Nothing is a private concern. Everything is affected with the public interest.

Under all other conditions, society and state are not identical. The state represents only the political aspect of society. Though the geographical boundaries of a state and a society are coterminous, and though the individuals who are members of the state are also members of the society, by reason of the fact that they live together in the same place, in the same country, it remains the case that the human beings who are members of the state also belong to associations or organizations that are not political, not creatures of the state, and not state-controlled.

They engage in many forms of activity which are not political in character and so do not involve their participation in the state. Their civilized life includes much more than that. It includes their domestic interests and their family life. It includes all their cultural activities that involve forms of leisuring. It includes all their business or professional associations through which they engage in work that is either toil or compensated leisure. It includes, above all, their private lives in which they seek, in addition to all other goods, their own personal perfections and their personal happiness.

When men voluntarily associate with one another for a common purpose, the purposes for which they associate differ in many ways. Only one of these purposes is purely political. It is that purpose and that alone which makes their association a state. When they associate for other purposes, they belong to communities or organizations that are parts of the all-embracing political society that is identical with the state.

What I have just said may appear to contradict the statement that state and society are not identical. It does not.

True, the political community or civil society, which is identical with the state, is all-embracing in the sense that it includes within its borders all other forms of human association that are entered into for nonpolitical purposes. But that truth does not conflict with the fact that the all-embracing society has many nonpolitical aspects. Nor does it conflict with the fact that its members engage in many nonpolitical activities.

Not everything that human beings do in a state is either prescribed or prohibited by the laws of the state. Much is merely permitted, still more lies totally beyond the scope of state-made laws— all the personal and purely private pursuits that affect only the individual engaging in them and no one else.

This, it must be added, holds true even in totalitarian states. No state can possibly be so completely totalitarian that it touches every aspect of human life and enters into its inviolably secret nooks and crannies. What is essentially private can never be totally transformed into something public.

Man, the Only Politically Social Animal

We learn from biological science that some animals lead solitary lives and that other animals live and act in groups that are more or less organized. The latter are called gregarious or social animals. Their individual survival and the survival of the species to which they belong depend upon their living with one another, instead of in isolation, and upon their acting, to some degree at least, in concert with one another.

There can be no question that the members of the human species are gregarious or social animals. They, too, cannot survive, nor can the species, unless they associate with one another in groups, the smallest of which is the human family, without whose care and protection human offspring would perish.

But is man gregarious in the same way that all other species of gregarious animals are? Or does the human race differ from other species of social animals by reason of the fact that its gregariousness gives rise to states as well as to other forms of societies? If so, then man is a *politically* social animal.

I have long persisted in the view that man is radically different from all other animals, different in kind, not merely in degree. This means that human beings have the ability to do what other animals cannot do at all. If what humans did, other animals also did to one extent or another, then the difference would be only a difference in degree. If other animals were simply less political than human beings, that would be so. But if other animals are totally nonpolitical, then the difference is one of kind, and man is the only social animal that is also political.

I have written a book on this subject, entitled *The Difference of Man and the Difference It Makes.* Since its publication in 1967, I have written many articles to confirm and reinforce the arguments it presents, countering the claims of students of animal behavior who think they have found new evidence to show that human beings only differ in degree from the higher mammals—the chimpanzees, the bottle-nosed dolphins, and other species, to which behavioral scientists incorrectly attribute syntactical speech and conceptual thought.

There is no need here to repeat arguments to the effect that only human beings have the power of conceptual thought and engage in speech that is syntactical. Only such speech is an expression of conceptual thought. What looks like speech on the part of other animals is nothing but a form of communication by signals that refer only to perceptual objects, not to objects that have never been perceived or are totally imperceptible.

The only point I wish to make here is that man is the only politically social animal *because* (1) only man has an intellect as well as perceptual intelligence; (2) only man has the intellectual powers of understanding, judgment, and reasoning; (3) only man has free will and the power of free choice; and (4) only human beings, through syntactical speech, communicate their thoughts to one another—their judgments and their arguments.

Not all human behavior is voluntary. Some human reactions issue from the reflexes with which human beings are endowed at birth. But all the rest, which do not consist in conditioned reflexes, are not only voluntary, but also a matter of free choice.

To say this is to say that man alone of all animals does not come into the world endowed with preformed instinctive patterns of behavior. His innate endowment does not program his behavior, except for a relatively small number of reflexes. All of his programmed behavior consists in the self-programming that is habit formation, and all habits arise from voluntary acts.

To say that human beings have no instincts, in the strict sense of that term, is not to say that all members of the species do not have, inherent in their specific (and therefore common) human nature, certain instinctual impulses or natural drives. Human gregariousness is a case in point. Human beings are instinctually driven or impelled by their natures to associate with one another. But an *instinctual drive* or *natural impulse*, such as this, is not the same as an *instinct*.

An *instinct* is an elaborate pattern of behavior that carries out an instinctual drive and reaches the goal at which the instinctual drive aims.

If man were instinctively social as well as endowed by his gregarious nature with an instinctual impulse or need to associate with his fellows, then all human beings, being members of the same species, would always form associations of exactly the same kind. No aspect of their association would be voluntarily determined, nor would it differ from one group of individuals to another.

On this score, the evidence is irrefutably clear. Human associations differ in an incredibly wide variety of ways, from time to time, from place to place, and from one human group to another. This simply could not be the case if all human association were determined by an instinct present in all members of the human species.

It follows from this that human associations are voluntarily formed, not instinctively determined. Otherwise they would not differ as we pass from one human group to another, or from one time and place to another, since the members of all human groups are members of the same species and would have the same species-specific social instincts.

The behavior of the social insects—bees, ants, termites, and others—lies at the opposite extreme of the spectrum. The hive built and organized by one species of bee, the mound built and socially structured by one species of ant, the colonies formed by one species of termite, are always and everywhere the same. They will remain so as long as the species survives. That sameness bespeaks the sameness of the species-specific instinct, which all members of the species possess by native endowment—*all without a single exception.*

In between the two extremes of the social insects at one end and the human species at the other, the different species of nonpolitical gregarious animals each have their own instinctively determined patterns of social behavior. These will be the same for all members of the same species. They will differ from one species to another. In addition, there will be some admixture of social behavior that manifests the operation of the perceptual intelligence, which all vertebrates possess and the higher mammals possess in a high degree. One need only observe the difference in dams constructed at different sites by different groups of beavers, all of the same species, to see that this is so.

At the outset of this discussion, I said that man is the only politically social animal because only man has an intellect, reasons, makes free choices, and communicates his thoughts and judgments by making sentences using words that are not just signals.

In the immediately preceding paragraphs, the argument took a different turn. We saw that the manifold diversity in forms of human association indicates that man's social behavior cannot be instinctively determined. It must be voluntary and influenced by reason.

When the argument moves in that direction, it applies to all types of human association—to the family and the tribe as well as to the state. Here we are saying that we can infer man's unique status as a rational animal with free choice from all the evidence we have about the highly various ways in which human beings organize their families, tribes, and states.

Is the State Natural, Conventional, or Both?

This question can be asked about other forms of human association as well as about the state. To call any of them conventional implies that they arise from voluntary, not instinctive, behavior. It would appear to follow, therefore, that an association or society cannot be both natural and conventional. They must either be voluntarily formed or the product of instinctive determinations.

I have already declared that all animal societies are natural, not conventional. All are the products, more or less, of instinctive determination—more in the case of the social insects, less in the case of the gregarious higher mammals.

We are acquainted with innumerable human associations that are purely conventional. Think of how our labor unions, our trade associations, our clubs and fraternal organizations, our business corporations and our professional associations, are formed. Individuals come together and voluntarily unite to act in concert for a common purpose.

Omitted from the preceding roster of human associations are families, tribes, and states. That they are natural is evident from the fact they are found everywhere on earth where human beings live; this is not so in the case of other human groupings.

It has already been asserted that the immense variety in the way these natural associations or societies are structured indicates the operation of reason and choice in their origination. Being conventional, they can also be natural only if the word "natural" can be used to mean something other than being instinctively determined, as bee hives and termite colonies are.

The clue to a solution of this problem lies in a point already noted.

While human beings do not have social instincts, as do bees, termites, and other gregarious animal species, humans are instinctually driven or impelled by their natural needs to associate in certain ways. Societies or associations that are formed in order to satisfy natural needs are natural in a sense of that word which is different from the sense it has when calling a society natural means that it is instinctively determined.

With regard to human families, the natural need is exactly the same as the natural need satisfied by instinctive associations on the part of the lower animals. The other gregarious species would not survive unless their members associated and acted in concert. The same is true of the human species. The existence of human families is coeval with the existence of the human species on earth.

The family came into existence to satisfy the animal needs inherent in human nature and to prevent human offspring from perishing. At different times and places, familial associations took on different forms. The human family is thus both natural (because it serves a natural need) and also conventional (because the various forms it takes are voluntarily chosen, not instinctively determined).

When, in the course of human history, families came together and united to form small villages or tribal communities, natural needs and voluntariness were again operative. The fact that a tribe or village involved more individuals than the number making up each of its component families allowed it to satisfy more than daily needs. The number of persons who toiled for the means of subsistence, and the division of labor among them, permitted them to accumulate more than they consumed from day to day and to store for some future time the excess that did not perish. The tribe or village was also better able to defend itself against outsiders and also to protect its members from the ravages of an inclement environment.

Both families and tribes or villages serve the same basic biological needs—survival and subsistence. The family was less self-sufficing and less secure than the tribe because it was a smaller, less populous, community. The crude implements used by the primeval family to eke out the means of subsistence from the natural resources available were improved and supplemented by other tools when families united to form tribes or villages. Some elements of culture—ritualistic practices, decorations, song, dance, and painting—also came into existence at this later stage of human social development.

At a still later stage, tribes or villages united to form the earliest cities. Once again the increase in population and a slightly more elaborate division of labor served better the same biological needs of survival and security. The larger society, now including families and tribes of associated families, was more self-sufficing and more secure against the inclemency of nature and the hostility of other social groups.

In addition, the elements of human culture proliferated, became more refined, and eventually gave rise to the arts and sciences, and to the institutions of religion and political life (i.e., city life).

The earliest cities were states—city-states. Being more self-sufficing and secure than isolated families and than families united in isolated tribal communities, the city-state was able to serve a natural need above the biological level—to serve the specifically human, rather than animal, need to do more than just stay alive, the aspiration to live well and to lead a civilized human life.

Let me paraphrase Aristotle's account of the origin of cities: "When tribes or villages united to form a community that was nearly or quite self-sufficing, the state came into existence, originating in the bare needs of life and continuing in existence for the sake of a good life. Therefore, if earlier forms of society were natural because they satisfied natural human needs, so too was the state natural."

In this account of the origin and naturalness of the state, no reference is made to two myths developed in the seventeenth and eighteenth centuries to explain how states came into being.

One was the myth that prior to the existence of states, human beings lived in total isolation from one another, in a condition that the modern mythmakers called "a state of nature." The other was the myth that they departed from a state of nature and entered civil or political society through a device that the mythmakers called "a social contract," to which the individuals who united to form a state gave their voluntary consent.

Rousseau, one of the mythmakers along with Hobbes and Locke, admitted that a state of nature is purely hypothetical, not historical. He should have said the same thing about the social contract.

The very phrase "state of nature" flies outrageously in the face of fact. Man being by nature a gregarious animal, a state of nature, understood to mean human beings living in isolation from one another, is not only mythical but also unnatural. If human beings never lived and could never have survived in this unnatural condition, they did not originate states by the voluntary act of isolated individuals contracting with one another to unite in a form of social organization that is a state.

The Aristotelian account of families uniting to form tribal communities and tribal communities uniting to form cities is much more in accord with all the facts. The acts by which these unions occurred were voluntary, but they were not of a character that can be properly described as entering into a contract.

Scholarly commentaries on Aristotle's *Politics* and Rousseau's *Social Contract* regard these two great political philosophers as starkly opposed to one another, with Aristotle insisting, on the one hand, that the state is purely natural and with Rousseau insisting, on the other hand, that the state is purely conventional. A more careful reading of the texts reveals that this is not so.

In the context of all the passages in Aristotle's *Politics* where its author asserts that the state is purely natural or a creation of nature, we can also find the sentence in which he says that "he who first founded the state was the greatest of benefactors." That reference to a founder of the state implies that the state is not purely natural in origin. It is not only a creation of nature, but also a product of human devising and innovation. What Aristotle had in mind when he referred to the founding fathers of states were innovators who drafted constitutions, the kind of constitution that Solon drafted for Athens and Lycurgus for Sparta.

Rousseau begins *The Social Contract* by saying that, of all human societies, *only* the family is natural because it serves the basic biological needs. The italicized word "only" implies that the state must be purely conventional. However, a few pages later, Rousseau tells us that mankind could not have survived in the isolated condition that he calls a state of nature. It was his natural need to associate for the sake of survival that led him to depart from a state of nature and enter, by voluntary contract, into civil society.

Two contradictions are plainly evident here. If the human family is a naturally necessary society, then human beings never lived in isolation in a state of nature. If the impulse to enter into civil society arises from the same natural need that caused human beings to live in families, then the state is as natural as the family, not purely conventional as Rousseau's earlier statement implies. In addition, if the family satisfied those biological needs adequately, there was no need for the state.

By saying that the state enables human beings not only to survive and subsist, but also to live well, Aristotle expands the natural needs that the state serves beyond the biological needs served by the family and the tribal community. From the passage in which Rousseau attributes the origin of the state to the merely biological needs of subsistence and survival, it would appear that some conflict is still present between Aristotle and Rousseau.

However, even that is not the case. A few pages later in *The Social Contract*, we find a passage in which Rousseau eloquently praises the state for enabling man to do more than merely survive and subsist—to live a civilized and good life, a condition accessible to no other species of animal, all of which associate instinctively only to serve their biological needs.

The only matter on which Rousseau and Aristotle remain opposed concerns the myth of the social contract, as opposed to the historical reality that Solon and Lycurgus brought states into existence by drafting constitutions for them.

What Must Be Included in the Definition of the State?

Aristotle's reference to the benefactors who first founded states by drafting constitutions for them would seem to imply that having a constitutional form of government is an indispensable element in the idea of the state. This raises a serious problem for us.

As we shall see in the next chapter, some of the human societies that we call states, both in the historic past and now, have despotic rather than constitutional forms of government. Is it, therefore, improper to regard ancient Persia, Babylon, and Egypt as states? Must we, for the same reason, withhold the attribution of statehood to the societies that, in modern times, lived under the absolute despotisms of the Bourbons, the Hapsburgs, and the Stuarts? Is it wrong today to regard Saudi Arabia, Argentina, Chile, and even, perhaps, the Soviet Union as states, or Germany under Hitler and Italy under Mussolini?

Before trying to answer these questions, let me first take a few preliminary steps toward a tenable definition of statehood.

(1) Families and tribes, as contrasted with states, are composed of individuals who, to a greater or lesser degree, are related by consanguinity or ties of blood—more so in the family, less so in the tribal community. This is not true of all the individuals who comprise the population of a state.

(2) Families may exist in independence of one another and as not subordinate to or included in any larger community. The same holds for tribal communities. Both may also exist as subordinate to and included in larger communities—families in tribes, and both families and tribes in states. But a state does not exist unless it is an independent community and one that is not subordinate to or included in any larger community. The point just made can also be expressed by saying that the state cannot exist unless it has sovereignty.

Much has been said on the subject of sovereignty, but the only thing that is relevant here is the note of supremacy which the term implies. States are supreme in the sense that, as independent communities, not subordinated to anything larger than themselves, they acknowledge no superior on earth.

This carries with it their claim to autonomy as well as to independence. As the word "autonomy" connotes, sovereigns are laws unto themselves. A sovereign state is not subject to laws imposed by others.

(3) In consequence of what has already been said, it should be added that states are more populous than families and tribal communities. The larger size of their populations, and the consequent greater division of labor, enables states to produce more wealth than families or tribal communities; and, in addition, to emancipate some portion of their populations from toil and give them time for the leisuring that produces the goods of civilization—the arts and sciences, together with social institutions of all sorts.

(4) From this distinguishing characteristic of states, it follows that states can serve more than the biological needs served by isolated families or independent tribal communities. Beyond the means of subsistence, they provide human beings with the conditions they need for a good or civilized life.

The fact that in all the states that have existed up to the present and in many of the states that now exist the conditions of a good life are enjoyed only by a privileged few does not alter the point under consideration. What matters here is that such conditions are not enjoyed by any individuals living in isolated families or small, independent tribal communities.

It may be regarded as a point of progress in human affairs that, when the earliest states came into existence, some individuals, if only a few, enjoyed such conditions. Further progress was made by later states in which the many, rather than the few, enjoyed the conditions of a good life. We can look forward to still further progress when this will hold true for all—the whole population of a state.

(5) Finally, we come to the criterion of statehood that appears to be problematic: its form of government. Not only Aristotle suggested that this criterion be employed in the definition of statehood. Locke wrote to the same effect when he declared that absolute monarchy is inconsistent with civil society, which is statehood. So, too, Rousseau when he maintained that the only legitimate form of government is that of a republic, and implied that only republics deserve to be called states in the full sense of that term.

The solution of our problem lies in the words "the full sense of that term." A definition can be either purely descriptive or it can be prescriptive as well. For example, we can define man-made laws as laws that any form of government makes and enforces, whether or not that government and its laws are just. Our definition is then purely descriptive because it falls short of considering what man-made laws *should* be.

The definition becomes prescriptive by requiring that, to be laws in the full sense, they must be made by a legitimate government, having the rightful authority to make laws as well as to enforce them, and also that the laws enacted be just. As Augustine and others have said, an unjust law is a law in name only, for it satisfies only the descriptive criteria in the definition of law. It fails to satisfy the prescriptive criterion.

Descriptively defined, the all-embracing large societies that include families and other subordinate communities and that have independence and sovereignty, can all be called states, regardless of the form of government under which their populations live. In a way that Aristotle pointed out, they carry over from tribal communities the kind of government appropriate to families and tribes— despotic rule by parents and by the elders or chieftains of the tribe.

In this sense, they appear to be extensions of the family and the tribe. To become fully different, states must satisfy the other descriptive criteria that distinguish states from isolated families and independent tribes. They must also satisfy the additional prescriptive criterion that requires a shift from the form of government appropriate to families and tribes to one that is distinctively appropriate to states—constitutional rather than despotic government.

In terms of this fuller definition of statehood, ancient Persia under Xerxes and ancient Egypt under its Pharoahs do not deserve to be called states. In contrast, ancient Athens and Sparta, under their adopted constitutions, were states in the full sense of that term.

The same discrimination between societies that are states only by a purely descriptive definition of states and societies that are states by an additional prescriptive criterion, applies to all later societies—in the Middle Ages, in modern times, and in the contemporary world.

Does the purely descriptive definition of statehood or the fuller definition apply equally to all the historic forms that states have taken?

For example, can a city-state have statehood in exactly the same sense of the term as a nation-state? Does this hold as well for imperial city-states and imperial nation-states that have colonies? And for unitary states, such as France and Sweden, as well as for federated states, such as the Soviet Union, Switzerland, and the U.S.A.?

I think the question can be answered affirmatively, both for the purely descriptive definition of statehood and also for the fuller definition of it. All the things that differentiate city-states from nation-states are accidental aspects of statehood and so do not enter into its definition.

Concrete applications of the point just made should clarify it. What differentiates a city-state from a nation-state lies in the role that a great city plays.

Consider such ancient city-states as Athens, Sparta, Thebes, and Corinth. Their domains embraced the surrounding countryside, but statehood resided principally in the city itself and secondarily in its immediate environs. The same can be said about certain of the great commercial cities in modern times—Venice on the Adriatic, and the cities of the Hanseatic League on the North Sea and the Baltic.

Though they were equally great commercial cities, London, Stockholm, and St. Petersburg were the capital cities of nation-states—England, Sweden, and Russia. The difference between being merely the capital city of a nation-state that includes other large cities and being an independent, sovereign city, dominating an adjacent countryside, justifies calling the latter city-states, but not the former. However, the nation-state that has a capital city and other large cities within its domains has statehood in exactly the same sense that independent, sovereign city-states do.

Similarly, it makes no difference to its having the properties of statehood whether a particular state does or does not have colonies and whether it has a unitary or federal type of organization.

Considering states that are federal in structure leads us to a distinction between two types of sovereignty, external and internal. All states have external sovereignty vis-a-vis other states. They also have internal sovereignty in the sense that they possess the supreme power to enforce the laws of the land. Everyone who belongs to the population of a state is subject to its laws; no one outside the state is.

In unitary states, that internal sovereignty is undivided. In federal states, it is divided between the states or provinces that constitute a federal union and the nation or nation-state thus composed.

For example, both the United States and the State of Massachusetts have internal sovereignty over the people of Massachusetts. The people of Massachusetts are subject to the laws of the federal government and also to the laws of the state in which they live. They live under a dual jurisdiction.

While Massachusetts has internal sovereignty over the population resident there, it has no external sovereignty whatsoever. It cannot make war or peace with other states. It cannot form alliances or conclude treaties. With minor exceptions, it cannot control commerce with other states or immigration from other states. It cannot do many other things that states with external sovereignty can do.

Must we not conclude, therefore, that the State of Massachusetts has statehood to a lesser extent because it lacks the external sovereignty that fully independent states possess? Yet it cannot be said that Massachusetts does not have statehood at all, in any sense of that term. Nor can it be said that the U.S.A. has statehood to a less extent because, being a federal rather than a unitary state, its internal sovereignty is restricted to certain matters, the rest being left to the jurisdiction of the several states in the federal union.

Considering the external sovereignty of states vis-a-vis one another, we can understand why states are sometimes thought of as moral or juridical persons. This attribution of personality to them derives by analogy from the things that real or natural persons and private corporations are able to do.

Individual persons can enter into contracts with one another, dispute with one another, engage in economic transactions with one another, and so on. Associated human beings, especially when their association creates a corporation, can do these same things. The laws that govern the activities of corporations and their interactions with one another recognize them as juridical persons for this reason.

For the same reason, states having external sovereignty regard themselves, metaphorically if not literally, as persons. This resembled literal truth more closely when absolute monarchs identified the states they ruled with their own persons, referring to themselves by the name of the state they ruled when addressing one another. Claudius, in Shakespeare's *Hamlet*, in a letter to the King of England, signed himself "Denmark." Louis XIV said, *"L'état, c'est moi."*

The consideration of external sovereignty leads us to one further insight. Sovereign states, like the sovereign princes who identified the states they ruled with their own persons, are always in a state of war with one another.

Their external sovereignty is inseparable from their absolute autonomy. No enforceable laws govern the conduct of sovereigns vis-a-vis one another. In the absence of enforceable laws, sovereigns resort to force, which is warfare, when they cannot settle their conflicts in any other way. Even when sovereigns are not engaged in warfare with one another, they always remain in a state of war, which consists in the necessity of resorting to force in order to settle disputes because other means of doing so are not available or sufficient for the purpose.

What this implies about the difference between war and peace, and especially about the meaning of genuine peace, which does not consist solely in the absence of actual warfare, I will reserve for the next chapter on the idea of government. There we shall see more fully that the state of war is a state of anarchy—the kind of anarchy, or absence of government, that exists in the relation of one autonomous sovereign to another.

The Goodness of the State

With respect to all the ideas treated in this book, the overarching idea, treated in a prior book, is the idea of goodness, of good and evil, of right and wrong. I cannot conclude this chapter without asking whether the state is good or evil.

Only philosophical anarchists look upon the state as evil, an evil that need not be suffered. They do so because they think all coercive force is evil. The state, through its internal sovereignty, has the power to enforce laws. It could not govern otherwise.

Philosophical anarchists mistakenly think that men can live in peace and harmony with one another without being subject to coercive government of any kind. In their view, the state and its coercive government are avoidable evils that do not have to be endured because another alternative is available.

Some, like Bakunin, advocate direct action to overthrow the state and abolish government. Others, like Marx, predict the ultimate withering away of the state in the future. The establishment of a communist economy, under the dictatorship of the proletariat, is the penultimate step in that direction.

By still others, the state is regarded as a necessary, not an avoidable, evil. It is to be suffered for the sake of certain benefits that cannot be obtained in any other way. It is the price one must pay for civil peace and for the protection of life and limb.

It would be better if these and other advantages could be obtained in the much smaller local community of a neighborhood, instead of the much larger, more extended society of the state, with its overwhelming concentration of power and its overpowering centralization of government.

Unfortunately, all but the most extreme advocates of decentralization admit that the benefits conferred by the larger society that is a state cannot be obtained without suffering certain disadvantages that follow in their wake. For them, the state is, therefore, a necessary evil, but one that is not totally devoid of redeeming features, which render it also good.

To whatever extent you concede that they have some justification for their complaints against the state, you minimize the good done by the state—the benefits it confers on its inhabitants. Be that as it may, you also affirm that the state is not totally evil and that it may, on balance, do more good than evil.

The greatest goodness inherent in the state, which in my judgment cannot be denied, lies in the ultimate end it serves, which no other form of society serves at all, or certainly not as well.

When the state is correctly conceived as made for man, not the other way around, it seeks to facilitate the pursuit of happiness. It does so both directly and also indirectly by promoting the general welfare, participation in which confers on individuals external goods they could not otherwise obtain for themselves.

When the state is correctly conceived as coming into existence not just for the increased satisfaction of man's biological needs, but preeminently to enable human beings to live well and to lead civilized lives, its goodness overshadows any of the evils that those who have complaints against the state can think of. If it is not an unalloyed good, it is at least more good than bad, and the goodness it does have is indispensable to the pursuit of happiness.

QUOTATIONS WITHOUT COMMENT

With Regard to the State and Other Forms of Society

Every state is a community of some kind, and every community is established with a view to some good; for mankind always act[s] in order to obtain that which they think good. But, if all communities aim at some good, the state or political community, which is the highest of all, and which embraces all the rest, aims at good in a greater degree than any other, and at the highest good. . . .

The family is the association established by nature for the supply of men's everyday wants, and the members of it are called by Charondas "companions of the cupboard," and by Epimenides the Cretan, "companions of the manger." But when several families are united, and the association aims at something more than the supply of daily needs, the first society to be formed is the village. And the most natural form of the village appears to be that of a colony from the family, composed of the children and grandchildren, who are said to be 'suckled with the same milk'. . . .

When several villages are united in a single complete community, large enough to be nearly or quite self-sufficing, the state comes into existence, originating in the bare needs of life, and continuing in existence for the sake of a good life. And therefore, if the earlier forms of society are natural, so is the state, for it is the end of them, and the nature of a thing is its end. . . .

Hence it is evident that the state is a creation of nature, and that man is by nature a political animal. And he who by nature and not by mere accident is without a state, is either a bad man or above humanity. . . .

Now, that man is more of a political animal than bees or any other gregarious animals is evident. Nature, as we often say, makes nothing in vain, and man is the only animal whom she has endowed with the gift of speech. And whereas mere voice is but an indication of pleasure or pain, and is therfore found in other animals (for their nature attains to the perception of pleasure and pain and the intimation of them to one another, and no further), the power of speech is intended to set forth the expedient and inexpedient, and therefore likewise the just and the unjust. And it is a characteristic of man that he alone has any sense of good and evil, of just and unjust, and the like, and the association of living beings who have this sense makes a family and a state. . . . The proof that the state is a creation of nature and prior to the individual is that the individual, when isolated, is not self-sufficing; and therefore he is like a part in relation to the whole. But he who is unable to live in society, or who has no need because he is sufficient for himself, must be either a beast or a god: he is no part of a state. A social instinct is implanted in all men by nature, and yet he who first founded the state was the greatest of benefactors.

Aristotle, *Politics*, Bk. I, Chs. 1–2 (4th cent. B.C.)

*   *   *

. . . A state exists for the sake of a good life, and not for the sake of life only: if life only were the object, slaves and brute animals might form a state, but they cannot, for they have no share in happiness or in a life of free choice.

Aristotle, *Politics*, Bk. III, Ch. 9 (4th cent. B.C.)

*   *   *

My nature is rational and social; and my city and country, so far as I am Antoninus, is Rome, but so far as I am a man, it is the world. . . . [For we must] look at things so as to see at the same time . . . what value everything has with reference to the whole, and what with reference to man, who is a citizen of the highest city, of which all other cities are like families. . . . If our intellectual part is common, the reason also, in respect of which we are rational beings, is common: . . . if this is so, there is a common law also;

if this is so, we are fellow-citizens; if this is so, we are members of some political community; if this is so, the world is in a manner a state.

Marcus Aurelius, *Meditations,* Bk. VI, Ch. 44; Bk. III, Ch. 11; Bk. IV, Ch. 4 (c. 175 A.D.)

★   ★   ★

The most ancient of all societies, and the only one that is natural, is the family: and even so the children remain attached to the father only so long as they need him for their preservation. As soon as this need ceases, the natural bond is dissolved. The children, released from the obedience they owed to the father, and the father, released from the care he owed his children, return equally to independence. If they remain united, they continue so no longer naturally, but voluntarily; and the family itself is then maintained only by convention.

Jean-Jacques Rousseau, *The Social Contract,* Bk. I, Ch. 2 (1762)

★   ★   ★

Since no man has a natural authority over his fellow, and force creates no right, we must conclude that conventions form the basis of all legitimate authority among men. . . .

I suppose men to have reached the point at which the obstacles in the way of their preservation in the state of nature show their power of resistance to be greater than the resources at the disposal of each individual for his maintenance in that state. That primitive condition can then subsist no longer; and the human race would perish unless it changed its manner of existence.

Jean-Jacques Rousseau, *The Social Contract,* Bk. I, Chs. 4, 6 (1762)

★   ★   ★

This public person, so formed by the union of all other persons formerly took the name of *city,* and now takes that of *Republic* or *body politic;* it is called by its members *State* when passive, *Sovereign* when active, and *Power* when compared with others like itself.

Those who are associated in it take collectively the name of *people*, and severally are called *citizens*, as sharing in the sovereign power, and *subjects*, as being under the laws of the State.

Jean-Jacques Rousseau, *The Social Contract*, Bk. I, Ch. 6 (1762)

★ ★ ★

The passage from the state of nature to the civil state produces a very remarkable change in man, by substituting justice for instinct in his conduct, and giving his actions the morality they had formerly lacked. Then only, when the voice of duty takes the place of physical impulses and right of appetite, does man, who so far had considered only himself, find that he is forced to act on different principles, and to consult his reason before listening to his inclinations. Although, in this state, he deprives himself of some advantages which he got from nature, he gains in return others so great, his faculties are so stimulated and developed, his ideas so extended, his feelings so ennobled, and his whole soul so uplifted, that, did not the abuses of this new condition often degrade him below that which he left, he would be bound to bless continually the happy moment which took him from it for ever, and, instead of a stupid and unimaginative animal, made him an intelligent being and a man.

Jean-Jacques Rousseau, *The Social Contract*, Bk. I, Ch. 8 (1762)

★ ★ ★

Though society is not founded on a contract, and though no good purpose is answered by inventing a contract in order to deduce social obligations from it, every one who receives the protection of society owes a return for the benefit, and the fact of living in society renders it indispensable that each should be bound to observe a certain line of conduct towards the rest.

John Stuart Mill, *On Liberty*, Ch. IV (1859)

★ ★ ★

The craving for universal unity is the third and last anguish of men. Mankind as a whole has always striven to organize a universal state. There have been a great many nations with great histories, but the more highly they were developed the more unhappy they were, for they felt more acutely than other people the craving for world-wide union.

Dostoevsky, *The Brothers Karamazov*, Bk. V, Ch. 5 (1880)

* * *

The teaching of Marx and Engels regarding the inevitability of a violent revolution refers to the bourgeois state. It *cannot* be replaced by the proletarian state (the dictatorship of the proletariat) through "withering away," but, as a general rule, only through a violent revolution. . . .

The replacement of the bourgeois by the proletarian state is impossible without a violent revolution. The abolition of the proletarian state, i.e. of all states, is only possible through "withering away."

Vladimir Ilyich Lenin, *State and Revolution*, Bk. I, Ch. 4 (1918)

CHAPTER 6 Government and
Constitution

READERS WILL HAVE OBSERVED that I could not avoid mentioning government in treating the idea of state. We saw that the most fundamental criterion in defining a state and differentiating it from other types of community consisted in the type of government that prevails. Nor could I avoid mentioning constitutions. One theory of the origin of the state, we noted, attributed its coming into existence to constitution-making.

In our consideration of state and society, the ideas of government and constitution lay in the background. When now they come into the foreground, they bring with them, as part of *their* background, two other ideas—democracy and citizen. As we shall see, the idea of citizenship is central to our understanding of constitutional government, and constitutional democracy is a pivotal idea in the classification of forms of government.

State and government are often thought to be interchangeable terms, sometimes even in scholarly treatises. The fact that all known states, past and present, have had governments and would not long endure without them, may be the source of this misunderstanding. But it should be quickly removed by attention to an equally obvious fact—that every organized community or human association (families and tribes certainly, and other types of society as well) involves the apparatus of government. They could not operate without it.

[157]

In addition, we are all aware that a particular state continues to exist and to maintain its identity, certainly vis-a-vis other states, while its form of government undergoes radical, even revolutionary, changes. One need only think of the continuing identity of France and of Russia as national states when they passed from the despotic regimes of their Bourbon and Romanoff rulers to the radically different regimes that followed in the trail of bloody revolutions.

It is not enough to be able to separate the ideas of state and government. We must also be able to understand the sense in which each idea covers more ground than the other.

That the domestic society we call a family and the kind of society we call a tribe has its appropriate form of government is one indication that the idea of government is broader than the idea of state. This is reinforced by the wide variety of corporations and associations with which we are acquainted—universities, trade unions, business corporations, and so on. In fact, so extensive is the ground covered by the idea of government that we shall restrict ourselves to the consideration of only three domains in which governments operate: families, tribes, and states.

It may be a little more difficult to catch the sense in which the idea of state is broader than that of government. However, one generally recognized fact brings this home to us. With few exceptions, perhaps only that of the United States, the titles "Head of State" and "Head" or "Chief of Government" belong to two different persons. A visit to our shores by the Queen of England and a visit by the United Kingdom's prime minister symbolize two quite different relationships—the former the relation between two sovereign states, the latter between the governments of those states.

This fact reminds us of an important distinction already made between a state's external and internal sovereignty. The head of state, actually or symbolically, represents a state's external sovereignty in its dealings with other states. The head or chief of government, in this case always actually, represents the state's internal sovereignty, its jurisdiction over its inhabitants.

We are further enlightened in our understanding of these matters by noting the susceptibility of states and governments to change.

An identifiable state can endure while its form of government changes; in fact, it may endure during a long span of time in which many changes occur in its form of government. A given form of government may also endure over a considerable period of time during which the administration of that government changes many times. In our century, changes in the administration of government occur more regularly and less frequently in Great Britain and the United States than in France and Italy.

Here, then, is another widely pervasive misunderstanding that needs correction. Most of us are given to thinking of an election as resulting in a change of government, when the only change that has occurred is in the administration of government. We also are given to referring to the government as if it were located in the nation's capital city, when what is located there are its principal administrators, not the government itself.

The importance of these simple points can, perhaps, be most forcefully driven home by the facts of American history. The celebration in 1976 of the two-hundredth anniversary of the birth of this nation was a huge, if colorful, mistake, a mistake almost as ludicrous as that of describing what emerged from the Civil War as the birth of a nation.

The only thing we could and should have properly celebrated in 1976 was the bicentennial of the signing of the Declaration of Independence, not even the beginning of the colonial rebellion against Great Britain, for that had started a year earlier. Still ahead of us lies the bicentennial of the birth of the United States of America and of its form of government, which has endured for almost two centuries while undergoing many changes during that span of time. The bicentennial anniversary of this nation's birth will occur in 1989, when we celebrate the ratification of the Constitution of the United States. Only after 1789 did we begin to have foreign policy, which determined our relation as one sovereign state to other sovereign states.

The closing paragraph of the Declaration of Independence begins with the words "we the representatives of the united States of America in general congress assembled." The reference would have been even more accurate had the word *States*, like the word *united*, not carried a capital letter. There was no *United States of America* at that time.

What came into existence with the signing of the Declaration was thirteen sovereign states, each of which had formerly been a colony of the British Empire. Those thirteen sovereign states, united in their effort to fight for the independence to which they declared their right, were as yet not even loosely united for the purposes of peaceful co-existence. That very imperfect union came into existence later, in 1783, after the victory at Yorktown, when the thirteen, now independent, states agreed to enter into a loose confederacy under the Articles of Confederation.

I speak of it as a loose confederacy and a very imperfect union because the thirteen confederated states each retained its external sovereignty intact, not only vis-a-vis European states, but also vis-a-vis one another.

The thirteen sovereign states were transformed into one sovereign state only after the Constitution, drafted in the years 1787 and 1788, was ratified in 1789. That transformation created what the Preamble to the Constitution called "a more perfect union"—a single state to which the thirteen federated states transferred all their external sovereignty. The states retained a portion of their internal sovereignty while conferring the rest upon the national government created by the Constitution they had ratified. The people of the thirteen federated states now began to live under two jurisdictions (two governments and two sets of laws)—that of the national government and that of the state in which they were inhabitants.

The Constitution's Preamble, containing as it does such phrases as "we the people," "a more perfect union," "to establish justice," and "insure domestic tranquility," presages three themes to which I shall return: the idea of constitutionality, the notion of popular sovereignty as the ultimate source of constitutional government, and the understanding of war and peace in terms of the distinction between the anarchy of sovereign states and the condition of a people living together under laws enforced by a sovereign government.

What Is Government and When Is Anyone Governed?

There are two questions here, not one, and the two are closely related.

Government consists in a relation between two parties, the rulers or governors and the ruled or governed. The two parties may be absolutely distinct, as is the case when an absolute monarch or a despotic regime of any other sort holds the reins of government and when those who comprise the governed are totally subject to their rulers or governors, with no participation in the government to which they are subject.

The absolute separation of the two parties may be, both historically and also in a majority of cases at present, the prevailing mode of government. But it is not the only mode.

Those subject to government may be governed with their active consent, not merely their passive or submissive acquiescence. They may also have a voice in their own government and participate in it in a variety of ways. They may, in different respects, be both rulers and ruled, both the subjects of government and its constituents.

When this occurs, we have, as we shall see, constitutional government. Then some, never all, of the governed are self-governing citizens. They are no longer merely or solely the subjects of government.

In addition to being ruled, they also participate in ruling in a variety of ways—always as consenting constituents of government, always as enfranchised citizens exercising a voice in government, and sometimes as citizens elected or appointed to public office and, thus, engaging in the administration of government.

The distinction between rulers and ruled, governors and governed, remains the same in both of those quite different modes of government, but the status of the two parties changes radically.

In one mode, the two parties to government are absolutely separate. One of the two parties exercises all the sovereignty of government. The other suffers total subjection to it.

In the other mode, the very same persons may occupy the position of both parties to government. The very same persons may have a share in the sovereignty of government as well as being subject to it. The very same persons may be at the same time both citizens and also holders of public office; or they may be both at one time and not at another.

When they are merely citizens, they are, in different respects, both rulers and ruled—both participants in government and subject to it. When they become citizens in public office, their role as rulers and as ruled does not change, but they acquire a new role—that of those entrusted with the administration of government.

This last point echoes what was said a little earlier about the mistake of locating government in the capital city of a state. This may be true when the mode of government involves an absolute separation between the two parties to government. Then the rulers may be in one place and the ruled in another. But in the other mode of government, the government is located wherever the self-governing governed are to be found. The only thing that has a special and separate location is the administration of the government, not the government itself.

Who are the governed? And to what extent are they governed? When the two parties to government are absolutely separate, embodied in different individuals, the parties occupying the position of rulers are totally ungoverned. They are completely autonomous.

Autonomy is the most extreme form that freedom of action can take. It is the unlimited freedom of *not* being subject to the enforceable laws of any government whatsoever. To be completely autonomous is to have no superior, to be a law unto one's self, to obey one's self alone.

The completely autonomous person can also be said to be completely ungoverned when the words "being governed" are understood, as they should be, to consist in being subject to government that is not *entirely* of one's own making.

Have completely autonomous and completely ungoverned individuals ever existed? Do they exist today? Yes, certainly in the past they were the absolute despots, the sovereign princes, and one does not have to look far afield to find replicas of them in existence today.

It is also true that wherever anarchy exists, there also can be found the complete autonomy of the completely ungoverned. According to the myth of the so-called state of nature, which is more properly described as a condition of anarchy, individuals living in isolation prior to the formation of civil societies and civil governments were completely autonomous because completely ungoverned. Being completely ungoverned is what the word "anarchic" literally signifies.

Anarchy, while mythical so far as human individuals are concerned, is a hard reality when we turn from human beings to the states of which they are members. All sovereign states, like the sovereign princes of yore, exist in a condition of anarchy vis-a-vis one another. To be a sovereign state in the full sense of that term is to be completely autonomous.

I say "in the full sense of that term" because when the thirteen loosely united states on our Eastern seaboard adopted the constitution which established their more perfect union, they retained a portion of their internal sovereignty while surrendering all their external sovereignty to the United States of America. The thirteen states that entered the federal union then ceased to be completely autonomous. The constitution was called "the supreme law of the land." Subsequently, it was held that laws made by the states in the exercise of their local, internal sovereignty could be declared unconstitutional by the Supreme Court of the United States.

The partial autonomy just attributed to the several states in our federal union also belongs to every individual who is subject to government. While some individuals may be completely ungoverned, no one is ever completely governed, not even those who suffer the most extreme forms of tyrannical despotism.

The reason for this is simple. It is, on the face of it, absolutely impossible, under any mode of government, for rulers to regulate every action or to prescribe every choice on the part of the ruled. Even those in a condition of abject slavery do many things each day and make many choices that elude governance. What holds for slaves tyrannically ruled holds to an even greater extent for everyone else who is subject to government of any sort.

While no one who is governed has complete autonomy (because being governed and being completely autonomous are incompatible), everyone who is governed has some measure or degree of partial autonomy. That is a statement of incontrovertible fact. But we are left with questions of principle.

How much partial autonomy do the governed have a right to possess? How much partial autonomy is it expedient for the governed to exercise? I shall return to these questions of justice and expediency when we subsequently come to consider which is the best of all possible forms of government.

Before we leave the subject of the nature of government and what is involved in being governed, two more distinctions must be noted. They are closely related.

One is the distinction between the authority of government, on the one hand, and its power or force, on the other hand. Most of us understand this distinction in terms of the difference between right and might.

When we go to a wise person for advice, we go to him out of respect for his authority—his special competence to tell us what is the right thing to do under certain circumstances. But his advice, whether we follow it or not, does not have the force of law nor the sanctions of government. Government without enforceable sanctions is a contradiction in terms.

It should be added that only the governments of states must exercise coercive force. That does not hold true universally for all other forms of human association. Some apply milder sanctions in order to govern, but all must employ sanctions.

The government of a state must exercise might whether or not it also claims right. It must exercise coercive force over the governed whether or not it elicits from the governed respect for its authority, an authority that resides in its rightness. It may combine both might and right, but it must have might to be a government at all.

The other distinction lies in the difference between two ways in which the governed are subject to government and obey its laws or other prescriptions and regulations.

When a government exercises might alone and has no rightful authority, everyone governed is subject to the coercive force of law and other sanctions of government. The source of their obedience resides solely in their fear of the consequences that ensue from disobedience.

But when a government has both might and right, then the governed fall into two groups. On the one hand, there are those whose compliance with the laws and regulations of government proceeds solely from their recognition of and respect for its authority. Just individuals who obey just laws because they are just are in no way coerced by the sanctions of government.

On the other hand, when criminals or non-law-abiding members in the community obey its laws, they do so only out of fear of the consequences. As governed, they are coerced by the sanctions that the might of government can impose upon them. They are constrained by government only to the extent that they calculate that they cannot get away with the infractions they are inclined to commit.

The Necessity of Government

If human beings could engage in their pursuit of happiness more effectively without living in states and under the auspices of government, then neither the state nor its government would be necessary as a means to the ultimate objective at which human beings should aim—living decent human lives.

In the preceding chapter, I argued that the goodness of the state or civil society lies in its being indispensable to living a civilized life and obtaining all the real goods that individuals cannot obtain by themselves alone or under the conditions of family and tribal life. The goodness of the state or civil society was thus seen to be inseparable from its necessity as an indispensable means to the ultimate good we should seek.

What holds for the state holds also for government. Its goodness resides in its necessity—in its indispensability as a means. But a means to what? Is it not possible for human beings to achieve good lives for themselves without the constraints imposed by government through its sanctions and the coercive force of its laws? Is not the road to happiness on earth more open to those who pursue that goal without being subject to government?

Those who call themselves anarchists—philosophical, not bomb-throwing, anarchists—answer such questions with resounding affirmations. When they call for the immediate abolition of the state or for its gradual withering away, they identify the state itself with government by might, that is, by the coercive force of its various sanctions. This is what they abominate.

They think that it is quite possible for human beings, either as they are now or as they might become under altered conditions, to live peacefully and harmoniously together in society and to act in concert for a common good in which they all participate, and to do this without the restraining force exercised by the state or its government. They do not see in the complete autonomy that everyone would have under anarchy any threat to the peace, harmony, and order of social life.

Why are they profoundly wrong? One answer was given by Alexander Hamilton when he said that if men were angels, no government would be necessary for social life. Spelled out in a little more detail, Hamilton's reference to angels expressed his understanding of angels as completely virtuous, and so obedient by free choice to just laws. When he rejected as illusory the attribution to mankind of angelic virtue, he did not thereby intend to deny that some men have sufficient, if not angelic, virtue to obey just laws out of respect for their authority and without responding to the threat of coercive force.

Some men, yes, but not all! That is precisely why some portion of the individuals living together in society must be constrained by coercive force from injuring their fellows or acting against the common good of all. Hence, government with its sanctions is as necessary for social life as that, in turn, is necessary for the pursuit of happiness.

Hamilton's argument is not only sound, but unanswerable by philosophical anarchists in the light of all the known historical realities. Their only out is to appeal, beyond the facts about human beings as they now are, to what human beings might become under radically altered future circumstances.

The hope for a new type of man, with a different human nature that has been altered by external circumstances, is bizarre and groundless. The specific nature of any living organism is gene-determined, not determined in any essential respect by external circumstances. Human nature may be overlaid by all the nurtural influences imposed by the environment, but that nurtural overlay does not alter the underlying nature.

There is one point with respect to which one must concede some soundness to the philosophical anarchist's position. The coercive force that is exercised by a tyrannical and despostic government is an evil from which human beings should be emancipated. But constitutional and just governments also exercise coercive force; and then, as Hamilton argued, that confers a benefit to be sought, not an evil to be avoided.

Sound and unanswerable as Hamilton's argument may be, it is not the only or complete answer to the position of the philosophical anarchist. The other part of the answer consists in seeing that the authority of government, quite apart from its exercise of coercive force, is necessary for the concerted action of a number of individuals for a common purpose.

Let us consider the simplest possible case of three individuals—scientists engaged in the exploration of the far reaches of the Amazon. Before they embark on their expedition, must they not all agree on the method by which decisions will be reached about matters upon which they, as reasonable individuals, can possibly disagree? Without such agreement, do they not stand in danger of having unresolved differences of opinion among them frustrate, even ruin, their concerted efforts?

Granted affirmative answers to these two questions, what are their options? Only two appear to be available. To insist upon unanimity

in the solution of all the problems they are likely to face is to deny
that reasonable differences of opinion are likely to arise. Grant that
likelihood and then the only options left are twofold: (1) the choice
of one of the three as the leader whose decisions about all matters
shall prevail; and (2) the adoption of the principle that decisions
will be reached by a majority of two against one.

Either principle of decision-making must be adopted unani-
mously on the part of the three explorers. It cannot be imposed by
one of them upon the other two; it cannot be selected by a majority
of two against one, because the problem of how matters should be
decided must first be solved by the agreement of all three. Lead-
ership by one can be set up by that one only through force. This
we have excluded in our imaginary case. The principle of majority
rule cannot be set up by a majority vote, not unless the majority
imposes it by force.

Decision-making can, of course, be avoided entirely by tossing a
coin. That, however, is an abdication of government, leaving everything to chance instead of putting reason to use.

Our hypothetical example of the three explorers setting up some
instrument of government for their expedition has excluded the use
of force either to institute government in the first place or to exercise it, once it has been set up. Here, then, we have government
with voluntarily established authority and with no recourse to might.
We also have government that serves a necessity other than that of
preventing or reducing antisocial or unjust conduct on the part of
some portion of society's population.

This picture portrays government as an indispensable means to
the concerted action of a number of individuals for a common purpose. That is the essence of social life. Many of the decisions that
have to be made may be morally indifferent; such as traffic ordi-
nances about driving on the left-hand or the right-hand side of the
road. There is nothing just or unjust about either alternative. But
when the circumstances are such that traffic control becomes necessary for the security of life and limb, one or the other alternative
must be chosen. Government is necessary to decide which, and to
render that decision with the requisite authority.

War and Peace

Implicit in the preceding pages are insights about war and peace that are the best fruits of thinking about the idea of government.

Our conventional and colloquial use of these two terms has for centuries obscured the difference between a state of war and warfare, and between civil peace and the mere absence of warfare.

In the vocabulary of daily usage, we speak of making war as an engagement in battle by the employment of weapons. When victory by one side or exhaustion on the part of both brings warfare to a conclusion, we refer to the cessation of violent hostilities as the onset of peace. Arrangements are then entered into by treaties or other devices to prolong the armistice which we think of as preserving peace.

To enlarge and improve our understanding of these matters, we need only remember what has been said in the preceding pages about the benefit that government confers upon any society by ensuring its domestic tranquility, which is the condition of civil peace. Civil peace is not just the absence of warfare, nor is it the absence of serious conflicts between individuals or groups of individuals who comprise the population of a society. It consists rather in the possibility of resolving all the conflicts that may arise in a society without resort to illicit violence and an illegitimate use of force.

There are only two ways in which human conflicts can be resolved: either by talk or by force. When talk fails, and the conflict is serious enough to demand resolution, resort to force—or the threat of force—is the only alternative. When the apparatus of government is adequate for the purpose, it provides the machinery for settling all conflicts or disputes by talk. It thus eliminates the need to have recourse to force and violence.

The adjudication of disputes in courts, the resolution of conflicts of opinion about public policy in legislative or other assemblies, the enforcement of the law, referenda, plebiscites, and elections, with one exception, are operations in which human beings talk about and talk away the differences that bring them into conflict.

The one exception to be noted is the enforcement of law. Here it would seem that talk alone does not suffice and the use of force must be employed. What force? Force employed by whom? The force that is vested in an arm of government, the force that a government employs, to prevent disruptions or breaches of the peace by criminal conduct that involves an illicit or illegitimate use of force.

A great German jurist, Hans Kelsen, pointed out that a de jure government, a rightfully established government, exercises a monopoly of authorized force. All other force, the resort to violence on the part of members of a society, either individually or in groups, is unauthorized force and, therefore, illicit or illegitimate.

As we have already observed, there are de facto as well as de jure governments—governments that rule by might alone, and rightfully established governments that have authority as well as power, an authority that includes an authorized use of force to preserve peace.

Do both modes of government provide adequate machinery for preserving peace? In one sense, yes; in another, no.

Government by might alone, without legitimate authority, preserves peace by means of an unauthorized use of force. It succeeds, of course, only to the extent that the force at its disposal has overwhelming weight as against the force that can be employed by any dissident groups in the population.

Furthermore, to the extent that the government itself lacks justice and rules unjustly, the peace that it establishes and preserves by illegitimate force is a fragile and unstable condition. Sedition, insurrection, riot, and rebellion are always seething below the surface in any society in which gross injustices are inflicted upon the population.

What appears to be peace is really a state of war between rulers and ruled, for when long-standing abuses and a train of injustices bring them into serious conflict with one another, actual warfare breaks out between them. A state of war is that condition in which actual warfare is always latent. It is the ever-present possibility of which warfare is the actualization.

Perfect peace, in contrast, is that condition in which the possibility of actual warfare is totally eliminated by the adequacy of governmental means for settling all disputes by talk, by lawful devices, by government's monopoly of authorized force, and by providing all dissident groups within the population with legal means of dissent so that, where injustices exist, the abused or oppressed can seek to redress their grievances without resort to violence.

Perfect peace is obviously an ideal that may never be fully realized on earth. But it is also an ideal that is realized in some degree wherever rightfully instituted governments exist. It is approximated to whatever extent such governments govern justly, provide machinery adequate for the purpose of resolving all disputes, and exercise authorized force.

Three great political philosophers—Cicero, Machiavelli, and John Locke—have pointed out, in almost identical phraseology, that there are only two ways of settling disputes. One is by talk, by law, and by law enforcement. The other is by force or violence.

The first is the uniquely human method of settling conflicts. The second is the method of brutes, of the beasts of the jungle.

When the first method prevails and succeeds, we have the civil peace of civilized life. When it fails or is totally lacking, we have a state of war in which actual warfare is always below the surface of a merely apparent peace that is nothing but the temporary absence of fighting, of bloodshed, of violence.

Another great political philosopher, Thomas Hobbes, completes the picture by pointing out that peace exists only within the boundaries of a state and among individuals living together under the benign auspices of a legitimate government. Between completely autonomous sovereigns—sovereign princes or sovereign states—there is always a state of war.

It is only in this century that we have come finally to recognize the soundness of his insight. We have invented the phrase "cold war" to refer to the state of war that sovereign states are in vis-a-vis one another. This is manifest in the conduct of foreign policy, in the actions of diplomats, in the subterfuges of espionage, and in the aggressive potency of the military installations that we call defense establishments. Lurking beneath the surface, ready to break out, is the hot war of the generals and the admirals, who are called upon to achieve the results that have been unsuccessfully sought by all the devices of the cold war.

Anarchy—the jungle in which all sovereign states find themselves—is identical with the alternatives of cold war and hot war. It is never a condition of peace, even when sovereign states appear to be friendly rather than hostile in relation to one another. What we miscall peace between states is nothing but the absence of actual warfare between them. Genuine peace exists only when government replaces anarchy.

From the beginning of history to the present time, there has never been world peace, but only a plurality of peaces—as many as, at a given time, there are separate societies. In each of these, some mode of government establishes some degree of civil peace by the machinery it provides for settling disputes without resort to violence. The plurality of peaces is smaller or larger according to the number of separate societies in which individuals live under government. The size or extent of each of these plural peaces varies with the size of the domain and of the population that is governed.

In the course of history, mankind has passed from tribal peaces and tribal wars to the peaces of separate city-states and the wars between them. When city-states became empires with colonies, the extent of the peace units became enlarged, and so also did the wars in which imperial dominions engaged. When in modern times, national states emerged from and replaced the anarchy that existed among the petty principalities of the feudal system, the size of the peace units once again enlarged, and enlarged still further as national states became empires with colonies under their dominion. What was called the *Pax Romana* in the ancient world and has been called the *Pax Britannica* in the modern world represent such enlarged peace units.

In the twentieth century, the first century in which anything that deserves to be called a world war first occurred, world peace has not yet come into existence, though its possibility is presaged by the occurrence of world wars. The creation of the League of Nations after the first world war and the formation of the United Nations after the second created inadequate devices for the establishment of world peace.

They may have served to inhibit the cold war, which always exists among sovereign states, from turning into the hot war that is always latently present. But precisely because the League of Nations was not and the United Nations is not a government with a monopoly of authorized force, neither can be regarded as an instrument for establishing and preserving genuine peace. That the United Nations is not a government and cannot be one is plainly indicated by the fact that its members are all sovereign states, each completely autonomous, each able to withdraw at will or to exercise a nullifying veto over any action taken.

The Charter of the United Nations is analogous to the Articles of Confederation, under which the thirteen sovereign states on our Eastern seaboard were associated with one another between the time they won their independence from Great Britain and the time they entered into a more perfect union by adopting a federal constitution. With that transition, the civil peace of the United States of America replaced the state of war that prevailed among the thirteen sovereign states under the Articles of Confederation.

The lesson to be learned should be patently plain. If government is the indispensable means for establishing and preserving genuine peace wherever it is found on earth in the plural peaces that exist (however small or large their extent may be, varying with the size of the domain and the population that is governed), then it inexorably follows that genuine world peace requires world government.

The obstacles to the establishment of world government are many and various. The probability of its being realized can be estimated in terms of the difficulty of overcoming those impediments. The two ways in which it may be brought about in the first instance are identical with the two ways available for resolving human disputes or conflicts—by talk and by force.

The first way would involve the framing of a constitution by a world constitutional convention and the adoption of that constitution by all sovereign states, which would then relinquish their external sovereignty vis-a-vis one another. The second way would involve a world war that resulted in world conquest without, at the same time, making the earth uninhabitable.

However unlikely the first way may appear to be, the second is even more unlikely. But the improbable, in whatever degree, is never the same as the impossible. However improbable may be the establishment and preservation of world peace by the institution of world federal government, its possibility remains untouched—for, since world government is *necessary* for world peace, and world peace is *necessary* for the survival and welfare of mankind, both must also be *possible*.

The Modes and Forms of Government

I have already called attention to the fundamental distinction between two modes of government. It springs from the difference between rule by might alone and rule by right or authority that is supported by a monopoly of authorized force. Each of these modes of government may take a wide variety of subordinate forms, the consideration of which let us postpone for a moment.

To understand all the differences between these two modes of government and their various forms, let us look at three archetypical relationships between rulers and ruled, governors and governed.

One is the relationship between human beings and the domesticated animals they employ or the tools and machines they use. We do not ordinarily think of this as a mode of government, yet we do recognize that this relationship consists in the human management of things.

Such management also occurs when human beings treat other human beings as if they were things to be managed and used for the good of the managers. The human beings thus managed are slaves ruled by masters. The rule is both despotic and tyrannical—*despotic* because it is government without the voluntary consent of the governed and without any participation by them in the government to which they are subject; *tyrannical* because the government serves only the interests of the masters, not the good of the slaves.

The second relationship is that between parents and children in the domestic community of the family. Here, so long as the children remain minors and so long as their immaturity requires that they be governed without their consent or participation, the mode of government is also despotic. When the children subject to such despotic government are not treated as slaves to be managed for the good of their rulers, but instead are governed for their own good and the good of the family, then the despotism of parental government is benevolent rather than tyrannical. It becomes tyrannical if it does not cease to be despotic when the children reach the age of consent and acquire the maturity that renders them capable of having a voice in their own government.

The third relationship is that which prevails among adult human beings who are associated for a common purpose and who, respecting each other as equals, live together and act in concert under a mode of government to which they gave their voluntary consent and in which they participate both as rulers and ruled.

This relationship did not exist in the domestic community when the marriage vow required the wife to obey her husband in all matters and thus made the husband a despotic ruler of the wife as well as of their offspring.

However, in very recent times, changes in the marriage relationship have brought about an acknowledgment of equality between husband and wife. This has resulted in family government in which both husband and wife participate as equals, each with a voice in the government of the domestic community, each being both ruler and ruled in deciding different matters.

When we go from the society of the family or that of the tribe to the political community or civil society, which we call a state, this third type of relationship comes into existence. Constitutional government replaces despotic rule. That mode of government is the government of equals, not of superiors over inferiors. It is a mode of government in which some of the governed have political liberty, the freedom that consists in being governed with one's own consent, with a voice in one's own government, and with all human rights secured.

Why only some of the governed, not all? Because, just as the mode of government we call despotic may take the form of tyrannical or benevolent despotism, so the mode of government we call constitutional may also take one of two forms: one in which only some of the governed are citizens with suffrage, while the rest remain subjects despotically ruled; and one in which all who are competent to be enfranchised citizens enjoy that status.

I shall postpone for the moment the question about the criteria of competency. In addition to those in a state of infancy before reaching the age of consent and to those hospitalized for feeble-mindedness or insanity, who shall be justly regarded as ineligible for enfranchised citizenship? The way in which this question is answered determines the line that divides the two basic forms of constitutional government—one with restricted suffrage, the other with universal suffrage. On one side of that line lie all the forms of constitutional government that are oligarchies; on the other side, all the forms that are democracies.

Postponing that basic division between forms of constitutional government until we deal, in the next chapter, with the idea of democracy, let us concentrate here on the more fundamental division between the two modes of government I have called despotic and constitutional. In addition to what has already been said on this score, what else differentiates them?

The answer is to be found in our understanding of the ideas of constitution and citizenship. That depends upon our eschewing the loose sense in which the words connected with these ideas are often used. Such usage obscures our understanding of these ideas.

Loosely used, the word "constitution" refers to any framework or form of government. Different forms of government are differently constituted. Some are constituted as absolute monarchies or despotisms, some as republics. Loosely used, the word "citizen" refers to the inhabitants or denizens of a state whether or not they are governed with their consent and with a voice in their government.

Properly conceived, a constitution, whether written or unwritten, is a framework of government that is adopted by the people who thereby become its constituents and who, as such, share in popular sovereignty. It is in essence an enumeration of the offices needed to perform the functions of government; an investment of each of these offices with certain limited authority and power; a determination of the relation of these offices to one another; and a definition of the criteria of eligibility for holding these offices. Last but not least, it creates citizenship as the status belonging to all members of the ruling class and as the prime requisite for holding any public office in the state.

A constitution may or may not include a bill of rights, protecting citizens from unjust encroachments on their political liberty, from unjust reductions of their partial autonomy, and from unjust invasions of their private lives. It may also provide for its own emendation and amplification by amendments to secure human rights, to safeguard individual liberties, and to promote the general welfare.

In any form of the constitutional mode of government, the primary office is that of citizenship with suffrage. To become a public official or an officer of government, one must first be a citizen. Public officials or office-holders do not hold the authority and power of government in their own hands. That resides primarily in the body of citizens; it is delegated by them to the elected or appointed officials, who do not have an unlimited power to govern.

Such limited power and authority as they have to administer the functions of government, they have only by virtue of the public offices they occupy. It consists in whatever measure of power and authority the constitution confers upon that particular office. When public officials exceed the authority and power of their constitutionally appointed offices, they commit usurpations that a well-devised constitution must be able to remedy by impeachment and dismissal from office.

In sharp contrast to office-holders who administer the functions of constitutional government, despots of every variety have unlimited power that is vested entirely in their own persons. They have no authority to govern at all, since such authority must be derived from the consent of the governed.

This fundamental distinction between two modes of government is recognized by everyone who has ever contrasted a government of laws and a government of men, and by everyone who has ever referred to limited, as contrasted with absolute, government.

A government of laws is one in which no individual is above the laws of the state, especially its most fundamental, formative law that is its constitution. Where such government exists, all are subject to the laws and no one can make laws, adjudicate legal disputes, or execute laws, except by virtue of the limited authority and power vested by the constitution in the legislative, judicial, or executive offices they occupy.

Two words are commonly used for those who govern by their personal might—always "despot" and sometimes "tyrant." They may be single individuals, and then they are called absolute monarchs. They may also be groups of individuals who exercise absolute and unlimited rule over subjects who are governed without their consent and with no voice in their own government. By extension of the terms, despotism, and sometimes tyranny, apply to the imperial government of colonies.

What words do we, or should we, use to name the administrative functionaries who hold office in a constitutional government, another name for which is "republic"? Since they hold political offices, we might be tempted to call them politicians, were it not for the fact that the word has come to mean an individual who uses any means to get and hold a political office rather than one who strives to discharge the functions of that office. Since they are officials of the state, we might be tempted to call them statesmen, were it not for the highly eulogistic connotation that is usually attached to that name.

These things being so, we had better settle for a more cumbersome but more accurate style of reference, calling them citizens who are also public officials or occupants of political offices. In no case should we call them rulers or governors, for they are never more than the administrators of governmental services. In the constitutional mode of government, the rulers are the citizens. They delegate to others the authority and power to administer the special functions of government. The sovereignty of a constitution derives from the sovereignty of its constituent people.

The Mixed Regime

In the history of political thought, the phrase "mixed regime" has been used in two senses. One is of slight importance. The other has great significance for our understanding of the two basic modes of government.

A form of government with one individual as king, president, or prime minister, with a senate or house of lords composed of patricians or nobles, and with some degree of popular participation, is said to be a threefold mixture, combining the elements of monarchy, aristocracy, and democracy.

In this use of the term, the governments of Great Britain and the United States can be called mixed regimes. However, to do so is to use such words as "monarchy," "aristocracy," and "democracy" in a way that distorts and confuses the classification of the forms of government. It ignores and obscures the fact that every form of government falls under one or the other of government's two basic modes, despotic and constitutional.

Our understanding so far of those two basic modes would lead us to think that their obvious incompatibility with one another prevents them from being combined in any fashion. The facts of the matter seem to be otherwise. Using the words "royal" and "kingly" as synonyms for "despotic," and the word "political" as a synonym for "constitutional," Aristotle speaks of governments that are both royal and political. In the late Middle Ages, that combination came to be called a *regimen regale et politicum*. How can these two modes of government be combined to create a mixed regime?

If we consider the nature of tribal government, we begin to discover the answer. The rules of conduct to which the members of a tribe comply are its immemorial customs—its customary laws that go back in time beyond the memory of any living member of the tribe. They have an authority that derives from their status as the accepted mores. The rulers of the tribe—its elders or chieftains— do not make these laws nor are they exempt from obedience to them. One of their principal obligations as tribal rulers is to uphold the customs of the tribe.

But the tribal customs must also be enforced when one or another miscreant individual runs amok. Individuals who are suspected or charged with such noncompliance must be judged. Since no body of laws or customs perfectly covers all particular cases, there is also the need for decrees, edicts, or ukases to decide what should be done when accepted customs prove inadequate to solve a problem at hand.

I have just named three governmental functions that fall within the province and the prerogatives of tribal leaders or chieftains. One is the enforcement of the laws; a second is the adjudication of particular cases that fall within the scope of the laws; and the third is the making of arbitrary decisions about matters that lie outside the scope of the laws.

Let us lump all three together as administrative functions of government, distinguishing all three from legislation and jurisdiction— making laws and promulgating them. In tribal government, no individual or group of individuals performs these latter functions. The laws of the tribe are known to all and their authority is generally respected because of their status as customs coming down from time immemorial.

The elders or chieftains of the tribe, in performing the aforementioned administrative functions, rule royally or despotically, not without the consent of the governed, but without their participation in these aspects of government. The established customs of the tribe which govern the conduct of all, that of the elders or chieftains included, represent the political or constitutional aspect of government. Thus, the two modes of government are combined to form a mixed regime, a *regimen regale et politicum*. It is a government that is, on the one hand, absolute and arbitrary; on the other hand, limited and lawful.

The slow development of constitutional government in England provides us with another example of the mixed regime. It makes its first appearance with the signing of the Magna Carta in 1215. A bridle was thereby put on the absolute despotism of King John. The barons swore a feudal oath of fealty to him on condition that he observe and respect the immemorial customs of the realm. The barons also drew a line around their rights to protect the partial autonomy each of them possessed as a feudal lord from being invaded or transgressed by undue use of the royal prerogative to settle matters by arbitrary decrees or edicts.

A second major step in the fencing in of the royal prerogative came with the enactment of a bill of rights by the revolutionary parliament of 1688. England was then still under a mixed regime, for the king still retained certain arbitrary power in the performance of the administrative functions of government, while parliament gained more legislative and jurisdictional power to make and promulgate the laws of the land.

Does the government of the United Kingdom today retain any vestiges of a mixed regime? It does symbolically, but not in actual practice. The throne, the crown, and the sceptre of the monarch still symbolize the royal aspect of Britain's government, to the authority of which the people generally give their consent.

The coronation ceremony involves the taking of an oath by the monarch to uphold the laws of the land, none of them made by the monarch and none susceptible to change from that source.* Few, if any, royal prerogatives remain and those that do are granted the monarch by parliament and limited by its enactments. All the functions of government are now performed by parliament and by the substructure of officialdom that is needed for the purposes of leg-

---

*Another manifestation of the constitutional aspect of a mixed regime comes down to us in the wording of the pledge entered into by the Spanish nobles at the coronation of the kings of Aragon: "We who are as good as you, swear to you who are no better than we, to accept you as our king, provided that you observe all our liberties and laws; but if not, not."

islation, adjudication, and the execution and enforcement of the laws and public policies.

The government of Great Britain today is conventionally called a constitutional monarchy, which is equivalent in meaning to the mediaeval phrase "political kingdom." But, apart from the vestiges of royalty that are symbolically retained, it is in actual practice no less a purely constitutional government than that of the republic of the United States.

Considering the stages in the transformation of government in Great Britain—from absolute despotism initially, through intermediate degrees of an admixture of both royal and constitutional elements, to a mode of government that is now completely constitutional—we can also see the difference between the unwritten constitution of the British government and the written constitution of the United States.

Except for the first step that is represented by the Magna Carta, all the rest of the constitutional developments in Great Britain have resulted from a long series of legislative enactments by parliament. The British constitution is an accretion of all these legislative enactments that determine the powers assigned to the various administrative offices of government and that secure the rights and liberties of the governed.

In contrast, the Constitution of the United States, and all the modern constitutions for which it has been a model, came into existence not by legislative enactment, but by the drafting of a single document in a constitutional convention and by the subsequent ratification of that document by the constituent people.

Analogous to the series of legislative enactments that altered and improved the British constitution is the series of amendments to the American constitution that have been formulated and adopted in accordance with a provision for innovations that is included in the original constitution itself.

The existence of a written constitution does not ensure the existence and operation of constitutional government. Without a constitution written in the American fashion, the government of Great Britain is now purely constitutional. With a written constitution (but one that was not framed by a constitutional convention representing the constituent people, nor ratified by them), the government of the Soviet Union (self-styled as a dictatorship of the proletariat) is as good an example of absolute despotism as anything we can find in the contemporary world.

Resistance to Government

Since despotic government is government by might or force, without the consent and participation of the governed, resistance on the part of the governed must always resort to the use of force against despotic rulers.

John Locke, who regarded encroachments on the rights of the people by an undue and arbitrary use of the royal prerogative as equivalent to a warlike use of naked force, called the despotic king a rebel, not the people who were compelled to use force to resist such encroachments. The word "rebellion" in his vocabulary (etymologically derived from the Latin word *"rebellare"*) literally meant a return to war or to forceful conflict, initiated by royal despotism and met by a forceful response on the part of the misgoverned, who were compelled by the actions of the despot to engage in rebellion.

When we pass from purely despotic governments, and from mixed regimes in which the despotic element becomes excessive, to purely constitutional governments, the word "rebellion," in the literal sense given it by Locke, no longer applies. In governments that derive their just powers from the consent of the governed, resistance to government that arises from grievances on the part of the governed should be feasible through due process of law—by legal and non-violent means of dissent.

One form of resistance to government need not concern us here, because it is common to both despotic and constitutional regimes. It is called "conscientious objection." It involves a refusal by single individuals to comply with man-made laws on the ground that they contravene the divine or the natural moral law. Conscientious objectors also comply with the laws they disobey by willingly accepting the penalty legally prescribed for disobedience. Their action is to this extent both lawful and nonviolent.

Resistance to purely constitutional government on the part of organized groups of individuals who, rightly or wrongly, regard themselves as treated unjustly can remain within the boundary of consent to whatever extent legal means are provided for dissent. When does organized dissent cross the boundary line and become insurgence or insurrection? When does it involve a withdrawal of consent and also latent or overt violence in response to the action of law-enforcement agencies? What failure or defect on the part of constitutional government explains and, perhaps, justifies these pathological forms of resistance to constitutional government?

If a constitutional government provided legal means of dissent that were entirely adequate for the purpose of redressing real or supposed grievances, and if recourse to such legal means could be effective within a relatively short period of time, so that long-suffered grievances would not appear to be irremediable within the immediate future, then there would be neither need nor justification for withdrawal of consent and recourse to unlawful and even violent measures.

Those who defend such resistance to constitutional government can justify it on either of the grounds mentioned above—the lack of adequate legal means of dissent or the prolonged delay in obtaining redress when the available legal means of dissent are resorted to. The appeal to these grounds indicates defects in constitutional government that should be corrected.

Whether or not they can be, whether or not constitutional government can ever be so perfected that no justification remains for riotous and violent resistance, is a difficult question indeed. I prefer leaving it for readers to ponder rather than attempting to answer it myself.

John Locke's justification of rebellion does not apply here, nor does Thomas Jefferson's espousal of the right to overthrow a government that has despotically violated the rights that the Declaration of Independence declares just governments should secure. Resistance to purely constitutional governments never need go to the extreme of violent rebellion and revolution, though organized and even violent political protests against the injustices that may be committed by such governments are justifiable if lawful and non-violent means of dissent are inadequate.

The Idea of Civil Police

Throughout the history of political thought, from antiquity to the beginning of the nineteenth century, there has been general agreement on the point that the exercise of coercive power to enforce the law and preserve the peace is an indispensable requisite for the effectiveness of government.

Unjust laws are laws in name only. It is equally true to say that unenforceable laws are laws in name only. The line that divides the condition of being governed from that of being directed by advice separates prescriptions and prohibitions that exact obedience by the sanctions of law enforcement from directions that can be disregarded without fear of any forcefully imposed penalties.

It is shocking, therefore, to discover that the formation of a police force, with constitutionally conferred and, therefore, limited power to act to prevent crime, to bring criminals to punishment, and to preserve civil peace, did not occur until the first quarter of the nineteenth century. One would certainly tend, on the contrary, to suppose that wherever constitutional governments existed and operated effectively prior to that time, there, too, one would find a constitutionally established police force as an agency or arm of such government.

That absolute and despotic governments—governments by might, not by right—have always exercised force to serve their purposes is beyond doubt or question. On this point, the historical evidence is ample and clear. But the force such governments have always exercised has either been the sheer military force at the disposal of the sovereign or, in modern times, the paramilitary force of what has come to be called "secret police."

It is remarkable that the republics of antiquity in the Greek and Roman city-states did not include in their constitutions an arm or agency of government adequate for law enforcement and peace preservation. This is not to say that there were no public officials at all who were empowered to function for these purposes. But the historical evidence of their existence and of their scope of operation plainly reveals their inadequacy as compared with the police forces that have been established, expanded, and perfected by republics or constitutional governments in the late ninteenth and twentieth centuries.

The idea of constitutional government is not a new idea, but it is an idea that has undergone a remarkable change in recent times with the birth of a genuinely new and related idea—that of a civil (and, therefore, a nonmilitary) police force as an indispensable arm of constitutional government.

To elaborate on this new idea and to survey the history that lies behind this very recent innovation in constitutional government would carry us far beyond the scope of this book. Readers interested in that elaboration and that historical background can find it in a treatment of the subject by the Institute for Philosophical Research, in an essay entitled, "The Idea of Civil Police."*

* Published by Encyclopædia Britannica in *The Great Ideas Today, 1983*.

QUOTATIONS WITHOUT COMMENT

With Regard to Constitutions and Constitutional Governments

A constitution is the arrangement of magistracies in a state, especially of the highest of all. The government is everywhere sovereign in the state, and the constitution is in fact the government. For example, in democracies the people are supreme, but in oligarchies, the few; and, therefore, we say that these two forms of government also are different: and so in other cases.

Aristotle, Politics, Bk. III, Ch. 6 (4th cent. B.C.)

★ ★ ★

Of forms of government in which one rules, we call that which regards the common interests, kingship or royalty; that in which more than one, but not many, rule, aristocracy; and it is so called, either because the rulers are the best men, or because they have at heart the best interests of the state and of the citizens. But when the citizens at large administer the state for the common interest, the government is called by the generic name [a polity].

Aristotle, Politics, Bk. III, Ch. 7 (4th cent. B.C.)

★ ★ ★

. . . To order anything to the common good belongs either to the whole people, or to someone who is the vicegerent of the whole people. And therefore the making of a law belongs either to the whole people or to a public personage who has care of the whole people.

Thomas Aquinas, Summa Theologica, Pt. I-II, Q. 90, A. 3
(c. 1265)

★ ★ ★

The basis of our political systems is the right of the people to make and to alter their constitutions of government. But the con-

stitution which at any time exists, till changed by an explicit and
authentic act of the whole people, is sacredly obligatory upon all.
The very idea of the power and the right of the people to establish
government presupposes the duty of every individual to obey the
established government.

George Washington, *Farewell Address* (Sept. 19, 1796)

★　★　★

There is, however, another important side of [Tom] Paine's conception of a constitution in which it might seem to differ funda-
mentally from the views of other opponents of arbitrary government
in his own time and before. One of Paine's most fundamental as-
sertions is that a true constitution is always *antecedent* to the actual
government in a state. If by the word "antecedent" he means prior
in time, he seems to be asserting a principle which can be true only
of constitutions "struck off" consciously by a people at a definite
time, as they had lately been formulated in the thirteen colonies in
America. On such an assumption the only true constitution would
appear to be a "written constitution" of a type familiar enough to
us since 1776, but scarcely thought of before, except perhaps for a
dozen years in the middle of the seventeenth century in England.
This narrow and novel definition of a constitution may have been
the one Paine had in mind, and the prominence in his political
thought of the notion of a definite historical compact between the
government and the governed makes it the more probable. . . .

Paine, in saying that a constitution must always be antecedent to
any rightful government, was laying down a political maxim, not a
rule of English law. . . . We must, I think, at least agree that the
analysis Paine made of the early American constitution was remarkably acute. The significant points in that analysis are these:

That there is a fundamental difference between a people's government and that people's constitution, whether the government
happens to be entrusted to a king or to a representative assembly.

That this constitution is "antecedent" to the government.

That it defines the authority which the people commits to its
government, and in so doing thereby limits it.

That any exercise of authority beyond these limits by any government is an exercise of "power without right."

That in any state in which the distinction is not actually observed between the constitution and the government there is in reality no constitution, because the will of the government has no check upon it, and that state is in fact a despotism. . . .

Paine's notion that the only true constitution is one consciously constructed, and that a nation's government is only the creature of this constitution, conforms probably more closely than any other to the actual development in the world since the opening of the nineteenth century.

Charles Howard McIlwain, *Constitutionalism Ancient and Modern*, Ch. I (1940)

With Regard to Government, Its Modes and Forms

When the government is personal, the ruler is a king; when, according to the rules of [a constitution], the citizens rule and are ruled in turn, then he is called a statesman. . . . The rule of a master is not a constitutional rule. . . . For there is one rule exercised over subjects who are by nature free, another over subjects who are by nature slaves. The rule of a household is a monarchy, for every house is under one head: whereas constitutional rule is a government of freemen and equals. . . .

But in most constitutional states the citizens rule and are ruled by turns, for the idea of a constitutional state implies that the natures of the citizens are equal, and do not differ at all.

Aristotle, *Politics*, Bk. I, Chs. 1, 7, 12 (4th cent. B.C.)

★ ★ ★

. . . The form of government is best in which every man, whoever he is, can act best and live happily.

Aristotle, *Politics*, Bk. VII, Ch. 2 (4th cent. B.C.)

★ ★ ★

. . . A man is not a king unless he is sufficient to himself and excels his subjects in all good things; and such a man needs nothing further; therefore he will not look to his own interests but to those of his subjects; for a king who is not like that would be a mere titular king. Now tyranny is the very contrary of this; the tyrant pursues his own good. And it is clearer in the case of tyranny that it is the worst deviation-form; but it is the contrary of the best that is worst. Monarchy passes over into tyranny; for tyranny is the evil form of one-man rule and the bad king becomes a tyrant.

Aristotle, *Nichomachean Ethics*, Bk. VIII, Ch. 10
(4th cent. B.C.)

★ ★ ★

. . . That rule is called politic and royal by which a man rules over free subjects who, though subject to the government of the ruler, have nevertheless something of their own, by reason of which they can resist the orders of him who commands.

Thomas Aquinas, *Summa Theologica*, Pt. I, Q. 81, A. 3
(c. 1265)

★ ★ ★

. . . A kingdom is the best form of government of the people, so long as it is not corrupt. But since the power granted to a king is so great, it easily degenerates into tyranny, unless he to whom this power is given be a very virtuous man.

Thomas Aquinas, *Summa Theologica*, Pt. I–II, Q. 105,
A. 1 (c. 1265)

★ ★ ★

A tyrannical government is not just, because it is directed, not to the common good, but to the private good of the ruler. . . . Consequently there is no sedition in disturbing a government of this kind, unless indeed the tyrant's rule be disturbed so inordinately that his subjects suffer greater harm from the consequent disturbance than from the tyrant's government. Indeed it is the tyrant rather that is guilty of sedition, since he encourages discord and sedition among his subjects, that he may lord over them more securely.

Thomas Aquinas, *Summa Theologica*, Pt. II–II, Q. 42, A. 2

(c. 1265)

★ ★ ★

It is evident that absolute monarchy, which by some men is counted for the only government in the world, is indeed inconsistent with civil society, and so can be no form of civil government at all. For the end of civil society being to avoid and remedy those inconveniencies of the state of Nature which necessarily follow from every man's being judge in his own case, by setting up a known authority to which every one of that society may appeal upon any injury received, or controversy that may arise, and which every one of the society ought to obey. Wherever any persons are who have not such an authority to appeal to, and decide any difference between them there, those persons are still in the state of Nature. And so is every absolute prince in respect of those who are under his dominion.

John Locke, *Second Essay on Civil Government*, Ch. VII,

Sec. 90 (1690)

★ ★ ★

As usurpation is the exercise of power which another hath a right to, so tyranny is the exercise of power beyond right, which nobody can have a right to; and this is making use of the power any one has in his hands, not for the good of those who are under it, but for his own private, separate advantage. When the governor, however entitled, makes not the law, but his will, the rule, and his commands and actions are not directed to the preservation of the properties of his people, but the satisfaction of his own ambition, revenge, covetousness, or any other irregular passion. . . .

It is a mistake to think this fault is proper only to monarchies. Other forms of government are liable to it as well as that; for wherever the power that is put in any hands for the government of the people and the preservation of their properties is applied to other ends, and made use of to impoverish, harass, or subdue them to the arbitrary and irregular commands of those that have it, there it presently becomes tyranny, whether those that thus use it are one or many. . . .

Wherever law ends, tyranny begins.

> John Locke, *Second Essay on Civil Government,*
> Ch. XVIII, Sec. 199–202 (1690)

★   ★   ★

I . . . give the name "Republic" to every State that is governed by laws, no matter what the form of its administration may be: for only in such a case does the public interest govern, and the *res publica* rank as a *reality*. Every legitimate government is republican.

> Jean-Jacques Rousseau, *The Social Contract,* Bk. II,
> Ch. 6 (1762)

★   ★   ★

A good government implies two things: first, fidelity to the object of government, which is the happiness of the people; secondly, a knowledge of the means by which that object can be best attained. Some governments are deficient in both these qualities; most governments are deficient in the first.

> Alexander Hamilton or James Madison, *The Federalist Papers,*
> #62 (1787–88)

★   ★   ★

The ends of government are as comprehensive as those of the social union. They consist of all the good, and all the immunity from evil, which the existence of government can be made either directly or indirectly to bestow.

> John Stuart Mill, *Principles of Political Economy,* Bk. V,
> Ch. II, Sec. 2 (1848)

★   ★   ★

I am far from condemning, in cases of extreme exigency, the assumption of absolute power in the form of a temporary dictatorship. Free nations have, in times of old, conferred such power by their own choice, as a necessary medicine for diseases of the body politic which could not be got rid of by less violent means. But its acceptance, even for a time strictly limited, can only be excused, if . . . the dictator employs the whole power he assumes in removing the obstacles which debar the nation from the enjoyment of freedom. A good despotism is an altogether false ideal, which practically (except as a means to some temporary purpose) becomes the most senseless and dangerous of chimeras. Evil for evil, a good despotism, in a country at all advanced in civilisation, is more noxious than a bad one; for it is far more relaxing and enervating to the thoughts, feelings, and energies of the people.

John Stuart Mill, *Representative Government*, Ch. 3 (1861)

★ ★ ★

There are, as we have already seen, conditions of society in which a vigorous despotism is in itself the best mode of government for training the people in what is specifically wanting to render them capable of a higher civilisation. There are others, in which the mere fact of despotism has indeed no beneficial effect, the lessons which it teaches having already been only too completely learnt; but in which, there being no spring of spontaneous improvement in the people themselves, their almost only hope of making any steps in advance depends on the chances of a good despot. Under a native despotism, a good despot is a rare and transitory accident: but when the dominion they are under is that of a more civilised people, that people ought to be able to supply it constantly. The ruling country ought to be able to do for its subjects all that could be done by a succession of absolute monarchs, guaranteed by irresistible force against the precariousness of tenure attendant on barbarous despotisms, and qualified by their genius to anticipate all that experience has taught to the more advanced nation. Such is the ideal rule of a free people over a barbarous or semi-barbarous one. We need not expect to see that ideal realised; but unless some approach to it is, · the rulers are guilty of a dereliction of the highest moral trust which can devolve upon a nation: and if they do not even aim at it, they are selfish usurpers, on a par in criminality with any of those whose ambition and rapacity have sported from age to age with the destiny of masses of mankind.

John Stuart Mill, *Representative Government*, Ch. 18 (1861)

★　★　★

A majority, held in restraint by constitutional checks and limitations, and always changing easily with deliberate changes of popular opinions and sentiments, is the only true sovereign of a free people. Whoever rejects it does of necessity fly to anarchy or to despotism. Unanimity is impossible. The rule of a minority, as a permanent arrangement, is wholly inadmissible; so that, rejecting the majority principle, anarchy or despotism in some form is all that is left.

Abraham Lincoln, *First Inaugural Address* (March 4, 1861)

With Regard to Law and Force, War and Peace

There are two ways of settling disputed questions; one by discussion, the other by force. The first being characteristic of man, the second of brutes, we should have recourse to the latter only if the former fails.

Cicero, *De Officiis*, Bk. I, Sec. XI, Ch. 34 (44 B.C.)

★　★　★

A private person cannot lead another to virtue efficaciously; for he can only advise, and if his advice be not taken, it has no coercive power, such as the law should have, in order to prove an efficacious inducement to virtue, as the Philosopher says. But this coercive power is vested in the whole people or in some public personage, to whom it belongs to inflict penalties.

Thomas Aquinas, *Summa Theologica*, Pt. I-II, Q. 90, A. 3 (c. 1265)

★　★　★

. . . A man is said to be subject to a law as the coerced is subject to the coercer. In this way the virtuous and the just are not subject to the law, but only the wicked. Because coercion and violence are contrary to the will; but the will of the good is in harmony with the law, while the will of the wicked is discordant from it. Therefore in this sense the good are not subject to the law, but only the wicked.

Thomas Aquinas, *Summa Theologica*, Pt. I-II, Q. 96, A. 5 (c. 1265)

★ ★ ★

The sovereign is said to be exempt from the law as to its coercive power, since, properly speaking, no man is coerced by himself, and law has no coercive power save from the authority of the sovereign. In this way then is the sovereign said to be exempt from the law, because no one is able to pass sentence on him if he acts against the law.

Thomas Aquinas, *Summa Theologica*, Pt. I-II, Q. 96, A. 5 (c. 1265)

★ ★ ★

Wherever there can be contention, there judgment should exist; otherwise things would exist imperfectly, without their own means of adjustment or correction, which is impossible, since in things necessary, God or Nature is not defective. Between any two governments, neither of which is in any way subordinate to the other, contention can arise either through their own fault or that of their subjects. This is evident. Therefore there should be judication between them. And since neither can know the affairs of the other, not being subordinated (for among equals there is no authority), there must be a third and wider power which can rule both within its own jurisdiction. This third power is either the world-government or it is not. If it is, we have reached our conclusion; if it is not, it must in turn have its equal outside its jurisdiction, and then it will need a third party as judge, and so *ad infinitum*, which is impossible. So we must arrive at a first and supreme judge for whom all contentions are judicable either directly or indirectly; and this will be our world-governor or emperor. Therefore, world-government is necessary for the world.

Dante Alighieri, *De Monarchia*, Bk. I, Ch. 10 (c. 1313)

★ ★ ★

World government . . . must be understood in the sense that it governs mankind on the basis of what all have in common and that by a common law it leads all toward peace. This common norm or law should be received by local governments in the same way that practical intelligence in action receives its major premises from the speculative intellect. To these it adds its own particular minor premises and then draws particular conclusions for the sake of its action. These basic norms not only can come from a single source, but must do so in order to avoid confusion among universal principles. Moses himself followed this pattern in the law which he composed, for, having chosen the chiefs of the several tribes, he left them the lesser judgments, reserving to himself alone the higher and more general. These common norms were then used by the tribal chiefs according to their special needs. Therefore, it is better for mankind to be governed by one, not by many; and hence by a single governor, the world ruler; and if it is better, it is pleasing to God, since He always wills the better. And when there are only two alternatives—the better is also the best, and is consequently not only pleasing to God, but the choice of "one" rather than "many" is what most pleases Him. Hence it follows that mankind lives best under a single government, and therefore that such a government is necessary for the well-being of the world.

Dante Alighieri, *De Monarchia*, Bk. I, Ch. 14 (c. 1313)

★ ★ ★

There are two ways of contesting, the one by law, the other by force; the first method is proper to men, the second to beasts; but because the first is frequently not sufficient, it is necessary to have recourse to the second.

Machiavelli, *The Prince*, Ch. XVIII (1513)

★ ★ ★

. . . It is manifest that during the time men live without a common power to keep them all in awe, they are in that condition which is called *war;* and such a war as is of every man against every man. For war consisteth not in battle only, or the act of fighting, but in a tract of time, wherein the will to contend by battle is sufficiently known: and therefore the notion of *time* is to be considered in the nature of war, as it is in the nature of weather. For as the nature of foul weather lieth not in a shower or two of rain, but in an inclination thereto of many days together: so the nature of war consisteth not in actual fighting, but in the known disposition thereto during all the time there is no assurance to the contrary. All other time is *peace.*

Thomas Hobbes, *Leviathan*, Ch. XIII (1651)

★ ★ ★

. . . Though there had never been any time wherein particular men were in a condition of war one against another, yet in all times kings and persons of sovereign authority, because of their independency, are in continual jealousies, and in the state and posture of gladiators, having their weapons pointing, and their eyes fixed on one another; that is, their forts, garrisons, and guns upon the frontiers of their kingdoms, and continual spies upon their neighbours, which is a posture of war.

Thomas Hobbes, *Leviathan*, Ch. XIII (1651)

★ ★ ★

Where the laws cannot be executed it is all one as if there were no laws, and a government without laws is, I suppose, a mystery in politics inconceivable to human capacity, and inconsistent with human society.

John Locke, *Second Essay on Civil Government*, Ch. XIX, Sec. 219 (1690)

★ ★ ★

Whosoever uses force without right—as every one does in society who does it without law—puts himself into a state of war with those against whom he so uses it, and in that state all former ties are cancelled, all other rights cease, and every one has a right to defend himself, and to resist the aggressor.

John Locke, *Second Essay on Civil Government*, Ch. XIX, Sec. 232 (1690)

⋆ ⋆ ⋆

There are two sorts of contests among men, the one managed by law, the other by force; and these are of such nature that where the one ends, the other always begins.

John Locke, *Letter Concerning Toleration* (1706)

⋆ ⋆ ⋆

War between two Powers is the result of a settled intention, manifested on both sides, to destroy the enemy State, or at least to weaken it by all means at their disposal. The carrying of this intention into act is war, strictly so called; so long as it does not take shape in act, it is only a state of war. . . . The state of war is the natural relation of one Power to another.

Jean-Jacques Rousseau, *A Lasting Peace* and *The State of War* (c. 1756)

⋆ ⋆ ⋆

With men the state of nature is not a state of peace, but of war; though not of open war, at least of war ever ready to break out. . . . Nations, like individuals, if they live in a state of nature and without laws, by their vicinity alone commit an act of lesion. . . . Though a treaty of peace [between them] puts an end to the present war, it does not abolish a state of war, a state where continually new pretenses for war are found; which one cannot affirm to be unjust, since being their own judges, they have no other means of terminating their differences.

Immanuel Kant, *Perpetual Peace* (1795)

⋆ ⋆ ⋆

To look for a continuation of harmony between a number of independent, unconnected sovereignties in the same neighbourhood, would be to disregard the uniform course of human events, and to set at defiance the accumulated experience of ages.

Alexander Hamilton, *The Federalist Papers,* #6 (1787–88)

★ ★ ★

Preamble

The people of the earth having agreed
    that the advancement of man
in spiritual excellence and physical welfare
is the common goal of mankind;
    that universal peace is the prerequisite
for the pursuit of that goal;
    that justice in turn is the prerequisite of peace,
and peace and justice stand or fall together;
    that iniquity and war inseparably spring
from the competitive anarchy of the national states;
    that therefore the age of nations must end,
and the era of humanity begin;

the governments of the nations have decided
    to order their separate sovereignties
in one government of justice,
to which they surrender their arms;
    and to establish, as they do establish,
this Constitution
as the covenant and fundamental law
of the Federal Republic of the World.

Preliminary Draft of a World Constitution, 1948.

As proposed and signed by

Robert M. Hutchins	*Erich Kahler*
G. A. Borgese	*Wilber G. Katz*
Mortimer J. Adler	*Charles H. McIlwain*
Albert Guérard	*Robert Redfield*
Harold A. Innis	*Rexford G. Tugwell*
Stringfellow Barr	

★   ★   ★

We are living in an international anarchy. There is no power whatever superior to the sovereign state today. That is the essence of sovereignty. . . . Something more than a world of separate democratic states is necessary for the survival of man in the nuclear age. . . .

What is necessary and indispensable for human survival is not merely the spread of democracy from one country to another until the world consists of democratic states. What is necessary, on the contrary, is *world democracy*. And I mean by this nothing less than the unification of the world under one democratic government.

John Strachey, *The Challenge of Democracy*,
Encounter pamphlet #10, Ch. X (1963)

CHAPTER 7

Democracy and
Citizenship

THE TWO CRITICAL TERMS in understanding the idea of democracy
are expressed by the words "people" and "citizen." The word "democracy" itself is of ancient lineage. Like most of the other words
that we use to name forms of government, it is of Greek origin.
From antiquity on down, the idea of democracy has been associated
with the notion of popular government—government by the people, by a multitude of persons who occupy the status of citizens,
with all the rights and privileges appertaining thereto.

Two things are called to our attention by the use of these two
words in talking about democracy. In the first place, when we identify *the people* with a *body of citizens*, we are, or should be, at once
aware that democracy does not mean lawless mob rule.

The term did have that meaning, among others, in Greek antiquity. We can find passages in both Plato and Aristotle in which they
classified democracy as one of the bad forms of government, just a
little less undesirable than tyranny. However, there are other passages in which they treat democracy as a form of lawful or constitutional government. When they do so, it is citizenship that makes
the difference: rule by the people is rule by a body of citizens.

Conceiving democracy as one form of lawful or constitutional
government, it is then the word "people" which deserves our attention. Its denotative reference is never the same as that of the word
"population." There never has been and never will be a form of

government in which the whole population is engaged in self-government, acting as enfranchised citizens or as citizen-office-holders.

Who, then, are the people in a constitutional democracy or who should they be? What portion of the population are citizens or what portion should be? These are the questions we must answer if we are to succeed in drawing the line between democracy and any other form of constitutional government.

Each of these questions is a double one. It makes a great difference whether we answer it by reporting what portion of the population were regarded as citizens at different periods in the last twenty-five hundred years of Western history, or answer it not historically as a matter of fact, but instead in terms of principles of justice and right. To answer it in the latter way is to say who should rightfully be citizens and what portion of the population should comprise a self-governing people.

I cannot stress this difference too much. If we ignore it, we are led to think that the idea of democracy is as old as the idea of constitutional government, as old as the Greek word *"demos,"* the people. We are prevented from recognizing that, of all the ideas treated in this book, democracy is of the most recent origin, even more recent than the idea of civil police.

This may be so startling for many readers that I am impelled to state at once that the question, "Who are the people?" was first asked in the seventeenth century; that the first (unsuccessful) appeal for the extension of suffrage to the unpropertied working class occurred in 1647; and that the first political philosopher who declared democracy to be the ideal form of government was John Stuart Mill in his *Representative Government,* published in 1863. In that book, he was also one of the first to argue for the enfranchisement of women.

If readers respond by pointing out that the Declaration of Independence declared that *all* men are created equal and that *all* have the same human rights, which include the right to political liberty, let me remind them that neither Jefferson nor any of his eighteenth century cosigners of the Declaration meant *all* when they used the word "all." They meant "all" with the exception of slaves, women, and the laboring poor. These exceptions were so taken for granted in the eighteenth century that no one thought it necessary to mention them when using the word "all."

That is why Lincoln, whose mind dwelt upon the words of the Declaration with the same reverence that is given to Sacred Scripture, said in one of his great public addresses that the Declaration must be read as a pledge to the future, not as the statement of an ideal that could have been realized at the time it was made.

But fourscore and seven years later, when Lincoln delivered his Gettysburg Address, concluding it by saying that "government of the people, by the people, and for the people shall not perish from the earth," did he imply that constitutional democracy then existed and should be preserved? He could not have meant that when the emancipated chattel-slaves had not yet been enfranchised, and when neither he nor any of his listeners thought that the word "people" included the female half of the population.

What Lincoln himself said about the Declaration of Independence, he should have applied to his own Gettysburg Address. We should not interpret it as a statement of accomplished fact, but only as a pledge to the future—the portent of an ideal still more than a half century away from the first faint blush of becoming a political reality.

If readers accept the facts I have just reported as historically accurate (which I think they are), must they not also agree with my further statement that the idea of democracy was first broached as a political ideal in the middle of the nineteenth century, and first became a political reality, even in the slightest degree, well on towards the middle of the twentieth century?

Doing so, they may still be puzzled about how we should properly use the word "democracy." Should we use it in such a way that it applies to the government of Athens under Pericles in the fifth century before Christ? Using it that way, should we say that that was when democracy began?

Should we then go on to say of democracy that, in the course of centuries of political progress and with many political reforms, it slowly developed into the kind of government Lincoln and John

Stuart Mill held up as a political ideal in 1863, an ideal still far from actualization in political reality?

My response is definitely and emphatically no. To use the word "democracy" that way is to confuse matters hopelessly and to confound our understanding of the idea and the ideal that the word should be used to express. Let me explain why I think so.

Pericles, in his great Funeral Oration at the end of the second year of the Peloponnesian War (an address that bears comparison to Lincoln's at Gettysburg), eulogized the Athenian government, of which he was then the leading statesman. In that address he eloquently declared:

> Our constitution does not copy the laws of neighboring states; we are a pattern to others rather than imitators ourselves. Its administration favors the many rather than the few; this is why it is called a democracy.

Pericles' use of the word "democracy" to mean a constitutional government by the many rather than the few gives us the clue we need to understand why we should not use the word as it was used by the Greeks.

Who were the many in Periclean Athens? The population of that city-state then comprised about 120,000 human beings. Of these, not more than 30,000 were citizens. The rest were slaves, artisans, barbarian aliens, and women.

The many consisted of the freeborn males who were relatively well-off, including those who owned land and slaves—an elite by birth and by property, the few the Romans later called the patricians in contradistinction to the plebian poor.

The Athenian government under Pericles was, in the Greek view, an extreme form of democracy by virtue of admitting to citizenship as many as 30,000 out of a population of 120,000. In its less extreme forms, the many were often much fewer than that. When did the reduction in numbers cross the line that divided what the Greeks called democracy from the form of government they used the word "oligarchy" to name? Without citing definite numbers, the answer is that they called a government oligarchical rather than democratic when the few who were citizens consisted of the very rich freeborn males. The exclusion from citizenship of the relatively poor freeborn males made it an oligarchy rather than a democracy. The few then could be as few as 500 out of the total population.

In all the centuries since the time of Pericles, right down to our own day, when the word "democracy" has been misused to signify government by the many rather than the few, the many has always been a number much smaller than the preponderant majority of the population. All such forms of government should have been called oligarchies, or perhaps aristocracies, if the many who were the few had some pretensions to being an elite by virtue of attributes other than simply being well-born males who were well-off.

Variations in the actual size of the number of self-governing citizens represented degrees of oligarchy, not degrees of democracy. As the ratio of the enfranchised to the disfranchised—of the self-governing citizens to those who were despotically ruled as subjects or treated as wards of the state—changed from time to time, constitutional government became less or more oligarchical, not more or less democratic.

I cannot refrain from reiterating the indisputable fact that during all these centuries when the word "democracy" was misused to name constitutional government by the many rather than the few, the many were always the relative few who comprised much less than half the population at that time.

It is for this reason that I think it right to restrict our use of the word "democracy" to signify that form of constitutional government in which the whole population becomes a self-governing people, with no exceptions except those that can be justified by the mental incompetence of infancy, extreme feeblemindedness, and insanity.

In that restricted use of the term, there can then be no doubt about the fact, however startling it may appear to be, that democracy is a brand new idea, conceived in the middle of the nineteenth century and, after more than a half century of painful and troublesome gestation, one that came to birth in reality only in our own time.

Why Did It Take So Long?

The answer, in a nutshell, lies in long persistent denial or misunderstanding of the truth that all human beings are by nature equal—that all are equal by virtue of having whatever properties belong to all members of the species; that all are equal in the sense, and only in the sense, that none is more or less human than another; that all equally have the dignity of being persons rather than things; and that all are equally endowed with the same human rights that derive from their having the same inherent human needs.

This truth in no way conflicts with another plain and indisputable truth, one that is generally acknowledged and mistakenly thought to be grounds for denying or rejecting the truth about human equality.

It is, and always has been, generally recognized that individuals differ from one another in a wide variety of ways that render them unequal in all the respects in which one has a certain native endowment or a certain acquired attainment to a greater or lesser degree.

Though all have the same species-specific properties that make them all equally human beings, they differ individually from one another in the degree to which they possess these properties. All the acknowledged facts of individual difference, and the individual inequalities that flow from them, do not require us to deny the sameness of the specific human nature to be found in all members of the species, or the one human equality that follows from that fact.

Nevertheless, over the past twenty-five centuries, the almost universally prevalent recognition of individual differences and individual inequalities resulted in the almost universally persistent neglect of the no less obvious fact that all these differing individuals are members of the same species and, therefore, have the same specific nature. When that no less obvious fact was ignored, for whatever reason, the almost universal acceptance of the truth about individual inequalities was accompanied by the almost universal denial of the truth about the equality of all human beings by virtue of their common humanity.

What reasons might explain this astonishing, persistent mistake?

The most profound and penetrating answer to this question was given by Jean-Jacques Rousseau in the eighteenth century when he explained the mistake Aristotle had made in the fourth century B.C. about the division of mankind into those who were by nature born to be free men and those who were intended by nature for slavery or subjection.

I have paraphrased Aristotle's view by speaking of those by nature intended for subjection as well as those by nature intended to be slaves. I have done so to include the female half of the population. Aristotle regarded them as naturally inferior to the male half. Consequently, he looked upon them as having no rightful claim to be self-governing citizens. Without that status, they must be left in subjection to despotic rule by the ruling class—the freeborn males whom he thought were qualified for citizenship.

The rest, male or female, were either those born into slavery or those bought or captured as slaves. All these, in Aristotle's view, were rightfully enslaved if, as a matter of fact, they were by nature intended for that status in society. Being tyrannically ruled by their masters did them no injury or injustice any more than the benevolent despotism to which freeborn women were subjected did them injury or injustice.

Rousseau's penetrating rectification of Aristotle's profound error concerning slavery consisted in pointing out that what Aristotle attributed to nature should have been attributed to nurture instead. Those born into slavery and reared as slaves took on the appearance of slavishness. Their apparent slavishness, due solely to the way in which they were nurtured and treated, concealed from view the underlying reality of their natural equality as human beings.

The apparent superiority of those nurtured and treated in one way and the apparent inferiority of those nurtured and treated in a radically different way accounts for the error to which all are prone who think that mankind is really divided into natural superiors and inferiors. In consequence, they attribute rights to one subgroup and deny them to another.

They were, according to Rousseau, so deceived by the appearances that they ignored or overlooked the fact that subgroups of mankind consisted of individuals, all of whom belong to the same species and who are, therefore, entitled to be called human beings. Even further, they were prevented from thinking that, if human rights exist, they must be rights possessed by all human beings.

The division of mankind into subgroups should not be limited to the division between freeborn and slaves. Everything that I have said about mistaking apparent inferiority (due entirely to nurture) for real inferiority (due solely to nature) applies in exactly the same way to the division of mankind by gender, as well as to racial and ethnic divisions of mankind into superior and inferior subgroups.

Chattel slavery was abolished in most of the civilized world long before male superiority was first challenged. It never occurred to Rousseau that his brilliant insight about nurture and nature applied to female inferiority. In spite of all the efforts of the women's liberation movement, male chauvinism still persists at present in the most enlightened countries, and goes unchallenged in the rest of the world. The same holds true of racism in all its protean forms.

This being the case, we should not be astounded, or find it unintelligible, that the idea of democracy has been so long in coming to birth. The archetypical Aristotelian mistake, made by many of the most eminent political theorists, has persisted in all quarters of the globe throughout all centuries down to the present. It still persists today, though it has at last been challenged and rejected by the more enlightened.

This explains why democracy, properly conceived, is so new an idea. It also explains why, in so many quarters, so many still refuse to acknowledge that the idea of democracy is inseparable from the political ideal of a form of government that is alone perfectly just.

One further step must be taken to make what has been said applicable to still one other subgroup that was thought unfit for citizenship and so remained disfranchised until the last hundred years or a little more. I am referring to the subgroup that Aristotle called artisans, who later came to be denominated the working or laboring class, and still later was called the proletariat.

To the extent that this subgroup included females as well as males, and to the extent that it included immigrant aliens regarded, on ethnic or racial grounds, as natural inferiors, it comprised an over-whelming mass of any population.

Quite apart from the mistake of regarding the female or immi-grant members of the working class as natural inferiors, why were the rest who belonged to this class thought unfit for citizenship? The first step in answering that question consists in remembering the disabling conditions under which they worked and the depri-vations that they suffered until the twentieth century.

It was not until quite recently that laborers toiled less than twelve or even fourteen hours a day. They frequently worked seven days a week. It was not until recently that children were legally prohib-ited from toil until they were fourteen or sixteen years of age. Many became laborers at much tenderer ages. It was not until recently that free schooling at the state's expense gave members of the working class some education and, with it, some preparation for citizenship.

When Jefferson in 1817 advocated three years of public schooling for those in society who were destined for labor, not for leisure and learning, it was rejected by the legislature of Virginia. It was thought to be too radical—and pointless. At the beginning of this century, most children of working class families went to school for six years, or at the most eight. The advance to twelve years of compulsory schooling came slowly after that.

Totally deprived of schooling or not given enough schooling to prepare them for citizenship, and lacking enough free time to en-gage actively in political life, the members of the working class, young and old, female and male, immigrants and native-born, appeared to be unfit for citizenship.

However, we must carry the explanation one step further by re-turning to the difference between nurture and nature, and the con-sequent difference between the appearances and the realities. Those who, from Aristotle right down to modern times, argued for the exclusion from citizenship of artisans, laborers, the proletariat, dis-missed them as inferiors in their natural endowments, not as infe-riors because of their nurture and the disabling conditions of life that society imposed on them.

Only when it began to be understood that theirs was a nurtural,

not a natural, inferiority, did social and economic reformers fight
for the amelioration or elimination of the disabling conditions and
the crippling deprivations that disqualified the working class for
participation in political life. Only then did the masses in the population of any country that enjoyed constitutional government become members of the ruling class. Only then did they form the
preponderant majority of any self-governing people.

The Only Perfectly Just Form of Government

The classification of the forms of government and the criteria for
judging their relative merits, which students are taught in college
when they take courses in the history of political theory, represent
flawed thinking about the subject.

This thinking derives from certain passages in the political writ-
ings of Plato and Aristotle, passages that are repudiated by insights
in other passages that anyone should be able to recognize as much
more fundamental.

In a dialogue called *The Statesman,* Plato uses the criterion of
lawfulness to make the one basic distinction in modes of government, putting all lawful or constitutional governments on one side
of the line, and all lawless or despotic governments on the other
side. Aristotle in the opening book and chapter of his *Politics* draws
the same line and declares it to be the most fundamental division.

Several books later, Aristotle introduces the sixfold classification
of forms of government. This became traditional in political theory
for thousands of years thereafter. It totally ignored the basic division of all governments into the despotic and the constitutional
modes. It put all forms of government in which the interests and
welfare of the ruled are served on one side of the line, and all forms
that serve only the interests and good of the rulers on the other side.
Ruling for the common good of the community thus became the
only criterion of just government. As we shall see, it is lamentably
insufficient.

The number of rulers served as the only criterion to differentiate
three forms of government on either side of the line that divides

good from bad forms of government—government by one, by few, or by many. The names attached to the three just forms of government are monarchy, aristocracy, and polity—government by one who is virtuous enough to rule for the good of the community, by the virtuous few, or by a more multitudinous middle class, neither the very rich nor the very poor.

On the opposite side of the line, we find a parallel differentiation of three unjust forms of government: tyranny, oligarchy, and democracy—government by one individual in his own interest, government by the few who are very rich in their own interests, or by the many who are relatively poor in theirs.

Among the just forms, the criterion by which they are appraised as good, better, and best is merely one of efficiency, with no reference to the more or less just. By this criterion, monarchy is said to be best; aristocracy, second best; and polity, the least good. By the same criterion, democracy is the least bad of the unjust forms of government; oligarchy a little worse; and tyranny the worst of all.

I have presented this totally unsatisfactory classification of types of government, together with its inadequate and confused criteria for appraising them, as background against which to contrast what I think is the correct account of the matter.

If readers wonder why flawed thinking about this subject has persisted so long and why the correction of its mistakes has been so long delayed, my explanation turns on the very same points I have used to explain the recency of the idea of democracy and the long delay in recognizing it as the ideal polity.

The one criterion of justice employed in the erroneous traditional account must also be employed in the account that corrects it. The least degree of justice that any form of government can have consists in its serving the common good of the governed, not the private, selfish interests of those exercising the power to administer government. By this one criterion, tyranny is totally devoid of justice.

If, now, we reinstate the truly fundamental distinction between modes of government, putting all despotic governments on one side of the line, and all constitutional or lawful governments on the other, we can employ this initial criterion to distinguish tyrannical from benevolent despotism. When a despotism is, in any degree, benevolent (that is, directed toward the common good), it is to that degree a minimally just form of government.

Its essential injustice consists in treating adult or mature human beings as if they were still children who need to be governed absolutely for their own good, without consent on their part and with no voice in their own government. It is better than tyranny by virtue of the fact that it does not treat persons, whose good should be served, as if they were things to be used for the good of their masters or managers.

The benevolence of despotism is always shortsighted. It fails to see that the good of the governed cannot be served by treating mature human beings as if they were still children, to be paternalistically governed in the way that well-meaning parents treat their offspring.

Even more important is the fact that it contravenes the truth that man is by nature a political animal, and so has an inherent human right to be a self-governing individual, participating in a government to which the governed give their consent.

It is by this additional criterion of justice that all forms of constitutional government are more just than the most benevolent of benevolent despotisms.

In all forms of constitutional government, the basic human right to political liberty is secured for at least some individuals who enjoy the status of citizenship. At this point, it makes no difference whether citizenship is restricted to the very few or to a larger multitude. If the multitude of citizens is, to any degree, less than all who are entitled to be citizens, the resulting form of constitutional government remains unjust.

It has met only two of the three criteria of justice. The first is that it avoids tyrannical injustice by serving the good of the governed. The second is that it secures the human right to participate in government for *at least some members of the community*. Herein lies the essential injustice of a constitutional government that is oligarchical. It restricts suffrage on grounds that do not justify the restricted franchise.

Unwarranted restrictions of citizenship made eligible only those having a certain amount of wealth or property; only those who are male rather than female; or only those who belong to a certain race, ethnic group, or a certain religious community. It may even include denying citizenship to immigrant aliens, affording them no opportunity to become naturalized citizens of an adopted country.

All of these prerequisites or qualifications for admission to citizenship are unjust by virtue of the fact that they violate the basic human right to political liberty and to self-government through political participation, which is no less inherent in the disfranchised individuals than it is in those who have been given suffrage.

Committing such injustice by its transgression of a basic human right, oligarchical government is nevertheless more just than any form of despotism, whether tyrannical or benevolent. It is more just because, in addition to being non-tyrannical, its constitutionality makes it a government by right as well as by might, a government having authority as well as exercising coercive force. At least some portion of the population governed comprises a self-governing people—human beings within the pale of political life, not pariahs excluded from it and governed as subjects, not as citizens.

To say, then, that constitutional democracy is the only perfectly just form of government is to say that it alone embodies all three criteria of political justice. The third criterion, which gives it superior justice to that of any constitutional oligarchy, consists in its securing for all (with the one justifiable exception of the incompetent by virtue of infancy or insanity) the human rights possessed by all. In a constitutional democracy, the self-governing people at last become coextensive with the whole population, subtracting therefrom only the aforementioned justifiable exceptions.

To be perfectly just, a constitutional democracy must go one step further. It must secure all basic human rights, not only the rights to political liberty and to enfranchised citizenship, but other political and economic rights as well. It must do whatever is possible to provide human beings with the external conditions of life that they need in their effort to pursue happiness. It must help them in their attempt to obtain all the real goods that enrich a decent human life, many of which, being external goods, they cannot obtain for themselves by their own unaided efforts.

Democracy, thus conceived, can also be defined as government of the people, for the people, and by the people, but only when two points are correctly understood.

One is that "the people" must be understood as coextensive with the whole mature population of the community—those who have reached the age of consent and who are not disabled by the mental pathology of either amentia or dementia. When this is understood, then government by the people involves universal suffrage, and government for the people involves government for the common good and one that secures all human rights.

The other thing that must be correctly understood is the phrase "government of the people." The significance of that phrase is misunderstood if the word "of" is interpreted to mean that the people are subject to the coercive force of government. Thus interpreted, every form of government, tyrannical, despotic, and oligarchical, as well as democratic, is government of the people.

The only interpretation of the word "of" that does not apply to all forms of government distinguishes constitutional from despotic governments. All constitutional, in contradistinction to all despotic, governments are governments *of* the people in the sense that they derive their authority and their just powers from the consent of the governed.

Government is government *of* the people only when the people are the constituents of a constitution—only when the sovereignty of the government ultimately resides in the sovereignty of the people. Popular sovereignty is to be found only in constitutional governments.

This mode of government takes the form of a constitutional democracy when the people who are the consenting constituents of government become coextensive with the population. Anything short of that is not popular sovereignty in the fullest sense of that term.

To complete the picture, one further point remains. A correct interpretation must be given the critical phrase "consent of the governed."

Does it mean the consent of all the persons in the community who are subject to government—the consent of justly disfranchised infants who have not yet reached the age of consent, the consent of justly disfranchised persons committed to asylums for the feeble-minded and the demented, the consent of resident aliens who have not become naturalized citizens? It cannot mean that. It must mean the consent of all the governed who are able to participate in government.

How shall we understand the giving of such consent on the part of those who were not alive at the time when a constitution was ratified or otherwise adopted by a constituent people? Only by the ratification or adoption of a written constitution can voluntary consent, not mere acquiescence, be explicitly and actually given. At all other times, and with respect to unwritten constitutions, such as that of Great Britain, the consent of the governed must be implicit or tacit. It cannot be explicit and actual.

How is such implicit or tacit consent given? By all the acts through which enfranchised citizens participate in government. Their every act of participation bespeaks their acceptance of the framework of government within which they act.

If they do not exercise the right to participate that a constitutional government secures for them, they have failed to discharge their duty as citizens. Like every other basic human right, the right to political liberty and to suffrage carries with it a duty to perform. Those who are derelict in the performance of their political obligations live under a government to which they tacitly give their consent only by virtue of the fact that they have not voluntarily chosen to emigrate elsewhere. They have, therefore, not completely withdrawn their consent. That is done only by those who, dissatisfied with the framework of government under which they live, either peacefully emigrate or violently attempt to overthrow it.

Is constitutional democracy, as I have defined and appraised it, subject to no weaknesses or infirmities? That cannot be so, for no human institutions, however good, can be altogether perfect. But the two infirmities to which constitutional democracy is subject are not peculiar to it. They are common to all forms of government that have justice to any degree, common to benevolent despotisms and to constitutional oligarchies as well as to constitutional democracies.

One weakness or infirmity in an otherwise just form of government lies in the degree of competence of the rulers (in despotic governments) or of the ruling class (in constitutional governments). In the case of despotic governments, this means the competence of despots to exercise the power in their possession to govern for the good of those subject to their absolute and arbitrary power. In the case of constitutional governments, this means the competence of the enfranchised citizenry, and especially of the public officials or office-holders who are entrusted with the authority and power that is vested by the constitution in the political offices they hold and administer.

The cure or remedy for this weakness or infirmity common to all forms of government is the same for all. It consists in the adequate preparation of individual rulers or of a ruling class for the governmental functions they perform.

We must concede that there is reason for thinking that the cure or remedy is more difficult to apply successfully in a constitutional democracy than in a constitutional oligarchy. The problem of adequate educational preparation for citizenship is more difficult to solve when, with universal suffrage, the requisite education consists in the schooling of the whole population.

It would seem to be much easier to solve when the people to be educated are only a small portion of the population. Then suffrage is restricted to those who have had the good fortune to grow up under conditions of life and the kind of nurturing that make it easier to educate them for citizenship.

I have not mentioned the preparation of despots for the exercise of power in their possession. The overwhelming evidence of history is that, whether by defects of nature or of nurture, most despotic rulers have lacked the moral and intellectual virtues requisite for a benevolent use of their power. Most have turned out to be tyrants instead.

This brings us to the second weakness or infirmity common to all otherwise just forms of government. They are all prone to some measure of tyranny, despotic governments most of all. Constitutional oligarchies may be tyrannical to the extent that their despotic rule of the disfranchised is not benevolent.

In constitutional governments, whether oligarchical or democratic, the will of the majority must initially prevail, either a simple majority or, with regard to certain matters, a two-thirds majority. How about tyranny on the part of the majority?

On this count, constitutional government can be superior to any type of despotism, but only if the constitution requires or allows for a judicial review of legislation or of executive action. Then the tyranny of a majority can be rectified by judicial nullification of legislative or executive acts, rejecting them as unconstitutional and unjust. Other methods have been proposed for preventing tyranny by the majority, but all end up by preventing majority rule itself.

All the civil rights cases that have gone to the Supreme Court of the United States in the recent past, where the Court has declared racist or sexist discriminations unjust, provide us with clear examples of how judicial review works to overcome tyranny of the majority.

The tyranny of despotic governments can be overcome only by the use of force against force. Nonviolent means are not available for the redress of tyrannical injustice. Only constitutional governments provide such legal and nonviolent means of redress, but only if their operation includes judicial review that can nullify the tyranny of a majority. There is no cure for that infirmity of constitutional government when, as in Great Britain, judicial review does not exist. There the only remedy for the tyranny of a parliamentary majority lies in an election that changes the character of the majority.

The Conflict Between Justice and Expediency

Justice, through the securing of all human rights for all, is not the only attribute of good government. Good government should also be efficient and effective. It was on this ground that many political theorists in the past preferred absolute monarchy or despotism, providing, of course, that the efficacy of such government did not involve tyrannical injustice.

Those who opposed the march toward democracy, from the time of the first efforts in the seventeenth century to extend suffrage to the unpropertied poor, did so on one or both of two grounds.

They denied the existence of natural rights. Hence, they were not moved by appeals that sought to give political liberty to the underprivileged portion of society. They were also concerned about the stability and efficacy of government. To give political liberty and power to those who, by virtue of the deprivations they suffered, could not exercise it effectively, seemed to them practically inexpedient.

In the nineteenth century, when the ideal of constitutional democracy first came into view, it was challenged by its opponents in the same two ways. They were unpersuaded about its superior justice because they denied the existence of natural or human rights. They also opposed it because it appeared to them to be patently inexpedient. It would result in government that was very bad indeed, because so ineffective in the performance of governmental functions. In addition, as representatives of one or another privileged elite that was then the ruling majority, they desperately feared the tyranny of the majority, for which they saw no remedy.

Even advocates of constitutional democracy and defenders of it as the ideal polity manifested the same doubts and fears—doubts about its effectiveness and fears about the character of the majority that would then be given the power to act tyrannically in their own special interests. They were reluctant democrats in the sense that, even though persuaded of the superior justice of democracy, they either sought to provide hedges against the tyranny of the majority, or to delay the constitutional enactment of universal suffrage.

Let us not march on precipitately toward democracy, they said;

let us wait until the time is ripe for it. Let us wait until it becomes expedient for us to be just.

The conflict between justice and expediency, which has led many reluctant democrats to espouse gradualist or delaying tactics, is clearly exemplified in the delayed extension of suffrage to the working class in England, to blacks in the United States after their emancipation from chattel slavery, and to the female half of the population in England, the United States, and other countries.

In all three instances, the argument against such advances conceded the justice of the constitutional change, but opposed it on the grounds of its inexpediency.

The working class in Great Britain was not yet ready for enfranchised citizenship under the deplorable conditions of industrial labor in the middle of the nineteenth century. The economic deprivations workers then suffered, especially their hours of work and their consequent lack of sufficient free time, together with the absence of any schooling for the young who went into the factories at a tender age, made it inexpedient to grant them suffrage.

The inexpediency of such a constitutional change was compounded by the fact that the very portion of the population least prepared for citizenship and for exercising political liberty in a responsible manner would also be the predominant majority in the population.

The enfranchisement of the blacks in the American South in the years immediately subsequent to their emancipation from chattel slavery appeared at the time to be inexpedient for somewhat similar reasons. Like the working class in England, they too were unprepared for citizenship. The economic conditions under which they lived and the deprivations of schooling and free time they suffered made it highly inexpedient to give them political liberty and power, even though these belonged to them by right.

The extension of the franchise to women likewise seemed inexpedient at a time when women were accorded the kind of nurture and treatment that made them deceptively appear to be inferior by nature. Their economic dependence on their husbands if they were not members of the working class, their economic deprivations if they were, their being barred from many occupations or professions, and their being given a different kind of schooling from their brothers—all these things militated against them. Even those who recognized the rightness of their cause counselled them to be patient and to suffer injustice until the time was ripe for rectifying it.

The resolution of all these conflicts between justice and expediency, which led the prudent to be cautious and the reluctant to try to slow up the march toward democracy by advocating gradualism, came about in the same way. Positive action on the side of justice was taken before the time became ripe—before the just action also became expedient.

It could not have happened any other way. The time would never have become ripe. The conditions that rendered the action inexpedient would never have become sufficiently improved to render the action expedient as well as just. Improved conditions could only result from taking the action at a time when it was inexpedient.

Granting the working class in England suffrage had to precede the factory laws and other economic reforms that improved the circumstances of their lives and removed the deprivations they suffered with regard to free time and schooling.

The constitutional amendment that extended suffrage to the emancipated blacks had to precede over a hundred years of persistent struggle on their part for other civil rights, for integrated schooling, and for economic conditions requisite for effective citizenship.

Similarly, the woman's suffrage amendment had to precede all the social, economic, and educational changes that the women's liberation movement has fought for since the first decades of the century. The fight for an equal rights amendment has not yet been won, but it could not have been initiated before the women's suffrage amendment altered the constitutional status of the female half of the population.

In all these instances, delaying tactics on the grounds of the inexpediency of action to redress injustices would have long postponed such redress. The rectification of injustice might have even been permanently prevented from occurring.

Two qualifications must be attached to that conclusion. One concerns the introduction of full-blown constitutional democracy in countries that are technologically, economically, and socially not yet ready for it.

When the Plimsoll line of a freighter is high above its water level, it is inexpedient for the ship to risk sailing into heavy seas. It had better be loaded first and the Plimsoll line brought down to the water level. A contemporary political commentator has pointed out that the ship of state has something analogous to the Plimsoll line. Its technological advances, its economic arrangements, and its social reforms must first make it ready to adopt political democracy. For a developing country to adopt democracy before it has become a technologically advanced, developed country is thought to be so inexpedient that the inappropriate institutions are doomed to be wrecked and thrown aside.

Nevertheless, the other view of the same picture remains. Unless a developing country moves steadily toward democratic institutions before such motion is sufficiently expedient, its development may be long retarded or permanently frustrated.

The other qualification to be added to what has been said on this score concerns technological progress itself.

The transition from a labor-intensive to a capital-intensive economy depends on a fairly high degree of technological progress in the production of wealth. Also dependent on a fairly high degree of technological progress is the production of enough wealth to eliminate severe economic deprivations in society. The same thing can be said of other changes that are needed for the economic substructure of political democracy.

Technological progress, now greatly accelerated, has been much slower in the past. When the labor-intensive agricultural economies of the past required the use of chattel-slaves to give the privileged few who were their masters enough free time to engage in politics, could the march toward political democracy have even been thought of, much less begun? The same question can be asked about other conditions inimical to thought about the idea of democracy or efforts to move toward its realization. All such conditions set up ob-

stacles destined to persist until sufficient technological progress had
been made to overcome them.

Will Democracy Survive, Spread, and Prosper?

Two other questions stand prior to the one just asked. *Should* democracy survive, spread, and prosper? *Can* it?

On the face of it, the question whether it should or not is the
easiest to answer. The difficult question is whether we can overcome the obstacles and impediments that block fully realizing the
ideal in practice. If these cannot be overcome, then we need not
pass on to the question that calls for prophecy or prediction about
the future.

Should constitutional democracy, which has little or no past, belong to the future? Should it, in the course of this century or the
centuries that lie ahead, become the form of government under which
all the peoples of the earth live and prosper?

Anyone persuaded by the argument set forth in the preceding
pages, to the effect that constitutional democracy is the only perfectly just form of government, must conclude, as I conclude, that
the ideal polity should be fully and universally realized in actual fact
and in political practice. To say this is to say nothing more than
that justice should be done, and that all human beings, obligated to
make decent lives for themselves, should be aided and abetted in
the pursuit of happiness by political institutions favorable to that
pursuit.

However, for justice to be done more is required than the justice
of a constitution that confers political liberty on all by enfranchis-
ing all. It is one thing to enjoy the advantages of self-government;
it is quite another to be justly governed.

Beyond the justice inherent in a democratic constitution lies the
justice of its laws and regulations. They are just to the extent that
they serve the common good; that they treat equals equally in all
significant respects; that they deal fairly with individuals in their
transactions with one another; and that they prevent one individual
or group of individuals from injuring others. Is anything more re-

quired for government to be just in its operation as well as just in its constitution?

Yes, to be fully just, it must in addition to all the other criteria of justice mentioned, leave the governed as free as they should be. How free is that? Everyone should have as much liberty as he or she can use justly; that is, without injuring anyone else or the welfare of the community. Anything beyond that? Yes, individuals and organized groups of individuals should have as much partial autonomy as befits their circumstances and the aims of government.

We have seen earlier that no one who is subject to government can have complete autonomy. Complete autonomy is compatible only with anarchy, not with being governed. We have also seen that no one who is governed totally lacks autonomy. No government, even the most tyrannical, can penetrate into all the secret nooks and crannies of an individual's private life. Even slaves or the subjects of tyrannical despotism exercise, in the course of their daily lives, freedom of choice with respect to many options that are not foreclosed by the prescriptions and prohibitions of the regulations under which they live.

But the amount of relative autonomy left to slaves or the subjects of despotic government is not enough for the citizens of a constitutional democracy. How much more should they have?

Thomas Jefferson asserted that that government governs best which governs least—which confers the largest amount of relative autonomy upon its people. This assertion not only went too far in one direction, but also ignored the proper criterion for appraising the justice of government. The opposite assertion—that that government governs best which governs most—would be equally at fault, and for the same reasons. The truth of the matter is that that government governs best which governs most justly.

Still the question remains: what quantity of government accords with justice? To what extent should a government that seeks to be just try to regulate the affairs of its people? What area of human conduct belongs within the provenance of just laws and what area of human conduct should be left unregulated and entirely at the disposal of free choice on the part of the governed?

Certainly, actions by individuals or groups of individuals that affect the good of others or the general welfare rightly fall within the sphere of government and legal regulation. Does that criterion suffice for drawing the line that must be drawn between the area of conduct that should be left for determination by free choice on the part of individuals or groups of individuals and the area that falls within the proper scope of government?

No; one further criterion applies. Abraham Lincoln defined it in a single sentence. He said that no government should do for its people what they, individually or collectively in subgroups, can do better for themselves. Lincoln's criterion, in the words of some political theorists, has been called the principle of subsidiarity.

It was also stated by John Stuart Mill, in the concluding pages of his great essay *On Liberty*, as the ultimate criterion for drawing the line between public matters that properly belong to government and private matters that should be left to decision by free choice on the part of the governed.

I trust that readers will appreciate at once the one further implication of this portrait of the ideal polity. It should give individuals or groups of individuals as much liberty as justice allows. At the same time it should establish as much equality of political, economic, and social conditions as justice requires. In this way it resolves what many have thought to be an insoluble conflict between liberty and equality.

When the ideal polity is thus delineated, it should be obvious at once that it does not exist anywhere in the world today. Constitutional democracy may now exist for the first time in the twentieth century and only at some places on this globe. But it exists mainly on paper, in political charters, constitutions, or enactments, but not in actual practice to an extent that can satisfy us as a full realization of the ideal. The idea of democracy has come to birth in the human mind, but it has so far barely seen the light of day in the practice of human affairs.

What obstacles or impediments must be overcome before that can happen? Let me enumerate five and describe them briefly.

The *first* requires us to solve a very difficult political problem—

the problem of a proper balance between (1) the direct participation in a democratic government by its citizens through elections, through the exercise of initiative and recall, and through referendums or plebiscites, and (2) the action of their representatives in all the administrative offices of government.

We are also called upon to solve the equally difficult problem of the proper *relationship* between members of the electorate and their elected representatives. To what extent should the decisions made by the people's representatives be subservient to the will of a popular majority? To what extent should the people's representatives, or a majority of them in legislative assemblies and in judicial tribunals, decide independently what is for the common good of the people and for the general welfare?

The *second* condition for the full realization of the ideal polity is the establishment of a truly democratic society as prerequisite for the effective operation of democratic government. The political institutions of democracy cannot come to full bloom in practice and prosper except in the environment of a society that is also democratic in its social institutions and its economic arrangements.

A rigidly class-structured and class-divided society throws roadblocks in the way of an effective operation of constitutional democracy. The people may be constitutionally granted an equality of political conditions, but if at the same time they are deprived of an equality of social and economic conditions, they cannot effectively exercise their popular sovereignty and their political liberty. They cannot participate in self-government as the citizens of a constitutional democracy should.

Alexis de Tocqueville, a young Frenchman visiting this country in the 1830's, wrote a book entitled *Democracy in America*. He was one of the first, thirty years earlier than John Stuart Mill, to hold up democracy as the ideal toward which all mankind, under divine providence, is destined to make progress.

Like Mill, he was fully aware of democracy's infirmities. Like Mill, he feared that the march toward democracy might lead to tyranny and oppression rather than to the harmonious maximization of both liberty and equality through just laws and regulations.

The tyranny he feared, and for which he could find no name, we have come to call a totalitarian democracy. Its citizens, who are in reality subjects of despotic government, are deprived of their political liberty. Their individual freedom, their relative autonomy, are severely curtailed. They are sacrificed in the name, not the fact, of social and economic equality.

A democracy in which liberty is sacrificed for the sake of equality would, in Tocqueville's view, be the worst form of democratic society that he feared might come into existence, as it has, not the best form that he hoped for, which does not yet exist.

The chief contribution made by Tocqueville was his conception of democracy in more than political terms. He used the word "democracy" to name a democratic society, not just a constitutional form of government in which universal suffrage is established and human rights secured.

A democratic society, in his view, ideally is one in which an equality of social as well as political conditions has been established, without diminution of liberty or of the relative autonomy that the people should have in deciding matters for themselves. Tocqueville envisaged the democratic ideal as a society at once both classless and free.

The *third* impediment to be overcome has already been intimated by the account just given of Tocqueville's conception of a democratic society as the environment requisite for the effective operation of political or constitutional democracy. It consists in eliminating the injustice of economic arrangements that divide the people into economic *haves* and *have-nots*, the latter being deprived of what anyone needs to lead a decent human life and to function effectively as a citizen.

All who are made citizens by universal suffrage can be regarded as political *haves*. They have the equal status of citizens with the political power vested in that most fundamental of constitutional offices. Some, as the administrative officials of government, have the additional, yet limited, political power that the constitution confers upon the administrative offices they occupy.

In the long march toward democracy from the seventeenth century on, the first battle begun but not won until much later was the struggle to extend the franchise to the poor—to the working class. It strove to achieve a just answer to the following question: "Should those who are economically unequal (divided by the chasm that separates the economic *haves* and the *have-nots*) be made politically equal as citizens with suffrage?"

In subsequent centuries, after the issue raised by that question had been resolved in favor of extending suffrage to the economically unequal, a second question arose: "Should not those who are now politically equal as citizens with suffrage also be made economically equal, by economic arrangements that make them all economic as well as political *haves?*"

The issue raised by that question has not yet been fully resolved in favor of the economic justice that can be achieved only by a socialist (not a communist) economy, in which all members of society participate in the general economic welfare to the minimal extent needed to eliminate economic *have-nots*.

The first constitutional step toward it in this country occurred in Franklin Roosevelt's message to Congress in 1944. In that message he proposed a bill of economic rights to supplement the original bill of political rights, enshrined in our Constitution by the first ten amendments. But the mixed economy or socialized capitalism of the United States has still a long way to go in order to achieve the practical fulfillment of what was then proposed.

Until that happens, the third impediment will not be surmounted. The economic substructure requisite for the effective functioning of political democracy will not be achieved.

The *fourth* obstacle lies in the moral and intellectual deficiencies that impede a very large proportion of those who have been made self-governing citizens from discharging well the obligations of citizenship.

One of the chief defects in such democracy as now exists on paper or in practice in the United States, and in other societies under constitutional government, stems from the failure on the part of a large majority of the citizens to understand, and their tendency to shirk, the obligations of the high office they hold—its privileges and opportunities as well as its duties.

Not only do they fail to understand what citizenship entails. They are also not helped by the way they are nurtured, under existing cultural conditions, to acquire the moral virtue, especially in its aspect of justice, that is requisite for the performance of their duties as citizens.

In saying this, I am not forgetting what was said in Chapter 4 about the insolubility of the problem that anyone confronts who tries to rear the young so that they become morally virtuous adults. Nevertheless, it remains possible to provide cultural conditions that tend to favor rather than disfavor the formation of moral virtue. While this by no means assures that all or even most will become virtuous men and women, it at least removes an obstacle to their becoming habitually disposed to act for the common good and for the good of their fellows.

With regard to the intellectual virtues requisite for effective citizenship, it should be immediately obvious that these can become the general possession of the people in a democratic society only to the extent that their schooling establishes genuine equality of educational opportunity—the same quality of schooling for all, not just the same quantity.

This was first accomplished in France by an educational enactment of its parliament in 1977. A system of public education that provides all children with the same quality of schooling does not yet exist in any other Western or Eastern constitutional democracy. No one should be deceived into thinking that it exists in the United States today. The factual evidence that it does not is overwhelming.

It would take much too long and be out of place here to state in detail what must be done to achieve a truly democratic system of education in the United States, or elsewhere for that matter. Instead, I refer readers to two books that have been recently published, written by me on behalf of a group of associates who engaged for several years in deliberation about how the educational impediment to democracy's fulfillment can and should be overcome. They are *The Paideia Proposal* (published in 1982) and *Paideia Problems and Possibilities* (published in 1983).

We come, finally, to the *fifth* obstacle that must be surmounted. It consists in the stresses and strains that deflect a democratic government from functioning as it should. The stresses and strains that I refer to arise from the encroachments on sound domestic policy that result from the intrigues of foreign policy.

The power politics that must be engaged in by the government of any sovereign state that is in cold war, even when not embroiled in hot warfare, with other states gives preeminence to might over right. It gives predominance to the Machiavellian principle of expediency as the guide to success in the struggle for power, even if putting that principle into practice results in serious injustice.

When a democratic government is compelled by the anarchy of sovereign states to engage in the Machiavellian machinations of foreign policy, on the one hand, while at the same time striving to do what is just in domestic policy, on the other hand, the latter effort is doomed to frustration. This is especially true when the right (the just) hand does not know what the left (the expedient) hand is doing.

Can this fifth and last impediment to an effective functioning of democratic government be surmounted? How?

I have, in the preceding chapter, suggested the only way I know for achieving the worldwide peace that constitutional democracies require in order for them to function as they should.

I am fully aware that the vast majority of persons think that the world federal government required for worldwide civil peace is a utopian fantasy, far beyond the reach of any attempt to embody it in the real world.

If they are right in their judgment that the means proposed lies beyond the bounds of possibility, or right in their assessment of its improbability, then this fifth impediment cannot ever be surmounted, or will not be in the foreseeable future.

How serious a flaw is this in our outlook for the future of democratic government, prospering in the benign environment provided by a democratic society? It is not fatal, as the failure to overcome the other four obstacles would most certainly be.

This brings us, in conclusion to the question with which we began: Will democracy survive, spread, and prosper?

An affirmative answer depends in part on our estimate of the likelihood that we can overcome the various obstacles we have been considering, if we are given the time needed by the difficulty of the problems to be solved.

An affirmative answer, especially with regard to the global spread of democracy, also depends in part on speeding up technological progress in developing countries. So far as the developed countries are concerned, further and even speedier technological progress will facilitate solutions of the economic and educational problems they still face.

Prudent prediction is one thing; reasonable hope, quite another. Whatever our predictions may be for the future of democracy, is it not reasonable to hope that both the idea and the ideal of democracy have favorable careers ahead of them?

Reasonable optimists, it seems to me, are justified in believing that what should be will come to pass—that what is necessary for the ultimate happiness of all mankind must also be practically feasible.

Such reasonable optimism is grounded on the belief that human beings will not forever endure unjust deprivations of liberty and equality, which stand in the way of their leading decent human lives.

Mankind will not long suffer injustice without seeking redress. Liberty and equality are goods the pursuit of which mankind will not abandon, if there is any way of achieving them.

The only alternative to the democratic government of a democratic society—a second best to the ideal proposed—involves the benevolent despotism of an oligarchical constitution—government of the people and for the people, *but not by all who should comprise the people.*

The second-best alternative to the ideal is simply not good enough to be endured for long or forever. Herein lies the hope of the reasonable optimist.

QUOTATIONS WITHOUT COMMENT

With Regard to Democracy

. . . In democracies of the more extreme type there has arisen a false idea of freedom which is contradictory to the true interests of the state. For two principles are characteristic of democracy, the government of the majority and freedom. Men think that what is just is equal; and that equality is the supremacy of the popular will; and that freedom means the doing what a man likes. In such democracies every one lives as he pleases. . . . But this is all wrong; men should not think it slavery to live according to the rule of the constitution; for it is their salvation.

Aristotle, Politics, Bk. V, Ch. 9 (4th cent. B.C.)

★　★　★

Of forms of democracy first comes that which is said to be based strictly on equality. In such a democracy the law says that it is just for the poor to have no more advantage than the rich; and that neither should be masters, but both equal. For if liberty and equality . . . are chiefly to be found in democracy, they will be best attained when all persons alike share in the government to the utmost. And since the people are the majority, and the opinion of the majority is decisive, such a government must necessarily be a democracy. Here then is one sort of democracy. There is another, in which the magistrates are elected according to a certain property qualification, but a low one; he who has the required amount of property has a share in the government, but he who loses his property loses his rights. Another kind is that in which all the citizens who are under no disqualification share in the government, but still the law is supreme. In another, everybody, if he be only a citizen, is admitted to the government, but the law is supreme as before. A fifth form of democracy, in other respects the same, is that in which, not the law, but the multitude, have the supreme power, and supersede the law by their decrees. This is a state of affairs brought about by the demagogues.

Aristotle, *Politics*, Bk. IV, Ch. 4 (4th cent. B.C.)

★ ★ ★

. . . A democracy, in effect, is no more than an aristocracy of orators, interrupted sometimes with the temporary monarchy of one orator.

Thomas Hobbes, *Elements of Law*, Pt. II, Ch. II, Sec. 5 (1640)

★ ★ ★

Were there a people of gods, their government would be democratic. So perfect a government is not for men.

Jean-Jacques Rousseau, *The Social Contract*, Bk. III, Ch. 4 (1762)

★ ★ ★

If we take the term in the strict sense, there never has been a real democracy, and there never will be. It is against the natural order for the many to govern and the few to be governed.

Jean-Jacques Rousseau, *The Social Contract*, Bk. III, Ch. 4 (1762)

★ ★ ★

A pure democracy, by which I mean a society consisting of a small number of citizens, who assemble and administer the government in person, can admit of no cure for the mischiefs of faction. A common passion or interest will, in almost every case, be felt by a majority of the whole; a communication and concert result from the form of government itself; and there is nothing to check the inducements to sacrifice the weaker party or an obnoxious individual. Hence it is that such democracies have ever been spectacles of turbulence and contention; have ever been found incompatible with personal security or the rights of property; and have in general been as short in their lives as they have been violent in their deaths. Theoretic politicians, who have patronised this species of government, have erroneously supposed that by reducing mankind to a perfect equality in their political rights, they would, at the same time, be perfectly equalised and assimilated in their possessions, their opinions, and their passions.

A republic, by which I mean a government in which the scheme of representation takes place, opens a different prospect, and promises the cure for which we are seeking. Let us examine the points in which it varies from pure democracy, and we shall comprehend both the nature of the cure and the efficacy which it must derive from the Union.

The two great points of difference between a democracy and a republic are: first, the delegation of the government, in the latter, to a small number of citizens elected by the rest; secondly, the greater number of citizens, and greater sphere of country, over which the latter may be extended.

The effect of the first difference is, on the one hand, to refine and enlarge the public views, by passing them through the medium of a chosen body of citizens, whose wisdom may best discern the true interest of their country, and whose patriotism and love of justice will be least likely to sacrifice it to temporary or partial considerations. Under such a regulation, it may well happen that the public voice, pronounced by the representatives of the people, will be more consonant to the public good than if pronounced by the people themselves, convened for the purpose. On the other hand, the effect may be inverted. Men of factious tempers, of local prejudices, or of sinister designs, may, by intrigue, by corruption, or by other means, first obtain the suffrages, and then betray the interests, of the people. The question resulting is, whether small or extensive republics are more favourable to the election of proper guardians of the public weal; and it is clearly decided in favour of the latter by two obvious considerations:

In the first place, it is to be remarked that, however small the republic may be, the representatives must be raised to a certain number, in order to guard against the cabals of a few; and that, however large it may be, they must be limited to a certain number, in order to guard against the confusion of a multitude. Hence the number of representatives in the two cases not being in proportion to that of the two constituents, and being proportionally greater in the small republic, it follows that, if the proportion of fit characters be not less in the large than in the small republic, the former will present a greater option, and consequently a greater probability of a fit choice.

In the next place, as each representative will be chosen by a greater number of citizens in the large than in the small republic, it will be more difficult for unworthy candidates to practise with success the vicious arts by which elections are too often carried; and the suffrages of the people being more free, will be more likely to centre in men who possess the most attractive merit and the most diffusive and established character.

James Madison, *The Federalist Papers*, #10 (1787–88)

★   ★   ★

To those for whom the word "democracy" is synonymous with disturbance, anarchy, spoliation, and murder, I have attempted to show that democracy may be reconciled with respect for property, with deference for rights, with safety to freedom, with reverence for religion; that, if democratic government fosters less than another some of the finer possibilities of the human spirit, it has its great and noble aspects; and that perhaps, after all, it is the will of God to bestow a lesser grade of happiness upon all men than to grant a greater share of it to a smaller number and to bring a few to the verge of perfection. I have undertaken to demonstrate to them that, whatever their opinion on this point may be, it is too late to deliberate; that society is advancing and dragging them along with it toward equality of conditions; that the sole remaining alternative lies between evils henceforth irresistible; that the question is not whether aristocracy or democracy can be maintained but whether we are to live under a democratic society, devoid indeed of poetry and greatness, but at least orderly and moral, or under a democratic society, lawless and depraved, abandoned to the frenzy of revolution or subjected to a yoke heavier than any of those which have crushed mankind since the fall of the Roman Empire.

Alexis de Tocqueville, *Letter to Eugene Stoffels* (Feb. 21, 1835)

★   ★   ★

We may naturally believe that it is not the singular prosperity of the few, but the greater well-being of all that is most pleasing in the sight of the Creator and Preserver of men. What appears to me to be man's decline is, to His eye, advancement; what afflicts me is acceptable to Him. A state of equality is perhaps less elevated, but it is more just: and its justice constitutes its greatness and its beauty. I would strive, then, to raise myself to this point of the divine contemplation and thence to view and to judge the concerns of men.

Alexis de Tocqueville, *Democracy in America*, Vol. II,
Bk. IV, Ch. 8 (1835–40)

★   ★   ★

We have seen above that the first step in the revolution by the working class is to raise the proletariat to the position of ruling class, to establish democracy.

The proletariat will use its political supremacy to wrest by degrees all capital from the bourgeoisie, to centralize all instruments of production in the hands of the state, i.e., of the proletariat organized as the ruling class, and to increase the total of productive forces as rapidly as possible.

Karl Marx and Friedrich Engels, *The Communist Manifesto*,
Ch. II (1848)

★   ★   ★

Democracy, of which the core is the establishment of representative government, is an extremely new and extremely bold, even revolutionary, experiment in the conduct of human affairs. The development of democracy, in this sense of the attempt at a significant degree of self-rule by large communities, is by far the most important and challenging thing which is happening in the world to-day. It is not certain to succeed; but on the success or failure of this attempt the fate of the world will turn.

After all, the attempt to establish democracy in this sense has been going on for less than two hundred years. For I have never been able to count the Greek City States of the ancient world as democracies. Even Athens at her zenith was, in fact, an oligarchy. The only people who had the vote were free male citizens of Athenian parents of two generations on both sides. The slaves, alone, formed something like nine-tenths of the population, and then there were a great many foreigners. The actual voters must have been much under one-tenth of even the total male population: that is oligarchy, not democracy.

> John Strachey, *The Challenge of Democracy*, Encounter
> pamphlet #10, Ch. I (1963)

★   ★   ★

Democracy in the sense in which I am describing it is a far more recent thing than is usually supposed. Britain is often thought of as "one of the oldest democracies in the world;" and it is true that some democratic institutions, such as the rule of law, a fair amount of freedom of speech, and some others, go back a good many years into British history. But real democracy, in the sense of a universal franchise by which all of the adult population of the country choose the kind of government they want, is a far more recent thing. As a matter of fact it has been finally established within my own political lifetime. One whole half of the British population, the women, were, after all, only given votes in 1918, an election which I remember quite well. And the younger women were, as a matter of fact, only given votes in 1929 during the election in which I was first elected to the British Parliament. Moreover, British trade unions have only become really powerful in the past twenty years. Democracy, in the sense in which I am using the word, is, then, a very recent thing, even in Britain.

> John Strachey, *The Challenge of Democracy*, Encounter
> pamphlet #10, Ch. III (1963)

★   ★   ★

I myself believe in the goal of a classless society as strongly as ever I did. It still seems to me that the organisation of an economic and social system which does not result in men being separated from each other by the barriers of class—peasants from landlords, wage-earners from the owners of the means of production, educated from uneducated, rich from poor—would be the greatest step forward that humanity could take. That is why I am and remain a socialist. . . .

The fact is that democratic political institutions are proving an even more important factor in socialist development than the ownership of the means of production. Do not misunderstand me. Both factors are extremely important. It matters a great deal who owns the means of production. At *certain* stages in social development this is the decisive factor. . . .

But in one way or another, the people of the advanced democratic societies will arrange the distribution of the national income to suit themselves. Experience shows that they can do this in a number of ways. The most obvious of these ways is so to arrange the tax structure that the main fruits of production do not go to the owners but are shared, directly or indirectly, with the mass of the population.

John Strachey, *The Challenge of Democracy*, Encounter pamphlet #10, Ch. VIII (1963)

★   ★   ★

What then are the pre-conditions for democracy? What makes a country capable of working democratic institutions? . . .

All one can really say is that a certain level of general civilisation seems to be necessary in order to enable a people to work democratic institutions. . . . There is an invisible "Plimsoll Line" to be drawn along the sides of all the countries of the world to-day. If the ship of state floats with that line above water, democratic institutions are workable; if the ship of state is so overloaded with difficulties that the line is submerged, democracy is not there possible. In countries below a level of general development, marked by this line, any attempt to establish democratic institutions will be at best futile, and will be, more often, actually harmful. In these cases, some form of arbitrary government, with all its disadvantages, is inevitable. . . . Well then, can democracy succeed in spreading throughout the world? I have conceded that democracy is not yet applicable in many parts of the world, but does this mean that democracy is only a passing phase of certain countries, mainly round the Atlantic seaboard, of countries which have had a particular historical development? Does it mean that democracy can never spread through the world? It does not.

For democracy *is* succeeding in, precisely, the decisive countries of the world. It is in the advanced, most highly developed, and therefore most powerful countries that democracy is proving a workable institution. This is the guarantee that democracy is the political system of the future.

John Strachey, *The Challenge of Democracy*, Encounter
pamphlet #10, Ch. IX (1963)

With Regard to Citizenship and Suffrage

. . . A state is composite, like any other whole made up of many parts—these are the citizens, who compose it. It is evident, therefore, that we must begin by asking: Who is the citizen, and what is the meaning of the term? For here . . . there may be a difference of opinion. He who is a citizen in a democracy will often not be a citizen in an oligarchy. Leaving out of consideration those who have been made citizens, or who have obtained the name of citizen in any other accidental manner, we may say, first, that a citizen is not a citizen because he lives in a certain place, for resident aliens and slaves share in the place; nor is he a citizen who has no legal right except that of suing and being sued; for this right may be enjoyed under the provisions of a treaty. . . . The citizen whom we are seeking to define is a citizen in the strictest sense, against whom no such exception can be taken, and his special characteristic is that he shares in the administration of justice, and in offices. Now of offices some are discontinuous, and the same persons are not allowed to hold them twice, or can only hold them after a fixed interval; others have no limit of time—for example, the office of dicast of ecclesiast. It may, indeed, be argued that these are not magistrates at all, and that their functions give them no share in the government. But surely it is ridiculous to say that those who have the supreme power do not govern. Let us not dwell further upon this, which is a purely verbal question; what we want is a common term including both dicast and ecclesiast. Let us, for the sake of distinction, call it "indefinite office," and we will assume that those who share in such office are citizens. This is the most comprehensive definition of a citizen, and best suits all those who are generally so called. . . .

He who has the power to take part in the deliberative or judicial administration of any state is said by us to be a citizen of that state; and, speaking generally, a state is a body of citizens sufficing for the purposes of life.

Aristotle, Politics, Bk. III, Ch. 1 (4th cent. B.C.)

★　★　★

. . . Since we are here speaking of the best form of government, i.e. that under which the state will be most happy . . . the citizens must not lead the life of mechanics or tradesmen, for such a life is ignoble and inimical to virtue. Neither must they be husbandmen, since leisure is necessary both for the development of virtue and the performance of political duties.

Aristotle, Politics, Bk. VII, Ch. 9 (4th cent. B.C.)

★　★　★

. . . We cannot consider all those to be citizens who are necessary to the existence of the state; for example, children are not citizens equally with grown-up men. . . . In ancient times, and among some nations, the artisan class *were* slaves or foreigners, and therefore the majority of them are so now. The best form of state will not admit them to citizenship. . . . We ought not to include everybody, for there must always be in cities a multitude of slaves and sojourners and foreigners; but we should include only those who are members of the state, and who form an essential part of it.

Aristotle, *Politics*, Bk. III, Ch. 5; Bk. VII,

Ch. 4 (4th cent. B.C.)

★   ★   ★

There never was any government so purely popular as not to require the exclusion of the poor, of strangers, women, and minors from the public councils.

Hugo Grotius, *Rights of War and Peace*, Bk. I, Ch. III,

Sec. 8 (1625)

★   ★   ★

For really I think that the poorest he that is in England hath a life to live, as the greatest he; and therefore truly, sir, I think it is clear that every man that is to live under a government ought first by his own consent to put himself under that government; and I do think that the poorest man in England is not at all bound in a strict sense to that government that he hath not had a voice to put himself under.

Debate in the General Council of the New Model Army of England concerning the Leveller's proposal for manhood suffrage: remarks of Major William Rainborough (Oct. 1647)

★   ★   ★

Every person in England hath as clear a right to elect his representative as the greatest person in England. I conceive that is the undeniable maxim of government: that all government is in the free consent of the people. If [so], then upon that account there is no person that is under a just government, or hath justly his own, unless he by his own free consent be put under that government.

Debate in the General Council of the New Model Army of England concerning the Leveller's proposal for manhood suffrage: remarks of Sir John Wildman (Oct. 1647)

★ ★ ★

Is it not . . . true that men in general, in every society, who are wholly destitute of property, are also too little acquainted with public affairs to form a right judgment, and too dependent upon other men to have a will of their own? If this is a fact, [then] if you give to every man who has no property a vote, will you not make a firm encouraging provision for corruption, by your fundamental law? Such is the frailty of the human heart, that very few men who have no property have any judgment of their own.

John Adams, *Letter to James Sullivan* (May 26, 1776)

★ ★ ★

What is the proportion of freemen possessing lands and houses of one thousand pounds' value compared to that of freemen whose possessions are inferior? Are they as one to ten? Are they even as one to twenty? I should doubt whether they are as one to fifty. If this minority is to choose a body expressly to control that which is to be chosen by the great majority of the freemen, what have this great majority done to forfeit so great a portion of their right in elections? Why is this power of control, contrary to the spirit of all democracies, to be vested in a minority, instead of a majority? Then, is it intended, or is it not, that the rich should have a vote in the choice of members for the lower house, while those of inferior property are deprived of the right of voting for members of the upper house? And why should the upper house, chosen by a minority, have equal power with the lower chosen by a majority? Is it supposed that wisdom is the necessary concomitant of riches and that one man worth a thousand pounds must have as much wisdom as twenty who have each only nine hundred and ninety-nine; and why is property to be represented at all?

Benjamin Franklin, *Representation and Suffrage* (1789)

★ ★ ★

The members of a civil society . . . united for the purpose of legislation, and thereby constituting a state, are called its *citizens;*

and there are three juridical attributes that inseparably belong to them by right. These are: 1. constitutional freedom, as the right of every citizen to have to obey no other law than that to which he has given his consent or approval; 2. civil equality, as the right of the citizen to recognise no one as a superior among the people in relation to himself, except in so far as such a one is as subject to *his* moral power to impose obligations, as that other has power to impose obligations upon him; and 3. political independence, as the right to owe his existence and continuance in society not to the arbitrary will of another, but to his own rights and powers as a member of the commonwealth, and, consequently, the possession of a civil personality, which cannot be represented by any other than himself.

> Immanuel Kant, *The Science of Right*, Part One of
> *The Metaphysics of Morals* (1796)

★ ★ ★

The capability of voting by possession of the suffrage properly constitutes the political qualification of a citizen as a member of the state. But this, again, presupposes the independence or self-sufficiency of the individual citizen among the people, as one who is not a mere incidental part of the commonwealth, but a member of it acting of his own will in community with others. The last of the three qualities involved necessarily constitutes the distinction between *active* and *passive* citizenship although the latter conception appears to stand in contradiction to the definition of a citizen as such. The following examples may serve to remove this difficulty. The apprentice of a merchant or tradesman, a servant who is not in the employ of the state, a minor, all women, and, generally, every one who is compelled to maintain himself not according to his own industry, but as it is arranged by others (the state excepted), are without civil personality, and their existence is only, as it were, incidentally included in the state. The woodcutter whom I employ on my estate; the smith in India who carries his hammer, anvil, and bellows into the houses where he is engaged to work in iron, as distinguished from the European carpenter or smith, who can offer the independent products of his labour as wares for public sale; the resident tutor as distinguished from the schoolmaster; the ploughman as distinguished from the farmer and such like, illustrate the distinction in question. In all these cases, the former members of the contrast are distinguished from the latter by being mere subsidiaries of the commonwealth and not active independent members of it, because they are of necessity commanded and protected by others, and consequently possess no political self-sufficiency in themselves. Such dependence on the will of others and the consequent inequality are, however, not inconsistent with the freedom and equality of the individuals *as men* helping to constitute the people. Much rather is it the case that it is only under such conditions that a people can become a state and enter into a civil constitution. But all are not equally qualified to exercise the right of suffrage under the constitution, and to be full citizens of the state, and not mere passive subjects under its protection. For, although they are entitled to demand to be treated by all the other citizens according to laws of natural freedom and equality, as *passive* parts of the state, it does not follow that they ought themselves to have the right to deal with the state as active members of it, to reorganize it, or to take action by way of introducing certain laws. All they have a right in their circumstances to claim may be no more than that whatever be the mode in which the positive laws are enacted, these laws must not be contrary to the natural laws that demand the freedom of all the people and the equality that is conformable thereto; and it must therefore be made possible for them to raise themselves from this passive condition in the state to the condition of active citizenship.

Immanuel Kant, *The Science of Right*, Part One of
The Metaphysics of Morals (1796)

★ ★ ★

The apprehended danger from the experiment of universal suffrage applied to the whole legislative department is no dream of the imagination. It is too mighty an excitement for the moral constitution of men to endure. The tendency of universal suffrage is to jeopardize the rights of property and the principles of liberty. . . .

The notion that every man that works a day on the road, or serves an idle hour in the militia, is entitled as of right to an equal participation in the whole power of the government is most unreasonable and has no foundation in justice. . . .

Universal suffrage, once granted, is granted forever and never can be recalled. There is no retrograde step in the rear of democracy.

> Reports of the Proceedings and Debates of the Convention
> Amending the Constitution of New York: remarks of
> James Kent (1821)

* * *

No man is good enough to govern another man without that other's consent. I say this is the leading principle—the sheet anchor of American republicanism.

> Abraham Lincoln, *Speech at Peoria, Ill.* (Oct. 16, 1854)

* * *

All human beings have the same interest in good government; the welfare of all is alike affected by it, and they have equal need of a voice in it to secure their share of its benefits. If there be any difference, women require it more than men, since being physically weaker, they are more dependent on law and society for protection.

> John Stuart Mill, *Representative Government*, Ch. 8 (1861)

* * *

Independently of all these considerations, it is a personal injustice to withhold from any one, unless for the prevention of greater evils, the ordinary privilege of having his voice reckoned in the disposal of affairs in which he has the same interest as other people. If he is compelled to pay, if he may be compelled to fight, if he is required implicitly to obey, he should be legally entitled to be told what for; to have his consent asked, and his opinion counted at its worth, though not at more than its worth. There ought to be no pariahs in a full-grown and civilised nation; no persons disqualified, except through their own default. Every one is degraded, whether aware of it or not, when other people, without consulting him, take upon themselves unlimited power to regulate his destiny. And even in a much more improved state than the human mind has ever yet reached, it is not in nature that they who are thus disposed of should meet with as fair play as those who have a voice. Rulers and ruling classes are under a necessity of considering the interests and wishes of those who have the suffrage; but of those who are excluded, it is in their option whether they will do so or not, and, however honestly disposed, they are in general too fully occupied with things which they *must* attend to, to have much room in their thoughts for anything which they can with impunity disregard. No arrangement of the suffrage, therefore, can be permanently satisfactory in which any person or class is peremptorily excluded; in which the electoral privilege is not open to all persons of full age who desire to obtain it.

There are, however, certain exclusions, required by positive reasons, which do not conflict with this principle, and which, though an evil in themselves, are only to be got rid of by the cessation of the state of things which requires them. I regard it as wholly inadmissible that any person should participate in the suffrage without being able to read, write, and, I will add, perform the common operations of arithmetic. Justice demands, even when the suffrage does not depend on it, that the means of attaining these elementary acquirements should be within the reach of every person, either gratuitously, or at an expense not exceeding what the poorest who earn their own living can afford. If this were really the case, people would no more think of giving the suffrage to a man who could not read, than of giving it to a child who could not speak; and it would not be society that would exclude him, but his own laziness. When society has not performed its duty, by rendering this amount of instruction accessible to all, there is some hardship in the case, but it is a hardship that ought to be borne. If society has neglected to discharge two solemn obligations, the more important and more fundamental of the two must be fulfilled first: universal teaching must precede universal enfranchisement. No one but those in whom an *a priori* theory has silenced common sense will maintain that power over others, over the whole community, should be imparted to people who have not acquired the commonest and most essential requisites for taking care of themselves; for pursuing intelligently their own interests, and those of the persons most nearly allied to them. This argument, doubtless, might be pressed further, and made to prove much more. . . .

However this may be, I regard it as required by first principles, that the receipt of parish relief should be a peremptory disqualification for the franchise. He who cannot by his labour suffice for his own support has no claim to the privilege of helping himself to the money of others. By becoming dependent on the remaining members of the community for actual subsistence, he abdicates his claim to equal rights with them in other respects.

John Stuart Mill, *Representative Government*, Ch. 8 (1861)

With Regard to Human Equality

. . . Some men are by nature free, and others slaves, and . . . for these latter slavery is both expedient and right.

Aristotle, *Politics*, Bk. I, Ch. 5 (4th cent. B.C.)

★   ★   ★

Aristotle . . . had said that men are by no means equal naturally, but that some are born for slavery, and others for dominion.

Aristotle was right; but he took the effect for the cause. Nothing can be more certain than that every man born in slavery is born for slavery. Slaves lose everything in their chains, even the desire of escaping from them: they love their servitude, as the comrades of Ulysses loved their brutish condition. If then there are slaves by nature, it is because there have been slaves against nature. Force made the first slaves, and their cowardice perpetuated the condition.

Jean-Jacques Rousseau, *The Social Contract*, Bk. I, Ch. 2 (1762)

★　★　★

There is a natural aristocracy among men. The grounds of this are virtue and talents. Formerly, bodily powers gave place among the *aristoi*. But since the invention of gunpowder has armed the weak as well as the strong with missile death, bodily strength, like beauty, good humor, politeness, and other accomplishments, has become but an auxiliary ground of distinction.

There is also an artificial aristocracy, founded on wealth and birth, without either virtue or talents; for with these it would belong to the first class. The natural aristocracy I consider as the most precious gift of nature, for the instruction, the trusts, and government of society. And, indeed, it would have been inconsistent in Creation to have formed man for the social state and not to have provided virtue and wisdom enough to manage the concerns of the society. May we not even say that that form of government is the best which provides the most effectually for a pure selection of these natural *aristoi* into the offices of government? The artificial aristocracy is a mischievous ingredient in government, and provision should be made to prevent its ascendancy.

Thomas Jefferson, *Letter to John Adams* (Oct. 28, 1813)

★　★　★

[That] equality of citizens, in the eyes of the law, is essential to liberty in a popular government is conceded. But to go further and make equality of *condition* essential to liberty would be to destroy both liberty and progress. The reason is that inequality of condition, while it is a necessary consequence of liberty, is, at the same time, indispensable to progress. . . .

These great and dangerous errors have their origin in the prevalent opinion that all men are born free and equal—than which nothing can be more unfounded and false. It rests upon the assumption of a fact which is contrary to universal observation in whatever light it may be regarded.

John C. Calhoun, *A Disquisition on Government* (1855)

With Regard to the Economic Substructure of Democracy

The first effect of the tendency to political equality was the more equal distribution of wealth and power; for, while population is comparatively sparse, inequality in the distribution of wealth is principally due to the inequality of personal rights, and it is only as material progress goes on that the tendency to inequality involved in the reduction of land to private ownership strongly appears. . . .

Where there is anything like an equal distribution of wealth . . . the more democratic the government the better it will be; but where there is gross inequality in the distribution of wealth, the more democratic the government the worse it will be; for, while rotten democracy may not in itself be worse than rotten autocracy, its effects upon national character will be worse. To give the suffrage to tramps, to paupers, to men to whom the change to labor is a boon, to men who must beg, or steal, or starve, is to invoke destruction. To put political power in the hands of men embittered and degraded by poverty is to tie firebrands to foxes and turn them loose amid the standing corn; it is to put out the eyes of a Samson and to twine his arms around the pillars of national life.

Henry George, *Progress and Poverty* (1879)

★   ★   ★

No man can be a good citizen unless he has a wage more than sufficient to cover the bare cost of living, and hours of labor short enough so that after his day's work is done he will have time and energy to bear his share in the management of the community, to help in carrying the general load. We keep countless men from being good citizens by the conditions of life with which we surround them.

Theodore Roosevelt, *The New Nationalism* (1910)

★   ★   ★

The prohibition of child labor.

Minimum wage standards for working women, to provide a "living scale" in all industrial occupations.

The prohibition of night work for women and the establishment of an eight-hour day for women and young persons.

One day's rest in seven for all wage-workers.

The eight-hour day in continuous twenty-four hour industries.

The abolition of the convict contract labor system; substituting a system of prison production for governmental consumption only and the application of prisoners' earnings to the support of their dependent families.

Publicity as to wages, hours and conditions of labor; full reports upon industrial accidents and diseases and the opening to public inspection of all tallies, weights, measures and check systems on labor products.

Standards of compensation for death by industrial accident and injury and trade diseases which will transfer the burden of lost earnings from the families of working people to the industry, and thus to the community.

The protection of home life against the hazards of sickness, irregular employment and old age through the adoption of a system of social insurance adapted to American use.

The development of the creative labor power of America by lifting the last load of illiteracy from American youth, and establishing continuation schools for industrial education under public control and encouraging agricultural education and demonstration in rural schools.

The establishment of industrial research laboratories to put the methods and discoveries of science at the service of American producers.

We favor the organization of the workers, men and women, as a means of protecting their interests and of promoting their progress.

The Progressive Party Platform of 1912

★   ★   ★

Every man has a right to life; and this means that he has also the right to make a comfortable living. He may by sloth or crime decline to exercise that right; but it may not be denied him. We have no actual famine or dearth; our industrial and agricultural mechanism can produce enough and to spare. Our Government formal and informal, political and economic, owes to everyone an avenue to possess himself of a portion of that plenty sufficient for his needs, through his own work.

Every man has a right to his own property; which means a right to be assured, to the fullest extent attainable, in the safety of his savings. By no other means can men carry the burdens of those parts of life which, in the nature of things, afford no chance of labor: childhood, sickness, old age. In all thought of property, this right is paramount; all other property rights must yield to it. If, in accord with this principle, we must restrict the operations of the speculator, the manipulator, even the financier, I believe we must accept the restriction as needful, not to hamper individualism but to protect it.

Franklin Delano Roosevelt, *Commonwealth Club Address* (1932)

★   ★   ★

In the President's message to Congress last year and this year he set forth eight self-evident economic truths as representing a second Bill of Rights under which a new basis of security and prosperity can be established for all—regardless of station, race or creed.

America led the world in establishing political democracy. It must lead the world once more in strengthening and extending political democracy by firmly establishing economic democracy. Let us not forget the painful lessons of the rise of fascism. Let us remember that political democracy is at best insecure and unstable without economic democracy. Fascism thrives on domestic economic insecurity, as well as on lack of or divided resistance to external aggression. Fascism is not only an enemy from without, it is also potentially an enemy from within.

We now must establish an economic bill of rights, not only out of common decency, but also to insure the preservation of our political freedoms. We must accord to this economic bill of rights the same dignity—the same stature—in our American tradition as that we have accorded to the original Bill of Rights.

Let us therefore affirm this economic bill of rights—and keep affirming it—until it is as familiar and real to us as our political bill of rights.

The economic bill of rights as embodied in the President's message to Congress last January is:

The right to a useful and remunerative job in the industries or shops or farms or mines of the nation;

The right to earn enough to provide adequate food and clothing and recreation;

The right of every farmer to raise and sell his products at a return which will give him and his family a decent living;

The right of every business man, large and small, to trade in an atmosphere of freedom from unfair competition and domination by monopolies at home or abroad;

The right of every family to a decent home;

The right to adequate medical care and the opportunity to achieve and enjoy good health;

The right to adequate protection from the economic fears of old age, sickness, accident and unemployment;

The right to a good education.

Henry A. Wallace, *An Economic Bill of Rights*,
New York Times (Jan. 26, 1945)

With Regard to the Tyranny of the Majority and Judicial Review as its Only Remedy

A majority taken collectively is only an individual, whose opinions, and frequently whose interests, are opposed to those of another individual, who is styled a minority. If it be admitted that a man possessing absolute power may misuse that power by wronging his adversaries, why should not a majority be liable to the same reproach? . . .

In the United States the omnipotence of the majority, which is favorable to the legal despotism of the legislature, likewise favors the arbitrary authority of the magistrate. . . .

If ever the free institutions of America are destroyed, that event may be attributed to the omnipotence of the majority, which may at some future time urge the minorities to desperation and oblige them to have recourse to physical force. Anarchy will then be the result, but it will have been brought about by despotism.

Alexis de Tocqueville, *Democracy in America*, Vol. I, Ch. 15

(1835)

*   *   *

As the restraining influence of tradition grows weaker, the danger of a tyranny of the majority comes nearer, and the time may arrive when convention must give way to law if the rights of minorities are to be respected and safeguarded as they have been in the past. A popular despotism must result if the omnipotence of parliament ever becomes in practice what it now is in law. Because it is not yet so, England is today an exception more apparent than real to the principle laid down by Thomas Paine, that in any state in which the government constitutes itself "with what power it pleases" there is in reality "merely a form of government without a constitution."

As a general principle I think we must admit the truth of Paine's dictum that "a constitution is not the act of a government but of a people constituting a government." And, if this be true, the consequence is that the forms and limits followed in this "constituting" become the embodiment of a "constitution," superior in character to the acts of any "government" it creates. If, for example, this constituent act of the people entrusts certain definite powers to their government, "enumerated powers" as we term them, it is a necessary inference that this government cannot exercise any powers not so "enumerated." All constitutional government is by definition limited government. We may not agree that these limits are necessarily "antecedent" in the sense of that term that Paine had in mind, but for everyone they must be in some sense "fundamental," and fundamental not merely because they are basic, but because they are also unalterable by ordinary legal process. . . .

The one conspicuous element lacking in Paine's construction

therefore seems to be the element of judicial review. Writing when he did, and as he did, to justify an actual rebellion, it is perhaps not strange that he was thinking primarily of politics rather than of law, that the "rights" he had in mind were the rights of man rather than the rights of the citizen, or that the sanction for these rights should be extra-legal action rather than any constitutional check. Paine, like many idealists in a hurry, was probably impatient of the slowness of legal remedies for existing abuses. But others, who were more constitutionally minded than he, had begun to feel that any such remedies, to be truly effective, must ultimately have the sanction of law.

Charles Howard McIlwain, *Constitutionalism Ancient and Modern*, Ch. I (1940)

CHAPTER 8 # Epilogue: Ideas with a Future

REFLECTIONS ABOUT THE PAST and present have a crucial bearing on the way we view the future. This plainly applies to the ideas treated in this book.

Readers, I trust, will find that what was promised at the beginning has now been fulfilled. The degree to which these ideas have greater concreteness and are more down to earth than the ideas in an earlier book has been manifest in the numerous references I have made to concrete examples of points under consideration. It was difficult to make things clear without reference to such examples.

Also evident throughout has been the historical background of these ideas, their present vitality, and the light they throw on so many aspects of contemporary life and society. But life and society on this planet, we all devoutly hope, will not end with us or our century. Our eyes, therefore, cannot help turning toward the future—a future that will take its shape, in part, from the future of these ideas in both thought and practice.

The thinking I have done about democracy over a period of fifty years suggested the title of this book. It was many years ago that I first understood that the word "democracy" names an idea that had its inception in the last hundred and fifty years, the first applications of which in human affairs came more than a half century later. I realized then that, with so little past to speak of and with so slight a hold on the present, this must be an idea that has a future.

In this respect, the idea of democracy does not stand alone. With

two exceptions, all the other ideas treated in this book are ideas with
a future. Most of them have deeper roots in the past than democracy. But all of them, including the two exceptions, have intimate
connections with the future of democracy, both in thought and in
practice.

The two exceptions are, of course, virtue and happiness. Little
of importance can be, or has been, added to the wisdom of antiquity on these two subjects.

The fundamental principles and insights of moral philosophy,
magnificently formulated by Plato and Aristotle, have not been affected by historical change. What is involved in leading a good human life is essentially the same today as it was twenty-five centuries
ago.

All the alterations in the external conditions of life in the twentieth century, and all the improvements in those conditions which
technological advances have bestowed upon us, do not affect in the
least our understanding of intellectual and moral virtues and the role
they play, along with external circumstances, in our pursuit of happiness. Nor do they make it any more difficult—or easier—for an
individual to acquire virtue and to succeed in the effort to lead a
decent human life.

When we turn from ethical to political thought, the situation is
otherwise. The manifold changes that differentiate the external
conditions of human life in antiquity, in the Middle Ages, and even
in recent times, from those that affect us in the contemporary world,
have occasioned improvements in our understanding of work and
leisure, wealth and property, state and society, governments and
constitutions. These improvements, in turn, have enabled us to
conceive democracy and citizenship in ways that are distinctive of
the twentieth century.

In many respects, the twentieth century is a turning point in history. It marks a great divide between the past and the future. What
Sidney Carton, the hero of *A Tale of Two Cities* by Charles Dick-
ens, said of the eighteenth century, we are inclined to say, even more
emphatically, of the century in which we live. He said: "It was
the best of times; it was the worst of times." Both remarks are

much more applicable to the twentieth century than to any of its predecessors.

We bemoan its being the worst of times when we contemplate, with fear and trembling, the threat of thermonuclear devastation and, with it, the uninhabitability of this planet and the end of life on earth.

We suffer the same dread and agony when we face the threat of environmental pollution, so extreme that it, too, renders the earth uninhabitable by us.

Less extreme, but no less serious, are the consequences of increased population and decreased food supply, of exhausting the available energy for our advanced technology, and of the massive unemployment that may be an unalterable consequence of technological advances.

All these things weigh heavily upon the conscience and consciousness of mankind for the first time in this century, and for the first time globally, not just locally. To remain an optimist in the face of these dire threats of doom requires us to believe that none of these problems is insoluble.

Human intelligence and rationality is capable of solving all of them, but *only on condition* that intelligence and reason are used for the good of the human race as a whole—for the salvation of mankind and for carrying forward into the future the extraordinary progress that makes the twentieth century a turning point in history.

Before I call attention to the distinctive steps of progress that enable us to say that our century is the best of times as well as the worst of times, let me qualify my optimistic hopes for the future.

If reason and intelligence are blocked or diverted from beneficent use by unenlightened self-interest; by blind passions; by the hatred of foreigners; by irrational prejudices or discriminations against other races and other ethnic groups; by the lust for naked might, uncontrolled by considerations of right; and by the short-term seeking of profits and gains at the cost of long-term losses, then whatever optimism about the future any of us may still harbor and cherish must be abandoned.

All the grave problems that confront us can be solved, as William

Graham Sumner said at the end of the nineteenth century, "if it were not for folly and vice." The problems we face today are more difficult to solve than the ones he contemplated then, but the qualifying condition of an optimistic hope for their solution remains exactly the same.

What makes the twentieth century the best of times? What distinguishes it, in that respect, from all previous centuries? In treating all the ideas with a future that are the subjects of this book, I have already called attention to the distinctive advances made in this century. They are as follows.

1. The extraordinary technological progress that has eliminated or alleviated much of the drudgery and backbreaking toil, which in the past barred a large part of the human race from even thinking about human happiness, not to mention engaging in its pursuit.

2. The same extraordinary technological progress that has made it possible to produce enough wealth to eliminate dire poverty and to distribute widely the ownership of productive property in capital-intensive economies.

3. The advent of the welfare state, which aims at the socialist ideal of enabling all its inhabitants to participate, at least to a sufficient, minimal degree, in the general economic welfare.

4. The occurrence of the first world wars, which are harbingers of world peace and indications of its possibility as well as its necessity. For the first time in history, human thinking about war and peace has ceased to be parochial and has become global. For the first time in history, our use of the word "world" as an adjective modifying such other terms as state, society, government, and citizenship, has drastically altered our understanding of all the ideas expressed by these words.

5. The first stumbling steps toward the realization in fact and in practice of the political ideal implicit in our understanding of the innovative idea of democracy. We have at last come to conceive democracy as an idea that is radically different from what was meant by the use of the word "democracy" to name a form of government in political theory prior to the middle of the nineteenth century. But it is only in the twentieth century that we have taken the first

steps toward making that ideal a reality. This alone would suffice to mark the twentieth century as a turning point in history.

6. Our recognition of the inadequacy of the steps we have so far taken, which may move us to take the further steps needed to fulfill the promise of universal justice for mankind, with liberty and equality for all.

As we look back at the centuries preceding our own, we cannot avoid seeing that, in all of them, the human inhabitants of every country were divided into a privileged minority and an oppressed majority—into the relatively few who were political and economic *haves* and the remaining multitude who were political and economic *have-nots*.

For the first time, in the twentieth century this has been reversed. In all technologically advanced, democratic societies today, we find privileged majorities and oppressed minorities. It remains for these advantaged countries to take the next steps—the further reduction and, ultimately, the total elimination of oppressed minorities.

Taking the world as a whole and thinking of the whole human race, we are compelled to say that the greater part of the earth's human inhabitants are still political and economic *have-nots*. Nevertheless, the fact that this is no longer the case in the technologically advanced, democratic societies holds out some hope that what has become the best of times for a majority of the population in the industrial democracies may before too long become the best of times for all human beings everywhere.

In everything I have so far said about the distinctive progress made in this century and the further progress to which it can lead, I have paid attention only to the external conditions of human life. While it is true that improvement in external circumstances, social and economic as well as political, is a necessary factor in moving toward a good life and a good society, it is also true that by itself it is not sufficient. The other factor, equally necessary but not by itself sufficient, is human virtue, both intellectual and moral, especially the latter.

I firmly believe that the educational reforms that must be accom-

1

plished to provide all with the kind of schooling needed to inculcate the intellectual virtues requisite for a good life and a good society can be achieved—not immediately, but in the foreseeable future. I wish I could say the same for the formation of moral virtue. Here I have many doubts about the likelihood that a sufficiently large portion of mankind can be aided, by any means with which we are now acquainted, to become adult men and women of good moral character.

If we ever discover how to solve the problem of directing the free choices individuals make so that right choices predominate over wrong choices and some measure of moral virtue results therefrom, the future of political democracy, where it now has come into feeble and fragile existence, would look much brighter.

For the same reason we might become more optimistic about world peace, about the survival of mankind, about the extension of the privileges and opportunities now enjoyed by the *haves* in the advantaged parts of the world to the *have-nots* that still remain there, and beyond that to the *have-nots* everywhere else.

In any case, whatever degree of optimism about the future we may still tenaciously retain depends upon our judgment about what is humanly possible and our estimate of the probability that what is genuinely possible can become actual.

Our vision today of what is possible in the future is controlled by our knowledge of past and present realities. In the light of what we have been able actually to accomplish so far, we tend to place limitations on what can possibly be accomplished in the future.

Our ancestors in remote centuries, and even in the recent past, drew a boundary line around the possible that fenced it in much more stringently than we are inclined to do. Our twentieth-century experience, the knowledge of what has been already accomplished in this century, much of it for the first time, has enlarged our vision of the possible. Much more now appears possible to us than could ever have been contemplated by our ancestors.

In an uprising of students of the Sorbonne in Paris at the end of the sixties, one student chalked up on a wall the following graffito: *Be realistic, attempt the impossible!*

On the face of it, considered soberly and strictly, the statement is, of course, outlandish. The impossible is that which cannot be done and, therefore, should not be attempted. To make the attempt is unrealistic. Nevertheless, the statement was a witty way of expressing the truth that the dividing line between the possible and impossible is extremely difficult to determine.

Drawing it correctly depends on our knowledge of past and present realities. The extent to which we know all relevant facts helps us to judge correctly what possibilities the future holds. The extent of such knowledge changes from time to time.

Our judgment about the limits of the possible is consequently better than that of our ancestors. Must we not, therefore, concede that succeeding generations will be able to make even more accurate judgments about future possibilities? Will they not have an enlarged vision of the possible?

The student who chalked that injunction on a university wall was trying to tell the world that anyone imbued with the spirit of progress should challenge those who seek to preserve the status quo by claiming that the changes called for by justice lie beyond the bounds of the possible. Our present view of the limits of the possible may be as woefully inaccurate as that held by our ancestors.

Plato and Aristotle in the fifth and fourth centuries before Christ discussed most of the ideas treated in this book. But they could not imagine, much less predict, the changes in our understanding of these ideas that came to pass in the centuries that lay ahead. If some seer had prophesied the occurrence of these changes and the consequent improvement in human affairs and institutions, they would have dismissed him as a dreamer. They would have been quite right to do so in terms of their very limited vision of the possible.

What I have just said about Plato and Aristotle in antiquity applies in the same way and for the same reason to the wisest thinkers of the Middle Ages and of modern times up to the end of the nineteenth century.

All of them were compelled by the facts they knew to entertain a much more limited vision of the possible than is entertainable by us who are alive today. None of them could have imagined or would have predicted what has become actual for us in the twentieth century.

It is in the light of such actualities that we are disposed to extend the boundaries of what may be possible in the future. This being the case, we dare not impute to our successors in the centuries that lie ahead the still too limited vision of the possible that we hold today.